FINDING THE REAL ME

FINDING THE REAL ME

True Tales of Sex and Gender Diversity

Tracie O'Keefe

and

Katrina Fox, Editors

JOSSEY-BASS
A Wiley Imprint
www.josseybass.com

Published by Jossey-Bass
A Wiley Imprint
989 Market Street, San Francisco, CA 94103-1741   www.josseybass.com

Jossey-Bass books and products are available through most bookstores. To contact Jossey-
Bass directly call our Customer Care Department within the U.S. at (800) 956-7739, outside the U.S. at (317) 572-3986 or fax (317) 572-4002.

Jossey-Bass also publishes its books in a variety of electronic formats. Some content that
appears in print may not be available in electronic books.

Library of Congress Cataloging-in-Publication Data
Finding the real me : true tales of sex and gender diversity / Tracie O'Keefe and
Katrina Fox, editors.
    p. cm.
  ISBN 0-7879-6547-2 (alk. paper)
  1. Transsexualism. 2. Transsexuals—Biography. 3. Transsexuals—Identity.
4. Gender identity. I. O'Keefe, Tracie. II. Fox, Katrina.
  HQ77.7 .F556 2003
  306.77—dc21   2002153518

Printed in the United States of America
FIRST EDITION
PB Printing   10 9 8 7 6 5 4 3 2

CONTENTS

FOREWORD

BEING A TRANSSEXUAL MAN (that is, someone born with a female body, but who has undergone a "sex change" and now lives his life as a man) I have been obligated to explore the complex understandings that give me my own knowledge of my gendered self. When I first sought help, there was a plethora of theories contained in the text books and medical papers. But none of them appeared to fit my, not fantastic but also not awful, experience of childhood and life. But I did get to know that in order to be, simply to exist, transsexual and transgender people, like myself, had to "pass" the "examinations" of the psycho-experts. They acted as the gatekeepers to the other medical professionals who would provide the hormones and surgery that I knew were essential to not only enhance my life but to keep me alive.

When faced with trans people, psycho-experts find themselves caught between the devil and deep blue sea. They are faced with individuals who simply are not whom they claim to be. How can a person born with a penis claim to be a woman, when to be a woman requires that you are not born with a penis (or vice versa)? Yet the vast majority of these people are plainly not mad, being able to function extremely well, and when they do have their "sex change" they clearly become the person they say they were all along. Trans people beg the whole question of human understanding as it currently is about gender and sex. Taking that challenge, over the past fifty years, the transsexual/transgender community through writing and theorizing has attempted to offer an "insider's" exploration of the ways in which trans people view gender issues. As this work progresses trans people have been among the first to acknowledge that gender, as we know it, is not a clear-cut issue.

Historically, gender, as a word, used to refer exclusively to an aspect of language (for instance the pronouns "he" and "she"). The change from referring to sex (biology) as gender (social role), to referring to gender as a set of social and cultural constructions came in the 1950s. Originally, the theory came about as part of the medical lexicon surrounding the treatment of intersex people. However it has not remained in the medical world, nor was it intended to. In the 1970s feminists and scholars appropriated the term to refer to "the social organization of the relationship between the sexes." Consequently nearly all of us now know that gender is clearly a separate entity from sex.

Part of the appeal of gender and gender identity theory is its contention that all of us have a gender identity and that it is somehow detachable from biological sex. But despite that understanding, "normal" development is still defined as congruent sexual anatomy and gender identity. To be gendered in "opposition" to one's sex is therefore a problem for society, despite the fact that sex and gender are, in the context of the modern world, analytically distinct.

Yet despite that analytical difference, sex and gender are still tangled together within the systems we use to organize our social world. When considering "sex" we group people according to whether someone has a vagina, breasts, ovaries, and so on, or a penis, testes, and so on. We maintain these distinctions in order to significantly reduce the potential pitfalls of what social gender roles people are supposed to play. Your place in society, your opportunity to join the women's luncheon group, the men's pool club, and a lot of other social positions become based on what you've got, and what you've not got. However the reality of people's bodies and people's real lives are not that easy. As science advances and our understandings of the complexities of the human body grow, in 2002 medicine recognizes over eighty intersex conditions as well as that there are real, sane, ordinary people who are transgender and transsexual. In truth, men and women take all sorts of forms, not just visibly—that is whether you are short or tall, fat or thin, blue eyed or brown eyed, but sex as a biological category needs far more categories other than those of "man" and "woman."

It is the same with gender. It is one thing to say someone has a vagina or a penis, it is another thing to assume that person is either female, feminine, or a woman. So what is gender and therefore gender identity? Gender as a conceptual idea aims to help us answer the question: "Am I a man or a woman or something else entirely?" Most of us do not think about this very much. We tend to let gender assignment (the label we were given at birth by a midwife who noted whether we had a penis or not) stand in for our gender identity. And we feel inadequate or confused on those occasions when we discover we do not feel very happy about the person we are expected to be in order to fit that label. But actually, our identity (and its gender) is personal; it's what we feel our gender to be at any given moment. This feeling may be influenced by biological factors that have a cultural tag sticking out of them. The feeling of being some gender might also have to do with sexual fantasy, or a preference for some role. There are as many good reasons for identifying with a gender label as there are people, but feeling comfortable when reconciling what is expected of you and what you desire is at the root of most of them. Our need to feel comfortable, and not to challenge or be challenged by our gender, will affect our life plans in many ways.

In the real world, outside of the antiseptic smelling corridors of the hospital, trans people are working at the raw coalface of the concept of identification. But it is against all the odds: the rigidity of a set of historical and cultural assumptions concerning sex-roles that pervades all discussion of gender—that the two, sex and gender, have an incorruptible sameness that makes them all pervasive. Yet gender, sex, and sexual orientation are fundamentally different for the trans community. We face the everyday reality of that difference in our lives, and our attempts to reconcile it have led to it being challenged in many unanticipated ways. We have moved to expressing a theory in which gender and sex roles are clearly separated (at least for a large number of people). What that means to the modernist view of gender theory is a challenge the trans community is not ignoring, nor is it prepared to come up with trite self-serving answers. Challenging our own sense of self, looking inward to find who we are, using the process of autobiography that we know so well, is producing some very interesting answers that challenge the very binary structure of the complacent world in which gender was invented, and by which it has become obsessed.

This book is a continuation of that process. It is not about justification, but it is an attempt at exploration and explanation. Sex and gender diverse people did not invent gender, yet they are experts in gender and what it means. This collection should lead the reader to understand that gender is merely a word to signify a concept of the human imagination that belongs within and supports the foundations of a patriarchal framework in which many, especially women, are daily oppressed. But the world outside the transgender world can take heart when they fail to understand what is going on. The fact is that within the sex and gender diverse communities there is no hidden answer as to what gender is. However there are answers to how it is experienced and what those experiences mean, and this collection should lead you further into the truths that come from that.

February 2003   STEPHEN WHITTLE

Dedicated to Vincent Keter (lawyer)

Vincent fought for many years in a case of sex discrimination that Tracie O'Keefe brought against several psychotherapists in the United Kingdom, after they attempted to halt the progress of her career when she came out as a transsexual woman in 1997. The effects of the discrimination were devastating to the lives of Tracie and her partner, Katrina, and Vincent went far beyond the call of duty in helping win the case and deliver justice. For his efforts, we are both eternally grateful.

ACKNOWLEDGMENTS

WE WANT TO THANK those people who have contributed their true-life stories. It has been a privilege working with them, and our admiration goes out to them. We are honored that they trusted us to deliver their stories to you, the reader.

Thank you to the many people throughout the international sex and gender diverse community who passed on e-mails, letters, and announcements that enabled us to get in contact with the contributors in the first place.

We would like to thank our publisher, Jossey-Bass, and in particular Amy Scott, who had the foresight to want to publish this specialist book. Thank you to them for their enthusiasm and for going bravely into the night and having the nerve to trust us with a small but ever-growing light.

Finally, we'd like to thank Xena and Gabrielle, our two cats, who let us know when we'd spent far too long hunched over in front of the computer screen, by walking across the keyboard, meowing, and looking cute.

Sydney, Australia
January 2003

TRACIE O'KEEFE, DCH
KATRINA FOX

Be all the positive things that you can be . . .
whatever they turn out to be.

Wonder at what you have become . . . again . . .
and again . . . and again.

Never ask anyone else to feel your pain for you
. . . only to share your good fortune.

Remember . . . life becomes the blessing you turn
it into.

INTRODUCTION

WHEN WE WERE APPROACHED to edit this book, we were thrilled. Why? Because we realized just how much the times really are changing in a positive way for so many sex and gender diverse people—that is, for those who identify as being transsexual, transgender, intersex, androgynous, or without any sex or gender identity.

This encouraging development is part of a growing political movement akin to that of women's and gay liberation in the 1970s. In the 1990s the seeds of sex and gender activism began to grow, as the Internet united those whose sex and gender identity falls outside the average male-female in a way never seen before. Websites, chat rooms, and e-mail helped begin to dissolve cultural and geographical boundaries, as previously small and sometimes isolated groups of people who challenge society's norms began to communicate, discuss, explore, and redefine themselves in positive terms. No longer willing to stay quietly in the background, often perceived as "freaks" or "perverts" unworthy of basic human rights, sex and gender diverse people all over the world began educating, campaigning, and lobbying to attain those rights.

As members of the sex and gender diverse community have become more visible and vocal, their increasing numbers have inspired others to come out in the sex and gender identity they feel is right for them. These are exciting times. The twenty-first century is seeing a proliferation of newly emerging identities, such as "spansexual" and "metagender." We are also rediscovering that third and fourth genders were acknowledged in many cultures in the past.

So who are sex and gender diverse people, and what kind of backgrounds do they come from? They come from all walks of life. In the book we meet people who are young and old, from a variety of ethnic and social backgrounds. They are someone's mother, father, daughter, son, friend, brother, sister, or work colleague—they could even be your next-door neighbor. In their own words, they share with us their feelings, emotions, opinions, and experiences on what it means to be different—to challenge some of society's most basic and fundamental norms. Some of the authors believe they were born "trapped in the wrong body" and have felt compelled to undergo surgery to physically alter their bodies to fit with the sex or gender identity they believe themselves to be; others were born with ambiguous genitalia, sex organs, or characteristics associated with their opposite sex; still others are sex and gender explorers.

When we put out an international appeal for contributions to this book, we were bowled over by the number and quality of stories we received. Many of the authors have never written anything before, and for some, English is not their first language. Their enthusiasm, pride, and achievement in making history by contributing their stories in this way matched our own joy at being part of such an important and groundbreaking work in the field of sex and gender.

You may laugh, cry, or be amazed as you read these stories, but you are sure to gain a sense of wonder, fascination, empathy, and inspiration. The heartfelt stories teach us to open our minds to the wondrous possibilities of sex and gender difference and how it can enrich our own lives. The stories also teach us about tolerance and respect for difference and offer us a window of understanding into the world of sex and gender diversity.

You don't need to have sex or gender "issues" to appreciate this book—it is for anyone who has even the remotest interest in human nature, as well as for clinicians, academics, employers, and the families and friends of sex and gender diverse people. Definitions of many of the terms used in this book can be found in the glossary at the beginning.

A book such as this would have been virtually impossible to put together ten years ago. The sex and gender diverse community had not gained the sense of pride it is now beginning to have, and those willing to share their stories would have been few and far between. What's more, no major publisher would have been interested in the idea. The 1990s saw a profusion of literature on the theories of sex and gender, as well as a smattering of autobiographies. But now we feel that it's time for something radically different.

So here is an extraordinary book and the first of its kind—an anthology of real-life stories told by a wide range of sex and gender diverse people in their own words, with no academic rhetoric or theory. That's right, just the stories. We made a conscious choice not to analyze or comment on the stories in the book, but simply to let them stand in their own right. We think it's about time for those who have often been pathologized by the medical profession, demonized by mainstream society, and ignored by lawmakers for years to speak their truths for themselves.

Reading this book will be a life-changing experience. You will never again be able to view humanity in terms of only male and female. You will be left with a sense of wonder at how inventive, adaptive, resourceful, and adventurous sex and gender diversity is. And as more people tell their stories of sex and gender diversity and teach us about themselves, perhaps we can all reeducate ourselves, dissolve our prejudices, embrace our diversity, and not be afraid of difference but remain in awe of its occurrence.

This is also a healing book—as the authors tell us their stories, we can be part of their journeys to self-acceptance and join the celebration of their lives. Come with us to learn, be inspired, laugh, cry, and appreciate these wonderful, courageous people and their journeys to be their true selves.

GLOSSARY

ALTHOUGH IT IS ACKNOWLEDGED by the editors that sex and gender diversity is much broader than the male-female bipolar model, some of the terms in this glossary have been defined within the confines of this model and therefore can be explained only in reference to it.

Anarcho Anarchist

Androgyne An androgynous person—someone who considers themselves to be both male and female. It can also mean someone who identifies as neuter.

BDSM Bondage/domination/sadomasochism.

Bondage Refers in this context to the consensual sexual practice where a person's movements are restricted and restrained. They can be bound, gagged, or trussed up in various ways.

Boston Marriage In the 19th century, this term was used for households where two women lived together, independent of any male support. Some of these relationships may have been sexual and others may not. Today, the term is sometimes used for lesbian relationships where two women live together but do not have sexual relations.

Crossdresser *See* Transvestite.

Domination (Dom) Domination, when used in its sexual context, refers to dominant and submissive role-play between two or more people. The shortened version "dom" can also mean a person who is dominant.

Fetish A fixation on an unusual idea. Someone with a fetish may have a sexual attraction to inanimate objects or unusual sexual practices.

FTM Female-to-male. Used as a noun, an FTM usually means a female-to-male transsexual.

Gender dysphoria (or Gender Identity Disorder) A sense of profound disturbance or unhappiness about one's gender identity.

GLBT Gay/lesbian/bisexual/transgender.

Hir Pronoun used by some people who identify outside the male-female spectrum, instead of *his* or *her*.

Intersex Someone who considers themselves to be in between the sexes. This term can refer to a person who is born with sex chromosomes, external genitalia, or an internal reproductive system that is not considered to be society's norm for either male or female. However, some sex and gender diverse people not born with obvious physical differences may also use the term to describe themselves.

LGBT Lesbian/gay/bisexual/transgender.

Metagender Someone who identifies as neither male nor female. Such a person also does not identify as being both male and female or as neuter. This is a new term that refers to a gender identity outside any current definitions.

MTF Male-to-female. Used as a noun, an MTF usually means a male-to-female transsexual.

Queer This term used to be a synonym for *homosexual*, but has now broadened to encompass anyone who believes they have a variant or interesting sex, gender, or sexual identity or who engages in sexual practices outside what is considered to be society's norm.

Sadomasochism (SM or S/M) Consensual sexual practices involving the taking and the relinquishing of power. They may include some or all of the following: the giving and receiving of pain, torture, domination of one person over another, ritual humiliation, and bondage. A person who inflicts these things on another is known as a sadist or "top," and the person receiving them is known as a masochist or "bottom" or "sub" (short for submissive). The term is often used as part of the acronym BDSM (bondage, domination, sadomasochism).

Separatist Someone who favors separation, especially for political or religious reasons. During the women's liberation movement of the 1970s, some lesbians chose to live and work in women-only environments, severing all ties with male family members, friends, and colleagues.

Sex positive Someone who is positive about sex. In the context of this book, a sex positive feminist is one who is not anti-sex. In the women's liberation movement of the 1970s, some feminists were against sex, particularly heterosexual sex, as it was seen as colluding with the enemy. Many were and some still are also against erotica and pornography and lesbian couples' use of sex toys. The term *sex positive* was coined by women who considered themselves to be feminists but who had an open attitude to sex and didn't want to be associated with the connotations of the word *feminist* on its own.

Sex reassignment or realignment surgery (SRS)   A surgical procedure that transforms a person's primary sex organs into the appearance of those of their opposite biological sex. Vaginoplasty and labiaplasty refer to the creation of a neo-vagina and neo-labia respectively; phalloplasty refers to the construction of a neo-penis, and metaoidioplasty refers to surgical enhancement of a clitoris.

She-male   Someone who identifies as between male and female, or as both male and female. The term generally refers to people born as biological males who later take on the appearance of females, sometimes through hormones, surgery, or both.

Sie, s/he, or zie   Pronouns used by some people who identify outside the male-female spectrum, instead of *he* or *she*.

SM   *See* Sadomasochism.

Transgender (TG)   This term can refer to someone who identifies as a member of their original biological sex but who, through hormones, surgery, or both, takes on the appearance of the opposite biological sex. It can also refer to someone who believes they live between the genders. The word is also used in some cases as an umbrella term to cover the whole of the trans community, but this can be offensive to some people, especially many transsexuals.

Trans man or trans woman   One who lives across the bipolar gender barrier from their original biological sex. The terms can refer to both transsexual and transgendered people.

Transsexual (TS)   A person who may begin life as one biological sex, but believes they are of the opposite sex. A transsexual person may attempt to transform their physical appearance into that of the sex they believe they are. They may undergo hormonal treatment and several surgeries to bring their body in line with their self-image. Transsexuals are often referred to as male-to-female (MTF) if they were born biologically male, or female-to-male (FTM) if they were born biologically female.

Transvestite or crossdresser (TV)   A person who dresses in clothes generally associated with their opposite biological sex, as defined by socially acceptable norms. An erotic transvestite is someone who gets sexually excited by wearing the clothes, whereas a social transvestite simply feels more comfortable wearing them.

Zie   See *Sie*.

FINDING THE REAL ME

PARADOX IS PARADISE FOR ME

Cynthya BrianKate

IT'S SO HARD COMING UP WITH WORDS for this book. I guess that's fitting, considering how hard most people find it to find words to describe me. I just don't fit the labels and categories most people use for things like gender. I'm not exactly a man or a woman; I'm somewhere in between, a bit of both and neither at the same time. Many people find this a paradox, a contradiction. We're taught to "stay in the lines" and that there's always a "simple, logical explanation" for anything. Well, that's not real life. What makes us who we are—our thoughts, feelings, emotions, and identities—are not simple, one-dimensional line graphs. We can have conflicting feelings, we can love someone and yet hate them, we can believe and yet not have complete faith, we can be sure of something and yet not be sure. People are not just all hot or cold, bad or good, total sunshine or total eclipse. That includes gender, and certainly includes my gender. I'm somewhere between or outside man or woman, and my body is too. And that may confuse a lot of people, but I'm totally happy with the way I've turned out, as are some really good friends and one potential partner. I like being confusing and hard to define. I like being not exactly this or that, one thing or another. To me, paradox is paradise.

Like my name: "Is that your real name?" people often ask. It's real to me, even if I made it myself. My mother named me Brian. I've always loved the name Kate, so I wondered, "Why can't I use that name too?" I ended up combining the two to make BrianKate. As for Cynthya, that goes back to my childhood. As a child of the 1980s who's always wanted to be and look as unusual as possible, I naturally fell in love with Cyndi Lauper. I used to dance and sing along with *Girls Just Wanna Have Fun* every day. And I certainly have a really strange fashion sense that most people describe as "something out of a Cyndi Lauper nightmare." I've always looked up to her because she's always been herself and has never tried to be mainstream. So I felt like naming myself after her . . . until I started feeling too unoriginal. So to take back some individuality, I dropped the "I" altogether—isn't that ironic? So I've made a name that's part boy, part girl, part I don't know what, but all me.

I don't think I can honestly say, "When I was a little boy . . ." or "When I was a little girl . . . ," as I never felt like either, even when I was little. My parents should've figured something out when I made them buy me the Miss Piggy puppet. I mean, my first toy was a girl played by a man . . . gee, no clues there. I would've loved to play with Barbie had I been given any of the dolls. At least I had plenty of aliens to play with; I've always been a science fiction junkie. This is how I got my first skirt, from my mom, at age six. For Halloween I'd picked this furry alien warrior mask, so my mom made what she figured an alien berserker would wear, not realizing that what she'd intended as either fur or animal skins ended up as a long skirt I kept tripping over. (It took me a few years to learn how to walk in one!)

Not Like Other Kids

I'd known I wasn't like the other kids as early as age four. While I played with my Darth Vader figure, I fell in love with the color of his lightsaber, magenta, which is still my favorite color. I knew I was expected, as a boy, not to like colors like pink and magenta. I saw that boys were expected to like certain things, such as cars and sports, and girls were expected to like other things, such as dolls and dressing up. When I was (expected to be) a little boy, I didn't feel like one, and I sure wasn't raised to know how to be a little girl. I've never known exactly what it means to feel like either. And I knew all this, even at age four while playing with Darth Vader's magenta weapons.

Growing up on Long Island, New York, I didn't know anyone who didn't seem to be all girl or all boy. I certainly knew nobody like me in my family. I was too afraid of other kids' reactions to ask them what they felt about themselves. Even in the media, I saw only those talk shows where people referred to themselves as "trapped in the wrong body." That wasn't me—I didn't feel anything "wrong" about being born with a penis, and the only things I felt trapped by were the expectations of how I "had to" act because I had one. I didn't want to get rid of my penis, so I didn't consider myself transsexual. The only other word I knew of—

transvestite—only covered the fact that I liked wearing dresses. It didn't seem to include my not feeling like a boy or a girl. Back then I knew nobody who seemed anything at all like me, which is funny, considering I had every Boy George album and lived two miles, though I didn't know it then, from the local *Rocky Horror Picture Show* theater.

It wasn't easy to make it through school. I got harassed and attacked from elementary to high school. I've never been into sports, always preferring books, so I was smarter than my enemies, but they were bigger, stronger, or sneakier. And even when I tried "being a boy," I didn't know enough about the role. So I got taunted, slammed into lockers, and kicked in the crotch a lot. I was even getting tormented for listening to the Pet Shop Boys—at the time I didn't even know the lead singer was gay, and I still don't get what the big deal was.

This kept up until around tenth or eleventh grade. Then half the football team realized they were friends with my brother, and the other half wanted to protect me because I was nice to them. I also had some large, scary girls who loved to fight on my side. One of them even asked me to the prom. I wish I'd had the courage to go with her—she might have even let me wear her dress.

The first time I heard anybody besides myself thinking about this was in twelfth grade. A girl in science class suddenly asked, "Any of you ever think of what it would be like to be the other sex?" The others just laughed it off, so I was too afraid of jeopardizing my newfound safety by discussing the issue with her, but I realized that somebody else at least thinks about this stuff. Which meant I wasn't the only person ever to not feel like what was expected of a boy or girl.

The first time I told anybody was during my first year of college. Jill, a friend from a history class, took me on a trip to a park for her photography class. We'd been talking about how phony MTV's appropriation of "grunge" music was, and then she said that Kennedy, an annoying MTV hostess, "always has perfect hair and makeup, and if they really wanted it to be a 'grunge' show they'd have a male host in a dress." I told her I'd been waiting for someone to be open to playing with gender. She was so supportive! I didn't even feel nervous talking about it all to her, even though I'd never opened my mouth to a single person before. She told me, "It's so sad that up until now you had to hide your feelings, it's like you were trapped in a huge iron ball." Which I had been until I found the courage to talk to her.

A semester later I met Lenore, my almost-first girlfriend, who gave me a lot more encouragement—hell, she even gave me my first pair of fishnet stockings and half her makeup collection. She even dressed me up like

Courtney Love and took pictures. She was a really great friend. I wish I
could have convinced her to leave her abusive boyfriend.

Around the time I knew Lenore, I told my mother about the whole gender thing. As she'd raised me on old sci-fi movies, I waited until we were
watching *Rodan*. I just turned toward her and said, "Uh . . . there's something I wanna tell you about . . ." And then told her in whatever words I
could find at the time. When I was done, she said, "Well at least you're
not hopping from bed to bed like your brother used to—just don't expect
anyone in the family to like it." She's been supportive, though she still
doesn't seem that happy to see her "youngest boy" in dresses and makeup.

I told my mother; a childhood ex-friend told my father. This girl I'd
known since I was eight or so goes running home to tell her whole family: "Guess what, I saw Brian all dressed up like Wednesday Addams, with
fishnets and everything," knowing full well this news would go right to
my family. I don't think it was any of her bloody business to tell anyone,
especially not to tell my family; especially what with all the arguments I
had with my father over my gender. I should have had the right to tell him
myself, rather than come home to that. At least my father and I are finally
starting to get along a lot more on this, though I don't think any of my
relatives get any of it.

Queer Youth

In my final semester of my first college I met Tracy, who took me to my
first queer youth center, which seemed great until I realized it was just gay
and lesbian rather than gay, lesbian, bisexual, and transgendered. I've
noticed this almost everywhere I've gone. Gay and lesbian groups seem
to sell themselves as LGBT or GLBT to seem more inclusive, but all the
added letters and titles in the world don't mean a thing if there are no services or groups, or even any significant numbers of people to represent
transgender people. It wasn't even that the center I went to was unfriendly
or hostile or anything like that. They just never did much on gender, never
had any real group for it (unless you count something that folded inside
of a week or two), and after a while they became "up to age twenty-one
only." Which makes no sense to me. Youth doesn't end at twenty-one. I
don't think I'm old just because I'm going to be twenty-six soon, though
I'm made to feel that way when everything I see for youth ends at twenty-
one. Like that old band Menudo—the one that kicked members out when
they turned sixteen. Even most gay youth I've seen don't seem to come
out until they've survived high school, which leaves what, four years until
you're too old. And as for trans youth, I don't know too many. I've a cou-

ple friends within a year or two of me, but most people I've met don't seem to figure out who they are on these issues until they're at least thirty or so.

Recently I saw renowned transgender author Kate Bornstein, who told me, "You're a lot further along than I was at your age—a whole lot." And it took me until I was nineteen to tell anyone else, let alone be anywhere near totally open about myself. At least before the youth center I went to got to be too ageist, I met a wonderful exception.

My friend Jamie "came out" at age seventeen, on the Sally Jessy Raphael show, no less. I met her just as I was going to give up on finding anybody openly gender-whatever on Long Island when she showed up at some Hawaiian theme party at the youth center. She thought I was "another angry young dyke" because of my Wednesday Addams dress, shredded fishnets, and combat boots. I saw her and thought she was the most ambiguous-looking person I'd ever seen. I somehow managed to go talk to her, and we knew that night that we'd be good friends, and we were right, as we're now sisters.

Right after I met her, my father tried pushing me to go out with her. We gave her a ride home during a storm and he tried making me do the whole chivalry thing of "open her door, help her out, look for puddles"—I'm sure he would have had me throw my flannel shirt over a puddle if there had been one. The whole ride home he told me, "That Lenore's friends are wacko, you should be going out with this girl." Hey, I never identified her as a "real" girl, he just assumed . . . and had a quite rude awakening five months later, screaming, "Ain't no way that's a guy!" Well, he was partly right. Jamie and I tried going out, though it didn't work out, and nothing we did amounted to too much past some (mostly) innocent feeling each other up. Still, we're best friends, and I've learned I'm most attracted to girls who were born guys.

Paradox

OK, I think that's enough of the "journey to where I am" for now, as I'm sure you're screaming, "Where's the whole paradox thing you mentioned?" Here goes.

I was born male, but I'm not a man. In fact, that's half of why it didn't work out romantically between me and Jamie, since she wants a guy, even if he's superfeminine, as long as he identifies as a guy. Just because I've got a penis doesn't mean that I'm a man, or that I should necessarily identify as one. I'm on the feminine side, though I also don't consider myself quite a woman. I was born male and I wear dresses and makeup, but I don't consider myself a transvestite, unless of course I'm at a performance of *Rocky Horror*. In case you haven't figured it out, especially if you haven't seen pictures of me (plenty on my homepage!), I can be much like Dr. Frank-N-Furter (the "sweet transvestite from transsexual Transylvania") when I feel like it. And for me, wearing either girls' or guys' clothes might be seen as crossdressing, since I don't really feel like either.

I don't see myself as a drag queen, though I have done some drag performance. Last year I was on a stage lip-synching to Jayne County, a transsexual punk rock star, singing Shania Twain's *Man I Feel Like a Woman* (like we didn't see that coming!) while dancing in a sequined dress and spinning a television aerial on a cowgirl hat. The performance is drag, and while I'm doing the performance it's drag, but I don't see myself as a drag queen. I usually get "all dolled up" just because I feel like looking pretty, and usually my performances are more about my material than my costume.

I don't know if "transsexual" applies either; I know the word doesn't fit me the way most people use it. I don't feel like "the opposite" sex— what's the opposite of me? I don't feel like a guy, and I don't feel like I'm going to be a woman. The only way "transsexual" applies is the way Kate Bornstein uses it, which is to include something like "anyone who does anything that breaks the accepted rules for gender."

I'm attracted to girls mostly, but the girls that do the most for me are the ones who were born boys. With me, gay or straight doesn't quite work. I'm somewhere in between guy and girl, and I go for girls who were born guys. I'm perfectly happy with my sexuality, though it confuses the living daylights out of people whose idea of attraction is based around opposite sex or same sex—now *that* would confuse me.

I'm not even sure if I'm male, female, or what. As I said, I was born with a penis, and don't feel like having anything done to it. Imagine my surprise about five years ago when out of nowhere I started growing breasts! I never expected to get them, so it was kind of scary. And it wasn't exactly painless. My chest just started throbbing, and my nipples started feeling like they were pushing outward. My friend Delilah says I was acting "like you had PMS" at the time, and she was as worried as I was when she saw me start grabbing at my chest. I was relieved, if confused, when soon after my shirts started bending out at the sides. Nothing was wrong with me . . . just really unexpected. I like my breasts—if anything I'm quite vain about them, especially since they've grown a bit since then, and I'm now somewhere between an A and a B.

So the question is whether I'm male, female, intersex, or what. I have no idea, because I've never looked into finding out. Maybe I will, just to find out what went right. I don't know what my hormone levels are, though I'm pretty hairy all over, and as I said I grew breasts. I don't know anything about my genetic makeup, chromosomes, or whatever. So the jury is still out as to which sex I am, because I could care less about supplying evidence.

I don't really care as much as people might think about finding out what I am. Why should I? I'm me. Whether I've got more estrogen, more testosterone, or if my chromosomes are XY, XX, or anything else doesn't matter. If I'm this or that, boy, girl, or whatever, it doesn't change my personality, doesn't change who I am. So it may seem contradictory, but I just don't really care that much about my biological sex. I'd rather live as I am and enjoy being me than try to figure out the reason I'm such a contradiction of not-quite-man-but-not-quite-woman. I care a lot less about theories of what gender is than I care about real life, my life as someone who doesn't fit the gender system. I'm not as concerned with why I'm neither as with how I'm treated because I'm neither.

I think a lot of people don't know what to make of someone like me, someone who isn't one gender or the other. To them it's just too much of a contradiction, too much of a paradox, since to them I "can't be both." And I don't know why, but things can still be pretty scary for me because these people don't see me. Instead of seeing me as a person, they see me as just a gender, and one that they're not used to or ready to handle. And that's the problem, that these people don't see me as a person. So they either want sex with me just because I'm so "exotic," or they want to banish me from their little universe, even if that means hurting or killing me.

Dangerous Liaisons

I've had at least five attempts made on my life in the past five years. The first two took place in broad daylight, in the middle of the afternoon, in the very park I used to go to for family picnics. The first time, me and this butch girl were jumped by mountain bikers because they couldn't deal with a "girl who looked like a guy" walking with a "guy who looked like a girl." That attack was funny because they didn't look where they were going and crashed into each other like something out of a 1950s sitcom. The second time, Jamie and I were attending a gay and lesbian picnic put on by the youth center where we met. Get that, we were attacked by bikers at a gay and lesbian picnic, who screamed "get the faggots"—couldn't they at least get their insults right? That's the point: they didn't see us, they only saw what they had been taught to hate. We escaped them by diving through thorn bushes.

The third time, a gang chased us through the streets of our hometown for the crime of walking as we are without fear, because they were afraid of us, because they saw us as posing some vague threat (I still don't see how) to their precious "manhood," though any real man wouldn't have to terrorize people to feel like a man. That was the closest I've come to actually dying just for my gender: they threw a bottle at us that almost smashed my head open—Jamie felt it whistle through her hair.

A couple of years ago at my school I interrupted a rape in the parking lot, and the guy tried attacking me. While that wasn't strictly a trans bashing, it certainly was a gender bashing, because he wanted to hurt or kill me because I wouldn't allow him to hurt the girl. The most recent incident involved some friends and I being chased by a carload of stupid teens who couldn't find anything better to do with their night, making me wonder if "freak" and "queer" bashing might not be replacing baseball as America's favorite pastime. And these are just the times I know about.

Some people have tried to hurt or kill me; others try to have sex with me, whether or not I want it. It seems like I can't check my e-mail or work on my homepage without having to get rid of some guy obsessed with having sex with me. Since they know nothing about people who aren't one gender or another, they put my gender into the realm of the exotic. And since so many people are still so ashamed of their gay or bisexual desires, sex with a genderqueer or transgender person reassures these men, because they can say, "I'm not really gay because it wasn't really a man."

Some of my friends have been raped by men like that for the forbidden allure of "trannie sex." I was almost raped a couple of years ago. I was walking down the street with Jamie when this huge creep grabbed me from an alleyway and tried pulling me into a doorway by my breasts. My childhood love of Miss Piggy helped save me from this thug. I spun around and smashed him with the Miss Piggy "hai-ya!" right through the ribcage and slammed him into a brick wall, then walked calmly on my way. The whole surreal thing played itself out in what seemed like an instant. One second we're walking down the street, next second I'm grabbed, then bam! I smash the creep, and we're on our way. Jamie didn't even see this, it was so fast. It takes longer to tell than it did to happen. This is what we have to worry about, just like any girl has to—as one friend said after the first of several times I had my breasts grabbed: "Now you know what us girls go through."

The Girl of My Dreams

At least I've finally found someone who's attracted to me in a real, romantic, healthy way. She's becoming the girl of my dreams, while she's becoming a girl. I met Lorrie about a year ago. I'd written an article for

Anything That Moves magazine, and she saw it and wrote to the e-mail address I'd included to let me know how much she'd loved it. We started e-mailing each other regularly, then we moved up to instant messaging. Then she sent me the first Valentine I've gotten in thirteen years—a little teddy bear with a sweater saying "e-mail me," which sits right on top of my computer. I certainly hadn't been looking for a long-distance relationship (she's in Michigan and I'm in New York), but that's what we seem to have started. We swapped phone numbers soon after Valentine's Day. Since we're both really into science fiction, and since she'd never been to New York, we agreed to meet up at my present college's sci-fi convention, I-CON. It's a huge convention, but we knew we'd know what each other looked like from our homepages. Just think, someone was interested enough in me to drive seven hundred miles, just to have a date!

Lorrie turned out to be every bit as great as I'd hoped, and we had an amazing date. Things got off to an excellent start. We went to a performance of our favorite musical, *Rocky Horror,* of course; I don't think I'll ever hear the song *Touch-a-Touch-a-Touch Me* the same way again. We spent the entire weekend together checking out the convention and getting to know each other, though she somehow found the time to introduce me to underground horror star Debbie Rochon. And she gave me the most beautiful gift at the end: my first real kiss, something I felt all over. I can't wait until the next time we can get together.

My family's reaction to my relationship with Lorrie is kind of weird. My father met her as he picked me up, and Mr. "I can spot a trans a mile away" still doesn't realize that he's encouraging his kid to go out with one. My mother is "trying to be happy" for me. She's glad I finally had my first date and first real kiss, and that I've found someone. She just doesn't know what to think about my having a girlfriend who was born male, but overall she just wants me to be happy.

And I am happy. I'm happy to have found Lorrie and to have hopefully started my first real relationship with her. I'm happy to have someone who loves me for who I am, and who I can be myself around, without having to have my gender be an issue every minute. And what's best is that I have friends who love me for who I am, like Jamie and Delilah, and a few others, like my friend John. When I'm around them I don't have to worry about whether they have a problem with my gender. With them, I'm just their friend. When I'm with them I can just be me.

Here's the final paradox to do with my gender. I want to create some awareness and education on gender issues, but I don't want to be defined just by my gender. There is so much more to me than just the fact that I'm not a man or a woman. I do things besides just sit here looking pretty and being "diversely gendered."

Obviously I write. Not just stuff like this here essay, I mean poetry, short stories, and anything I can. I've written a short, thirty-minute film, and Lorrie and I are trying to do some collaborative projects. I draw. I'm nowhere near as good at it as my brother, but as he's an art teacher I guess I wouldn't be; still my work is interestingly strange. I occasionally illustrate my writing, though most of my best work can be seen only in my room.

I perform. Mainly this means poetry reading and some occasional comedy. I've done quite a few readings. I read annually at a little gathering called the Be-In, which is a singers/songwriters/poets gathering and the best modern-day hippie party. Recently I played a third of the voices in my friend John's radio play *The XX, XY Files,* a sex spoof of the show *The X-Files.* Not only do I perform poetry, comedy, and whatever at the I-CON, but I'm also going to be joining John next year as Fun Stuff Coordinator, which means that we'll get to pack the performance lists with our own wacky friends and fellow performers, so I guess I'll be on both ends of that one.

I act. I'm taking some acting courses at my college, but I seem to have picked up the basics by acting out bad slasher skits with Jamie. I starred in a music video of hers called *Love, Neutered.* I'm trying to get into filmmaking. I learned my way around a video camera when I helped with the camera work on *Love, Neutered,* and as soon as I can get hold of my own camera I've got some ideas, most of them documentaries. Hey, I could make a ton of projects just off interviewing the people in my life.

I help rescue animals. Between me and my parents, we've helped save anywhere between five hundred and seven hundred animals from all sorts of situations, ranging from people who just had to move, to outright torture. And we've had something like an 80 percent success/survival rate, especially good considering the condition some of them were in. I'm not involved with any organized groups, as I'm looking for one that won't force me to turn vegetarian or else. Right now I have a dog, some rabbits, chinchillas, and hamsters, and I share my room with a hedgehog and a magenta tarantula.

I hope you like this story about me and that it doesn't leave you too confused, though I also hope it isn't too straightforward . . . otherwise where would the fun be?

○

LESSONS OF LIFE

Nero

MY MOM ALWAYS SAYS that we go through lives like lessons. Before we're born, we pick the lesson, and that life is dedicated to teaching ourselves, or teaching someone else. I guess the idea is that once we learn everything we're supposed to know, we get to some kind of heaven, some kind of Nirvana, but until then we're stuck in the repetitive cycle of reincarnation. Personally, I think I slept in the day the Great Karmic Entity passed out assignments.

I'm Nero. I live in Ireland with my mom, my boyfriend, and our cats. I'm a writer, Web designer, and actor, looking for some minimum-wage job to take care of necessities. I smoke too much, stay up too late, and like loud music. I'm obsessed with video games (*StarCraft* is great, and *Final Fantasy*'s the best), comic books (definitely the Sandman series), and movies. Poppy Z Brite, Neil Gaiman, and Charlie Parker are my own personal gods. I love music, everything from Smashing Pumpkins to Mozart, Nine Inch Nails, and the Beatles. My boyfriend and I are writing a book that's going to be the Greatest American Novel some day. And I honestly believe that one day, cats will rule the world. Just your average, not-so-normal, geeky eighteen-year-old boy, full of sarcasm, profound knowledge, and wit.

Except for the fact that I haven't always been a boy. Like being a teenager isn't hard enough, right? Add bisexuality, living in a foreign country, and transsexuality to that, and it seems almost unbearable. Well, sometimes it is, and sometimes it isn't.

I'm one of the lucky ones. I've got a boy who adores me and will do anything to make me happy. My mom's my best friend and always has been. The few friends I've told about being transgendered simply accepted it without question. And I get an entirely new city to be me, the real me. I'm making new friends here. I'm getting identification documents stating me as male, and no one even thinks twice about the American boy walking down the street. I've got a great psychologist who I've been seeing for a few months now, and pretty soon I'm going to start seeing the endocrinologist to start hormone therapy.

Sounds almost perfect, huh? It is, pretty much. It wasn't always like this, though, and despite how easy it seems sometimes, every day is just as hard as the last.

Ireland Versus the United States

OK, let's go back in time a little bit to September 1998. I was fifteen and had just moved to Ireland for the first time. Why did we pack everything up and go to an entirely different country? I'm still not sure exactly why, although life in small-town West Virginia wasn't so great for my mom and me. I was unhappy, there weren't any jobs for her, and generally, I think we needed a change. Mom had fallen in love with Ireland, and thus we boarded a plane, all worldly possessions strapped on our backs or in suitcases, and flew across the Atlantic. The move didn't really seem to make me any happier, so four months later, I flew back to the United States to live with my father and finish up my freshman year.

That, in short, was a disaster. We didn't get along at all. He didn't allow me as many freedoms as Mom, and treated me like a much younger person, rather than someone capable of making my own decisions. By summer break, I couldn't stand being near him anymore, and once again boarded a plane and flew back to Ireland, where I spent my entire sophomore year from 1999 to 2000.

School has always been a problem for me. I'm just one of those people the educational system isn't designed to accommodate. For as long as I can remember, school has always been extremely tedious and a waste of time for me, despite random teachers trying to encourage me by giving me extra assignments or special projects to work on. The Irish school system was no different, and by the time I finished my sophomore year, the prospect of another two years of schooling made me seriously consider dropping out. I didn't really want to do that, since I've always been a little too ambitious, and I honestly enjoy learning, so once again, I decided to go back to the United States and connive every means possible to graduate in one more year, which was something I just couldn't do in Ireland.

So, in spring 2000 I moved back in with my father, once again enrolled in high school, and set about meeting with the principal and secondary education coordinator to facilitate my early graduation. The principal didn't want me to graduate early, and even told me it was illegal for me to do so. The secondary education coordinator, however, believed different and made the decision that I would, in fact, be allowed to graduate early, provided that I fulfill all requirements for my graduating class, which, because of a new bill, were slightly different than those for the graduating class above me.

I got a summer job working at a folk arts center and used the money I earned to buy my first car. The situation with my father was even more stressful than it had been before, and my car was a necessity to maintaining my sanity. I started my junior year of high school, which was the equivalent of a semester, or four months, at seventeen, and continued the battle between my high school and the board of education over whether or not I would graduate at the end of the year.

Branching Out on My Own

Everything seemed to be in place and heading in the right direction, until November 2000. At 2:00 A.M. on Thanksgiving Day, my mother called from Ireland to tell me my uncle had died suddenly and she needed to get to the United States immediately. Two days later, my father and I picked her up at the airport.

With her help, I was able to move out of my father's house and into my own apartment. I got a job working at the burger place Wendy's after school and began looking forward to the new semester, when I would no longer be a junior, but among the ranks of seniors.

Everything around me felt right, but I still felt out of place. Throughout my entire remembering life, I'd always identified as male, though I'd never really told anyone this, not even my mother. At first I'd thought I was just crazy—that no one else felt like this, and for whatever reason, there was something wrong with me. Through the Internet, I'd managed to scrape up a small bit of information about other guys in my situation (female-to-male transsexuals or FTMs). I discovered two things: first, I wasn't alone, and second, the amount of information on FTMs is incredibly limited compared to our counterparts, male-to-females, let alone the fact that there's very little readily accessible information on transsexuals in general.

So, I knew I wasn't some sort of freak. That was nice, but what was I going to do next? At the time, I lived in small-town West Virginia and didn't have many friends to begin with. When it came right down to it, I had only two I really trusted—Megan and Jay, both of whom I'd known for five or six years and had increasingly confusing relationships with. I wasn't sure if I wanted to go through with the whole transitioning process then; it'd be hard and expensive and painful, emotionally as well as physically. All I knew was that my body and my self were two entirely different creatures, so I started referring to them as such. There was the "girl," the physical, superficial persona, and then there was Nero, embodiment of all personality, intelligence, and emotion. My close friends took my divided personality as just another quirk. I always was the weird one. So, gradually my confidence grew, and I started dropping even more obvious hints.

Telling My Best Friends

During December 2000 I mustered my courage and told Megan and Jay the truth. Maybe because Megan was bisexual, maybe because she spent more time with me, maybe a million other reasons, I don't know, but with her, it was OK. Jay, on the other hand, was a disaster waiting to happen. I told him and he flipped out. He told me I was crazy, evil, not real, and any other variant on those themes he could think of. Obviously that was pretty much the end of our relationship. For me, his reaction symbolized the foretold reaction of every other person I trusted and cared for. I pulled back from all my friends and kept myself and my little secret locked away in my own personal hell. I didn't want anyone else to get close to me. I convinced myself no one could ever love me, and if anyone found out, I'd always be alone. I became increasingly depressed, and that's putting it mildly. It was also around this time, January 2001, that Mom had to return to Ireland. I still hadn't had the courage to confide any of this to her and, as had become my habit, tried to pretend it didn't exist.

In February, just two months after telling Jay, I planned out my suicide. It seemed so incredibly simple. Just go to school one day, go to work after, make a quick run to the supermarket, and come home and die. I didn't feel anything or really think about it, except in the most basic terms. I could've been running to pick up milk or crackers for all I cared. I didn't do any of it, though, and you know what? It turned out pretty good, considering.

Why didn't I do it? Hmm. Well, I'm sure there are a million reasons why people change their minds about suicide at the last minute, but I don't think any of them apply to me. The Great Karmic Entity running my life had other plans—it's as simple as that. All right, we'll backtrack a little bit.

Nik

The day after Valentine's Day, 2001. The day when Nero's going to die. The day Nik decided to run away. Nik was a new boy who had started going to our high school in the beginning of February 2001. He was perfect—beautiful, intelligent, gothy, gay. I loved him from the first time I ever saw him. Immediately, the dynamic duo that was Megan and I became a trio, and school became synonymous with Nik. I skipped classes to see him, got cigarettes and lighters for him whenever I could, hung around after senior bell just to talk to him. If Nik wasn't around, I wasn't interested.

The combination of a chance conversation before last period, the advantage of having my own car and my own apartment, and Nik desperately wanting to get out of his situation, and suddenly I had a new roommate and all thoughts of suicide were forgotten. Everything happened so quickly after that. The day after his great escape, Nik said, "Y'know, it's kinda ironic, but I think I'm falling for you," and before the weekend was over, I had a boyfriend.

It took a while for reality to set in. Nik was dealing with falling for a "girl"; I was dealing with whether to tell him about my transsexuality or not. I wanted to tell him I wasn't really a girl. I wanted to tell the whole world I wasn't really a girl—Nik more than anyone, but I didn't have the vaguest idea how. The idea terrified me. After all, who could love me?

In the end, I didn't have to. That year during spring break, I went to Ireland to visit my mother, and Nik stayed at the apartment. While I was gone, he found Internet links to FTM resource pages on my computer. Before asking me about it, he asked Megan, presuming that she would know the answer to his question: "Is Nero transsexual?"

Nik didn't say anything about it until I got back. It was the simplest conversation I've ever had about being transsexual. He told me what he'd found, what he'd asked Megan, and that she'd told him I was transsexual. He told me I didn't have to talk about it if I didn't want to, or wasn't ready, but that he'd like to know. So I told him the truth, and he said the one magic phrase that made everything seem possible: "Well, that explains a lot."

The Parent Trap

My parents . . . I think out of everyone, telling your parents something like this is the hardest. You love them and hate them, fear them and fear for them. They made you; they've known you your entire life. They're supposed to know you better than anyone. And in five seconds, you can completely turn their world upside down.

My dad still hasn't got it. I've had the same conversation with him a hundred times, and it never gets through. But you know what? That doesn't bother me. Well, OK, maybe a little. But in the great scheme of things, what my dad thinks isn't all that important to me. He's back in the United States, so I don't have to deal with him much, and never face-to-face. We're not close and haven't been since I was a little kid. I've had a while to get used to the idea of my father not being in my life.

Mom was a different story. I was terrified of telling her. I was so scared she'd hate me, or yell at me, or . . . I don't know what else. I think mostly I was afraid she'd be disappointed in me, and that is something I never could bear. Anyone else can think what they want, but disappointing my mother has always been able to break me. My great solution was to get really drunk one night and send off an e-mail to Ireland, telling her rather incoherently about being FTM. I wouldn't recommend it for any of you considering that particular option.

I ended up having to tell her again, sober and in person when Nik and I moved to Ireland at the beginning of 2002. Not knowing what else to do, I basically just threw the situation at her without much of an explanation. Needless to say, this also was not a very good approach. She didn't take it well at first. She was angry, scared, frustrated, confused. She thought somehow it was her fault, and everything she read only confirmed that fear. In every way she could, she resisted accepting this as real.

Where I'm at Now

Back to the present . . . June 2002. Well, Mom gets the pronoun right about half the time. She's joined a couple of mailing lists for parents, although, like me, she's discovering there aren't many resources for someone in her situation. She gets excited with me and is interested in what I'm doing, the people I'm meeting in similar situations. She's adapting. Considering she only found out about four months ago, I think she's doing pretty well.

When I think of all the places I could've chosen to transition, Ireland was probably the stupidest place to go. There's one endocrinologist and one psychologist in the entire country, both of whom are a six-hour round-trip train ride from me. There are no legal provisions in terms of rights and protection against discrimination for transsexuals, and only recently was a provision put in to protect gay people from discrimination. In other words, say I get a job here as male, then somewhere down the line one of my coworkers or my employer finds out I'm FTM, technically I can be fired and there's no law to stop it. And, if I were Irish, I couldn't change my gender on my birth certificate after transitioning, which also means that, hypothetically, I couldn't get married, either.

But yeah, I've got some advantages the other transgendered people here don't have: I'm American; I can change my gender on my birth certificate. If I want, I can always go home and at least get some protection. But even then, laws aren't unbreakable.

It's hard. It's always been hard and it's always going to be hard. Some days I wake up and wonder why I keep going. Every month I have to deal with a very obvious reminder that I don't have a male body. I look at pictures of phalloplasty (penis construction) and metaoidioplasty (enhancement of the clitoris) surgeries and wonder if the results are ever going to be any better. Because I'll tell you right now, with both of them, the results are sickening. I think about the fact that I'm going to have to take hormones for basically the rest of my life. I've got at least two, maybe three surgeries looming in the hazy, distant future. I don't know what the final result is going to be once I fully transition, if I ever make it that far. I don't know what it's going to do to my relationship with Nik. And to be honest, those questions scare me. A lot.

Is it worth it? Yeah, I think it is, but you know what? If I could wake up tomorrow and be perfectly content to have a female body, I'd do it in an instant. Of course, if I could wake up tomorrow and be completely, biologically male, I'd do that even faster.

Life as a Lesson

It's not an easy lesson to have, this life. People you love will disappear. Very few will try to help you, and even fewer will actually understand what you're going through. I'm not one of the brave ones. I'm not one of those people you'll see on TV or read about in the newspaper advocating for transgender rights. If I have it my way, no one'll ever know I wasn't born male. Although I guess you could say even writing this is brave in its own way, even if I don't use my real name or the names of those close to me.

So why am I doing it if I don't want to be found out? Because I remember what it was like to be so scared and alone, where the only option I saw was death, and no one deserves that. I know kids three, four, five years younger than me going through what I'm going through now. I remember what it was like to be that age, to feel incredibly and totally insufficient and just *wrong*, and I remember how little support there was.

I want people to understand it isn't bad but that it isn't easy either. Nothing in life is easy, when it comes right down to it, especially if you're not "normal." Especially if you're alone.

So maybe some kid will read this and realize there are others out there like him (or her, I'm not forgetting you girls). Or maybe some parent will realize their son or daughter isn't crazy or throwing away their life. It's OK to be special; it just makes you work a little harder.

My advice? Be patient, and keep your sense of humor. Sometimes people will surprise you. Parents, in terms of coping with transsexuality or, well, anything weird with their kids, have it almost as hard as their kids do. They have to deal with the social implications, who to tell, who not to tell. They have to realign their perception of this creature they created, someone they raised and know better than anyone else, supposedly. They have to deal with the realization that their child's life is going to be that much more difficult, more dangerous. They have the fear and guilt that somehow they're responsible for their child being this way. They have the knowledge that for your entire life, something was wrong and they never noticed, or maybe they did and tried to hide it. Of course, how each parent reacts to these things is an entirely different story, and entirely up to them.

And just because someone can't accept you immediately doesn't mean they don't still care. Sometimes they just need time. I know. That seems like an odd concept. It's easy to forget that even though you've had your whole life to get used to this, no one else has.

I've learned a lot since coming back to Ireland, talking with my mother, talking to others in my situation. (I always did hate the word *transsexual* and only use it when I have to.) The days when I don't even want to get out of bed get fewer (except before noon, then I'm not getting out of bed, period). It gets easier to forget I'm not a "real" boy. And if my mom is right, and every life is a lesson learned, then that Great Karmic Entity owes me big for this one.

---
o

A ROSE IN BLOOM

April Rose Schneider

APRIL 12, 1951, DAWNED over the town of Dayton, Ohio, like any other spring day. A few wisps of clouds, a light breeze, and plenty of sun. Generally speaking it was a day without distinction—unless you happened to be Roland or Doris Schneider. For them this day was portentous. This was the day of the birth of their first child. Doris wanted a boy, Roland a girl. Everything seemed normal as they took their first tentative steps toward building their all-American postwar baby-boomer family. In 1951 life was good, and the future looked even better. The fifties were pregnant with possibilities, so Roland and Doris could afford to have high hopes for their firstborn. Boy or girl, the Schneiders didn't care that much, as long as it was a healthy, happy child. What they did produce would inevitably far exceed their parental expectations.

My name is Rosie Schneider, and the first five years of my life were the happiest I've ever known. I was too young to understand the contradiction that would eventually haunt me. Unaware of the shame that would eventually be heaped upon me, I lived a relatively normal childhood. Societal judgment had not yet been internalized. Happily ignorant of the struggles for life and sanity that lay ahead, I lived in prophetic dreams. It was in these dreams that I felt most comfortable, because in my special dreamtime I was a little girl.

In early Native American culture, the kind of dreams I began experiencing in early childhood would have been a sign from the Great Spirit that I was destined to be a "two-spirited person." Most indigenous Native American tribes believed that the Great Spirit chose certain special members of the tribe to be two-spirited. These people exhibited preferences for behavior outside the boundaries of the normally gendered early in life. The most convincing indicator of their special status was revealed to the young person in the form of dreams. These dreams set in motion a specialized regimen of training designed to guide the young person toward their future roles, which ranged from healer to mediator to substitute wife. Their legacy, now largely forgotten, was one of value and honor in their respective tribes. By comparison, my experience would be the very antithesis of theirs.

My dreams have always been a part of my consciousness. From an age before I could understand their significance or future importance, they were the mainstays of my nightly bedtime routine. For the years prior to entering elementary school, they were the means by which I achieved sleep. Each night I would put on my pajamas, clutch my stuffed dog to my chest, close my eyes, and become a little girl in a perfect world. In the bliss of my youthful innocence, there was no contradiction, no shame, no guilt. I dreamed I was a little girl, and I was happy. At first it never occurred to me to tell anyone because it was such a natural part of my consciousness. Just a few years later I realized that to reveal this component of my personality would lead to most tragic consequences. What if they tried to make me stop? What if they sent me away? The possibility was too much to bear. I kept the dream to myself.

Dancing with Madness

My adolescence was filled with swirling, powerful, wordless emotions, much like a tornado whose fury I first sought to suppress, then fled from in fear of disintegration. As my childhood progressed, so did my awareness of some apparent contradiction between the way I felt and the way I was perceived. Identifying as a little girl seemed quite natural until I gazed at my reflection in the mirror. As my self-awareness progressed I would spend much time crossdressing and posing in front of a mirror. And eventually all mirrors became my unforgiving captor. No matter how hard I tried, no matter what frilly thing I wore, the mirror was a constant reminder that regardless of what I felt in my heart, the reflection was that of a little boy. Here was the dark genesis of my dance with madness. Here was the first sign of stress fractures in my fragile eggshell personality. As I matured, the stress fractures eventually combined to create one huge schism that threatened psychic destruction.

On the first day of my first year in kindergarten, September 1956, I experienced the first assault on my innocence. I learned my first lesson in social intercourse when it became necessary for the class to be divided into boys and girls. It immediately became obvious to me that a really big mistake had been made when I was put into the little boys' group. I was mortified, and vowed to take action at the first opportunity. I saw my chance at naptime. Laying my head down on my desk, I dramatically beseeched God to change me into the proper feminine form by the time I woke up. Profoundly disappointed upon awakening, I saw that my wish had not been granted. At that moment a young atheist was born. I would gradually give up all hope that this god cared a pittance for the misery of a young transsexual.

By the age of ten, I had developed a growing fascination with girls and all things female. This fascination would create in me a keen observer of human behavior. I found myself studying the girls in my peer group with a passion. I felt inexplicably drawn to them. Way deep down in my young psyche I secretly shared their adolescent need to express themselves in the way that only girls were permitted: to skip rope, wear dresses, grow their hair, and attend pajama parties. This was my secret passion. This was the real desire that dare not speak its name.

An Epiphany

Then on one particularly poignant spring afternoon around 1962, I experienced a profound epiphany that seemed to certify my status as a pariah. I remember it as clearly as if it was yesterday. I had been experimenting with my mom's clothes and makeup for a couple of years. I used any and every opportunity to stay home alone and indulge myself in the contents of her closet. I never questioned my behavior, and my parents never suspected. I had begun crossdressing as a natural progression of the dreams.

On this particular day my mom was at her therapist and my father was at work. I was sitting on the floor of our living room in my favorite full-length crinoline petticoat—the kind often worn under a poodle skirt. The sun was shining, and a warm breeze blew in through the window, carrying the sound of boys playing. As I sat there and listened to those happy sounds, sadness overwhelmed me. I remember thinking, "That's what it must be like for normal kids." Slowly my gaze dropped to the petticoat, then returned to the scene outside. Sudden realization raised the veil of youthful innocence from my vision, and tears fell from my eyes. How melancholy I felt to be so different.

At that moment I felt the first inkling of the isolation that would eventually both protect me and drive me to the brink of suicide. I was struck by the gravity of my predicament. The sun was still bright overhead. Breezes still blew and birds still sang. But for me a subtle shift had occurred in my self-perception. I was a little boy whose idea of fulfillment was staying home alone and wearing my mother's clothes. And from that day forward, a part of me knew for certain that I was headed for stormy seas in a leaky dinghy.

Thus the strangeness of my neophyte transsexual life had begun in earnest. Without fanfare or ticker tape parade, with shaky faltering steps, I had embarked on my transsexual path toward an inevitability that I could not have imagined. And this benign ignorance was perhaps the kindest gift that cruel fate would ever bestow upon me. Painted on the canvas of my future was a portrait of despair, confusion, fear, and loneliness. Somewhere it is written that the easiest way to rob a person of their humanity is to place them in permanent isolation. Transsexualism is the epitome of isolation. It is the transsexual's body that betrays the spirit. It is the body that imprisons and isolates our true selves. It was my body that offered the pretense of masculinity, forcing me down a path I would gladly have forsaken.

As I look back to my earliest realizations, two things stood out. I knew there was something very different about the way I felt and that I was the only person in my little world who felt the way I did. I did not question for a minute the rightness or wrongness of my "unusual" impulses. I did what I did for the same reasons that fish swim—it felt right and natural to do so. But as I was also a product of my environment, wherever I encountered moral judgment and bigotry I internalized those feelings. Tragically then, at such a tender time in my life I was doomed by a paradox of staggering proportion. What I felt to be completely right and natural was perceived by my society to be immoral and perverted. Eventually an expression would be coined that put all of this misery into a neat little box. The name for my particular brand of madness is gender dysphoria. I still believe it to be a measure of my parent's infinite capacity for denial that they never once suspected or perceived anything untoward in my unusual behavior. I also believe that it was one of my innermost desires to be found out. As dangerous as it seemed at the time, discovery still seemed preferable to living in fear and isolation. As I entered my teens, I began nursing an invisible little emotional bruise. But as with all wounds that do not get proper attention, what had begun as a tiny little innocuous hurt had begun to fester. The gnawing pain in my heart would eventually find expression in a litany of neurotic behaviors that ranged from alcoholism to near-fatal risk-taking behavior.

At the apex of adolescent need for attention I went into a department store, grabbed four or five baby-doll nighties and brazenly threw them over the door of a locked dressing room. I then asked an attendant to let me into the room, where I stuffed the nighties under my coat. If this was not a cry for attention, then I don't know what would qualify. Naturally I was apprehended as I exited the store. The security guard was a little confused, but he sent me home with a promise to notify me of a court date. Terrified as I drove home, I quickly came to the conclusion that the best course of action was to tell my parents so they would know why I would be summoned to court. Admittedly they did appear momentarily perplexed. They asked some superficial questions, such as, "Why women's lingerie?" But I mumbled a few "I don't knows," and the issue was quickly forgotten. Ironically, for whatever reason, I was never called upon by the justice system to explain my heinous behavior. The whole incident did teach me another valuable lesson—apparently my parents' capacity for denial far exceeded my need for parental attention.

Dante's Inferno

High school. Or Dante's Inferno, as I have come to think of it. While so many of my peers were apparently adapting to this final stage of their public education, I was becoming obsessed with my pubic frustration. The full onset of testosterone signaled the real beginning of my darkness. From a male-to-female transsexual's point of view, nothing epitomizes hopelessness like the burgeoning presence of virilizing hormones as they invade our bodies, creating all the wrong changes in all the wrong places. I had always been at odds with my male body. I appreciated it as a pretty decent male body, it was simply the wrong one for me. If I was condemned to live in this male body, so be it, but the chest hair would have to go. Thus began a thirty-year struggle to rid myself of body hair.

High school for me felt like being tortured on that famous device known as the rack. Drawn and quartered by forces I barely understood at the time, I often feared my own dissolution in the midst of a psychic tug of war. With no real self to operate from, I did the best I could to fake it. My grades were above average, my teachers liked me, and all together I'm quite sure they had no clue as to my inner turmoil. The only exception to the rule was a psychology teacher to whom I shall be forever grateful. It was the tenth grade. The stress I was feeling was so great that I can only assume that my subconscious was operating on its own when I wrote an "anonymous" note to this teacher. In my pain and confusion it never occurred to me that he could match my handwriting with other papers I had written. When he approached me about it the next day after class and asked me if I wanted to talk about it, I froze in terror. I was paralyzed by the desperation to speak my truth and by fear of the consequences of telling the wrong person. I quickly denied authorship. The subject, to my relief, was never brought up again.

As I eased, or uneased, into the eleventh grade, I felt hormone-driven changes happening all around me but not to me. For me, sexual development was an abstract concept. The big lesson I learned about sexuality was that it could not exist when the body and soul are at odds. My hormones only forced me deeper into despair. Hopelessness grew daily. I knew, based on observation, that certain behaviors would be expected of me. I knew that most of these behaviors were masculine in essence and that I had better start studying, and fast. The two male behaviors that I passionately abhorred were concerned with various aspects of male aggression: fisticuffs and sex.

The matter of physical confrontation was not as much of a concern as matters of the heart. I was not physically imposing in any sense of the word, nor was I inclined toward aggression. So keeping my head down and staying out of the line of fire would be fairly easy. The other problem, though, was going to be a bitch, plain and simple. Behaving like a male was the toughest role I would ever attempt. The consequences of being found out in the enemy camp were unpleasant to say the least. But like the dedicated actress that I was, I studied hard and succeeded. Some might even say that I overdid it, but I survived. Looking back now, I often joke that I was a double agent, an undercover transsexual agent stranded behind enemy lines. Deep cover, for I alone knew my real identity. There were no reinforcements, no manuals, no maps, and no survival kit that described the intricacies of being a male impostor. I studied hard and faked it.

For the next two years until my graduation in June 1969, I was the consummate actress. I played my part as if my life depended on it. I ingratiated myself into the company of men and listened to their boastful speech. I tolerated their young sexism with tacit disdain, nodding and occasionally grunting for effect. But my sympathy inevitably lay with the recipients of their crude, unpolished advances. The young women who were the subject of so much salacious gossip could never have guessed that I listened for them and defended them when possible. To them I was just another high school boy trying to find his way through the morass of sexual vagaries that boggled the mind. I even went as far as to date a couple of girls who seemed to like me. I tried really hard to do the "right thing," but the truth is that I was lost at the moment when most men seemed unstoppable. I simply did not have what it took to do the manly thing, and I knew it. I just didn't have the words or the heart to tell them.

So to all the girls I've known before, I would like to take this opportunity to apologize. I knew from the look in your eyes, the smile on your lips, and the sensual toss of your hair that you were ready for me to do what came natural to a boy. How could you have known back then that I was dying to be one of you? How could you have seen that the only lust in my heart was to be one of you, and that everything that happened between us only reminded me of the hopelessness of my situation?

As my senior year came and went, I glided through the halls of college like a cipher, bereft of hope, friends, or plans for the future. There was a period of months during the latter half of the year when I thought I had a friend, knowing full well that friendship with a ghost like me was impossible. Still, for a short time friendship seemed possible, and then like everything else in my young life, it too faded away into the mist of disillusionment. As my peer group focused on their plans for the immediate future, graduation found me surrounded by family turmoil, seething neurosis, enough self-hate to float an armada, and a really bad case of hives. I wanted to die.

Sword of Damocles

Fortunately I remained alive long enough to learn another really important life lesson. In the absence of positive planning, fate can throw a monkey wrench or two into the proceedings. One of those wrenches turned out to be my personal Sword of Damocles. At first it appeared more like a panacea for every single thing that I thought was standing between success and me. Then it would become the noose with which I almost succeeded in committing suicide. Alcohol and I began our twenty-five-year affair in the summer of 1969, not coincidentally immediately following graduation from high school. We got close really fast. So fast in fact that I would become a burden to the few people who could tolerate me until they embarked on their own life. I took to drinking like a drag queen takes to high heels, and it did for me something that no one or nothing had been able to do up to that time: it erased my pain. Unfortunately, it also exacted a toll on my self-respect, integrity, honesty, physical coordination, and memory.

Alcohol was also the culprit responsible for a most egregious case of bad judgment on December 31, 1970. That's the day I got married. In a state of screaming denial, I married the first person to come along with a car and a job. All I wanted was to leave home, but it cost six years of my life to escape the marriage. I'll not waste precious words on the debacle, save to describe it as odious from beginning to end. Remarkable in one and only one respect—that a reasonably intelligent, responsible woman would voluntarily marry a neurotic, confused, unmotivated, unemployed,

alcoholic, drug-abusive, self-loathing transsexual. Then incomprehensi-
bly produce two children using my drunken sperm, divorce me, and then
keep the children away from me. Nuf said!

It isn't always darkest just before the dawn, but it certainly seemed that
way to me. As bad as my marriage had been, it had also functioned as a
flotation device. But by 1976 huge gaping leaks had sent it plummeting
to its briny demise. The next year found me adrift on the streets of my
hometown. Everything seemed so unreal. I felt as if I was outside a bubble
looking in, the warmth and spirit of life denied me. Again I was the
specter on the outside, where cold wintry blasts rattled my bones, ever
reminding me of my isolation and my frozen heart.

On the Road

Perhaps it was a death wish or the desperate need to flee from the forces
of imminent psychological and spiritual collapse that propelled me on a
three-year hitchhiking odyssey that would eventually cover approximately
twenty-five thousand miles. Between 1977 and 1980, I ranged from Ohio
to San Francisco, from Los Angeles to Fort Lauderdale, then back to
Ohio. With my personal demons ever hot on my trail, I sought nothing
more than surcease on the open road. For a few years the plan worked. I
found necessary distraction in long-distance travel. My existence was sim-
plified to primal elements. I slept outside in ditches, in fields, and on
mountains. I ate out of cans, was chased by wild dogs, and passed out
pleasantly drunk under a million stars. I got into a car with anyone who
would take me anywhere. Looking back now on my abandon, I realize
that I was lucky just to survive.

In 1979, at my wits end, I found myself standing on the Golden Gate
Bridge. I truly had nothing but the clothes I wore. I gazed longingly at the
water over four hundred feet down and tried to will myself to jump. But
something stopped me, and I experienced a sudden epiphany. I had
found something that I thought was lost forever. Hope. Nothing else had
changed. There was no real reason to be hopeful, but I had found its
essence within, and I would not question its arrival. Considering the state
of my consciousness, just finding this little glimmer of hope was miraculous enough to keep me going.

So I went back to the only home I had. My family had all eventually
moved to Florida, and the climate was perfect for the life of a beach bum.
I hitched to Fort Lauderdale and lived for a year by selling my plasma, eating happy-hour cheese crackers, and sleeping on the beach or wherever I
could. Ah, the good life! For a while it seemed as if the past would repeat

itself. There were more itinerant jobs, more nights sleeping anywhere, and more drunkenness. In fact, I had unconsciously changed my self-image from tragically transsexual to sadly besotted. I was a reprobate who wanted nothing more than to drink my life away in my favorite bar. That's exactly what I was doing on a balmy night in April of 1980 when, ever so subtly, my whole life changed forever in the time it takes to open a door.

My new adopted home was an earthy sort of drinking establishment called the Draft House. Anyone who saw me sitting in that bar would have typecast me as just another beer-drinking, pool-playing, rock-and-roll biker type. My consummate disguise had become my reality. I had long hair, a beard, and bad teeth. I wore dirty jeans and a cutoff T-shirt, and I carried a knife purely for the sake of image. A twenty-nine-year-old drifter, I had no friends, no money, no job, and no prospects. I was interested only in replacing a lifetime of pain with alcohol. In the program of Alcoholics Anonymous this is referred to as the jumping-off place.

As I sat there with one eye on my beer and one eye on the entrance, I noticed a young wild child as she opened the door and glided in. I quietly watched her as she lit the place up with an inner fire I had not seen in quite a while. She left after a short while, but I was still in the same seat when she came back in two nights later. We struck up a conversation, and I finally got around to asking her for a ride to my apartment. She stayed for a drink, then she stayed the night. And the night turned into weeks, and the weeks turned to months. Miraculously, we recently celebrated twenty-two years of marriage.

The Power of Love

In a fairy tale, she would have kissed me early on and I would have turned into a princess, but the truth is far less dramatic. It took all of those twenty-two years to explain to her that I was really a girl in disguise. For her to have come so far philosophically, from a Pentecostal upbringing to living as an agnostic lesbian married to a transsexual, is a miraculous feat and a tribute to the enduring power of love. She now says that she always knew I was "special." She just didn't know how special! In 2001, she supported me while I worked and saved and flew to Bangkok, Thailand, for sex reassignment surgery (SRS). She is my one and only love, my soulmate.

Yet some dreams refuse to die. Previously in this text I alluded to the only person in high school with whom I felt any kinship at all. His name was Paul. He was 5'8", fair skinned, slight build, and blond. Paul and I spent hours talking about everything. I felt a closeness with him, a trust that transcended words. With Paul I experienced a degree of emotional intimacy that I shared with no one else. I was fairly certain that I knew why. Paul was gay, or at least he was destined to be gay. It was a moot point in 1967. Don't ask, don't tell was the ethos. No one had to tell me. Paul was gay, and I was a closet transsexual happy to have found an unwitting ally. Then one day, inexplicably, Paul pulled away from me, and I lost the only friend I had in those troubled times. Later I would see him pal around with a female schoolmate who I assumed was a lesbian. I thought Paul was in youthful denial.

In May of 2002, five months after SRS, I was visiting a website that provides a cyberplace for alumni of high schools all over the country to find each other. When I saw the name that I had kept in my memory for thirty-five years, my heart leaped with happiness. Finally a small chance for even a tiny bit of redemption. Expectantly I sent him my e-mail address, using my high school name of course. Within days I received an enthusiastic return from Paul. My inhibitions were overwhelmed by my passionate need for resolution. My correspondence began, "Dear Paul, there's no easy way to say this, but I'm a transsexual."

Oh, to be a fly on the wall! When the poor man recovered from his seizure, we began a period of torrid correspondence that rekindled the flame of our youth and fanned it considerably. The story that emerged is a clear case of mistaken identity and unrequited love. In a convoluted plot befitting Agatha Christie, desire drew us in at intersecting tangents. As it turned out, Paul had a monumental crush on me back in high school. At first he thought I was straight, then he thought I was leading him on. I personally didn't have a clue. I just couldn't fathom the idea of having sex while stuck in the wrong body. Paul took it hard. He felt rejected. That's when he faded out of my life.

As we reconnected from adult perspectives, our realization of what had happened and not happened propelled us to a greater understanding of the sacrifices we made in the name of self-preservation. Somehow amid the social facades of our youth revisited, we emerged with a finer perception of the paths we had traveled together and apart. And while thirty-five years hadn't diminished our affection for each other, there was one little matter that still required closure. And this was the most delicate issue of all. Apparently neither time nor space nor gender had assuaged his ardor for the person he knew thirty-five years ago. I must admit that I was flattered, yet puzzled. I thought he was gay, but then he explained that he was bisexual. Oh! Even so, it seemed to me that he was taking a big chance. Though I had sent him a picture, I knew there was a recently emerged version of me that he was not at all acquainted with.

His next communication to me was the apex of resurgent passion. We finally spoke on the phone, and it must have been disconcerting for him to hear me as a girl. He said that he had a question to ask me via e-mail and that he hoped I wasn't shocked. Shocked indeed! Paul suggested that perhaps if our partners "loved us enough" they might understand our desire to consummate our long-lost lust. Mostly his lust. So I decided that the least I could do would be to ask my partner. When wisps of steam began to exit her ears, I adroitly retracted my question. Paul took it hard but made a speedy recovery, and has promised to visit soon.

The year 2002 is the year of my rebirth and a celebration of the first year of my new life. The ominously dark cloud of fear that once hounded me has broken apart, and now sun shines on my life every day. My self-image is radically improved. I am a spiritual warrior on my own path to a greater understanding of myself. By virtue of my life as a transsexual, I have learned many lessons about the world I live in. I am fiercely proud of what I am and what I have accomplished. I held fast to my dream, nurturing and protecting it from forces that threatened destruction. I never gave in to fear, even as I clung desperately to a tiny ray of hope. I survived drug and alcohol abuse, murderous sexism, religious intolerance, inept psychiatry, legalized bigotry, and socially reinforced oppression. And despite all these threats to my sanity, I have emerged victorious. With the reconciliation of mind, body, and spirit, my focus now rests heavily on the development of spiritual principles: integrity, humility, compassion, and gratitude. Especially gratitude. For today I am so very grateful to have something that I thought was lost forever. Today I have myself.

A JOURNEY TO ANDROGYNY

norrie mAy-welby

I WAS BORN IN 1961 in Paisley, Scotland, the second child of a Presbyterian working-class family with Freemason ties. On my birth certificate my middle name was "Norrie," from my mother's maiden name. My first name, however, was a boy's name, for that was what I appeared to be at birth. My father worked as a plumber, and also taught this at a technical college.

As a young child of preschool age, I was unhappy with the rough-and-tumble play of my older brother and of my peers, who seemed to enjoy violence, mud, and the cold outdoors. I preferred solitude, learning to read by age four, and playing with my best friend, my teddy bear.

In early primary school, I enjoyed schoolwork, the classroom, and the teachers, but felt awkward and lost on the playground. In first grade, on my way home, I was forced through a barbed-wire fence by some older children. I arrived home in tears with blood streaming from multiple lacerations, expecting that this would gain my mother's sympathy. However, she gave me the clear message that my "sissy" behavior would not be tolerated. Thereafter, I walked the long way around to and from school. Where previously I had some company walking along the grasslands and stream (where the barbed wire fences were), I walked alone around the roadway, making up adventures in my head for entertainment.

In those adventures, I played different characters, including a good witch (inspired by the TV show *Bewitched*), a jungle girl (inspired by the *Tarzan* TV show), Supergirl, and a boy superhero. His powers derived from his all-enclosing costume, and he led a group of uniform boy-heroes. The female characters' powers were inherent, and they were independent operators. As I saw it, girls were treated with care and affection, without being expected to accept being bullied, or being yelled at for crying. Men were nice to them, and allowed them their sensitivity and compassion, while a little awed by their difference. In my fantasies, I was seeking to not be chastised for my own character traits. The boy hero was how I saw males, clad in the power of masculinity and surrounded by their peers. Only in fantasy could I fit this ideal.

I did not, however, dislike my own small male body. Indeed, I remember being quite comfortable with my "naughty bits," playing games of "rudies" with another four-year-old boy under the stairs. This involved no more than exposing our privates in defiance of (and beyond sight of) all adult authority. I did, however, sometimes dress up as a girl when I was very young. I remember being seven and wrapping my school tie around my head to simulate a girl's long hair. This was entirely in secret, for I knew my parents would have disapproved. I was barely four when my mother chastised me for playing with my female cousin's dolls.

Somewhere around puberty, I realized that my female fantasy identities were not "appropriate," and developed a script in which the jungle girl was in fact the costumed boy hero, who had been turned into the jungle girl by a wicked witch, and then the witch was defeated, and the boy managed to change back again. Before long, however, I became another jungle girl, and she sometimes had adventures by herself, and sometimes she was friends with the boy hero. I was scripting the gender journey to androgyny that I would later live out.

Moral Values

The family migrated to Perth, Western Australia, in 1969 when I was seven. We were a regular churchgoing family, my father being an elder of the parish, and I used to quite enjoy Sunday school. Then, as a young teenager, I began reading the Bible, and was horrified to read the directive in Leviticus to kill homosexuals. The killing of people for various victimless "crimes," and the dreadful strictures placed on women in the Pentateuch repelled me from my parents' faith. I scripted a superhero fantasy in which a being claiming to be God tried to impose his will on earth, and the superhero was morally bound to oppose this evil and murderous being. As I saw it, the Creator had no more right to abuse His creation than parents have to abuse their children.

While I rejected the God of Moses, I realized there were Christian faiths not bound in a literal reading of the Old Testament. I felt there was some truth in the psychedelic "God is Love" stickers of the time. Many of the writers of the Bible, I decided, were just deceitful men who had put their own words into God's mouth for their own selfish or (in Moses' case) megalomaniacal ends.

Yes, I knew what the word *megalomaniacal* meant when I was thirteen. I read Superman comics. And it was from comic books that I learned my morals and values, having rejected the Bible. Superman was one of my role models, a being who was clearly not descended from Adam and Eve, yet who tried to do the right thing and avert evil more than any descendant of Moses.

I was appalled at what my older brother told me about sexuality. He hit puberty a couple of years before me and tried to impress on me the importance of "conning chicks," that is, manipulating women into progressively more sexual acts, without regard to the women's own feelings or desires. He told me that at puberty I too would turn into a hormone-driven sex-obsessed teenager, compelled to ruthlessly pursue sexual conquests, before eventually settling down when adolescence petered out.

I duly underwent puberty at thirteen, and gradually got the hang of masturbation, but my desires for others remained more romantic than carnal. I was disappointed in a budding relationship with the daughter of a family friend, seeing clearly how she was trying to treat me as a foolish male to be manipulated. At sixteen, I fell passionately in love with a boy in the school band, because he had fallen asleep with his head on my shoulder on a bus tour. This was completely unrequited, although I visited him daily after school until I graduated from high school two years later. While at university, I returned to the school band, ostensibly to help coach the percussion section, but really just to be near him. He eventually addressed my infatuation and told me he was straight. I contemplated seeking a sex change then, but told myself that this was not a good enough reason for it.

I was enticed to go to the university because of their annual anarchistic newspaper that was sold for charity. The atmosphere there was one of freedom and rebellion, and I was cheered by the gay lib posters that greeted me on my first day. Though I was an unkissed virgin with no interest in unromantic sex, I blossomed from a shy bookworm into a flamboyant androgyne, wearing frilly blouses, tight stretch jeans, and a flower in my hair. No one thought I was really gay, however, for I was so over the top they thought I was just taking the piss [mocking gays].

Getting into Politics

In my first term, I helped campaign successfully against a ticket of serious young socialists in the Faculty of Arts' students' association elections and was rewarded with editorship of the association's magazine. Seizing the opportunity to make an icon of myself, I dumped my old boy's forename as being too ordinary, and used my former middle name in its place. The embittered young lefties had not forgotten my presumptuous victory, and I returned from the first term break to find posters everywhere denouncing "Norrie" as a right-wing fascist, English, upper-class, heterosexist male. I was overjoyed by their promotion of my notoriety, and privately amused at how wide of the mark they were!

At the end of my first year at uni, I wore a red "Mao" cap and ran for the Council of the Guild of Undergraduates as a Rasputinist (Dismemberist faction). I lampooned both the left- and right-wing candidates, pouting on my campaign poster with the slogans "Comrade Norrie Loves You" and "Think: this'll get the vote from both gay lib and the drunk engineer students who think it's a chick!" I was not only elected to the Guild Council, but scored a junket, flying to Melbourne for the annual conference of the Australian Union of Students. The serious gay lefties were a little surprised when I turned up at the gay caucus meeting there.

Part of the tradition of the day the university students sold their satiric newspaper was various student stunts and lampoonery. For my part, I dressed up as a girl and returned to my old high school, selling the newspaper in the classrooms and addressing my former teachers by their forenames, so that they would know they were supposed to know who I was. My music teacher, when he finally recognized me, said he hoped this wasn't permanent. I joked that it was just a stage I was going through.

I had become frustrated at having unrequited crushes on straight boys, and joined the student drama society because there were obviously gay students in it. I figured, if none of them fancied me, then perhaps through them I could meet other gay guys. My strategy worked, and they introduced me to Perth's only gay nightclub. After a few visits, I finally, awkwardly, kissed a boy at the nightclub, our spectacles tinkling together. He invited me home with him, but once there, fear got the best of me, and I couldn't get aroused.

Since I had been a failure with a boy, I succumbed to a female friend's advances. There was no romantic meaning for me this time. Without the impediment of nervousness, everything worked as expected, and I lost my virginity. I had only just told all my friends I was gay, and now it seemed that I was a closet heterosexual after all! But, for me, the heterosexual act was emotionally hollow and compared poorly to solitary masturbation.

I went back to the gay nightclub, brazenly picked up an attractive young man, and took him to my place. In a passionate nightlong session of mutual oral stimulation, I discovered that my sexuality was actually worth something to me. But I was still driven by romantic longing, and it broke my heart when I realized he didn't want to see me again, despite his promises.

Sheltered by the freedom of university and the gay nightclub (where I had scored a part-time job during my university years), I was very comfortable being colorfully camp and ambiguously gendered. Then, a year out of university, deciding that I needed a career and thinking that it would provide a haven from discrimination, I joined the public service.

Discrimination

I was careful not to draw undue attention when I started as a probationary officer in a regional office of Social Security, and my work was commended in the three-month probationary report. However, shortly before the six-month report, in which permanent appointment is the usual outcome, I was "sprung." An article I had written for the local gay bar rag was pinned up in my office by a coworker. This was without malice, I'm sure. They just thought it an amusing article and didn't realize the dire consequences its placement would have. The six-month report recommended extension of probation, without any clear reason. I knew the office manager had arranged this out of prejudice, for my coworkers were happy with me and my work. I read the *Personnel Management Manual* and resolved to give the manager enough rope to hang himself.

I began dressing as I pleased, no longer restricting myself to the drab colors and styles worn by the men in the office. I became flamboyant, with knee-high white boots, "new romantic" makeup, and crew-cut hair with patterns cut and colored into it. In the final eleven-month probation report, the manager recommended my dismissal, citing a list of my dress "violations," alleging shaved legs and false eyelashes. I responded that my legs were waxed, not shaven, and while I wore mascara, those long lashes were my own, thank you very much, and what does this have to do with my work performance? Further questioned on this point by the personnel manager, the office manager admitted he had no evidence of poor work performance, other than a "gut feeling" that my "progress would not be sustained."

Since work performance was the only criteria allowed for not doing so, the personnel manager confirmed my appointment. I then lodged official complaints against being passed over for promotion in the regional office, in favor of those I had trained. Despite the clear proof in the probation reports, the department determined that there was no evidence of unfair discrimination.

The day after I was notified of this, I couldn't face the office. I had lost the ability to function in the face of adversity. I had fought the system for two years, winning a permanent appointment, but losing the fight against unfair discrimination. I was devastated that the rules and evidence written in black and white were no protection. I hand-delivered a letter of resignation, but colleagues persuaded me to withdraw it. I took three months' leave, suffering from reactive depression.

The very night after submitting the resignation, I entered a talent quest at the gay pub, winning approval and acclamation in female persona. As a result of my performance, I joined the regular drag show troupe, and another icon was born. La Contessa Norrishka became my presentation to the world, replacing bureaucratic warrior Master Norrie, who, it seemed to me, had been an abject failure.

Two months later, as I was preparing my makeup at the home of a transsexual friend, I realized there was a woman's face looking back at me in the mirror. She wasn't just a drag show character. She was a sane, confident, strong, adult woman, and this, I realized, was my true self. After contemplating this for three days, I asked my doctor for hormones. My former gender ambiguity had been ruthlessly persecuted by the straight world, and, unable to change the feminine aspects of my character, I saw changing to a female identity as the solution. I saw no need to change my name, for it was so rare I figured it could easily pass as a girl's.

An older postoperative transsexual solemnly told a group of us young trannies, "If you don't want it cut off, you're just wasting your time." I knew my newfound female self was no mere delusion. I wanted sex-change surgery as soon as possible. Completely blanked out were all the memories of enjoyment I had experienced with my male genitals. Instead, I projected onto them all the persecution I had experienced from the straight world as an effeminate boy. And then all the persecution I experienced as a transsexual.

I was a very shy and reserved young woman, terribly embarrassed about my transsexuality. Over the next four years, although my features had changed to reflect an attractive young woman, I was lonely and loveless, expecting and receiving rejection when the awful truth about my genitals was known. The closest I came to intimacy was with a lesbian who took me home and made love to my breasts, respecting my need to keep my genitals covered.

I returned to the public service a couple of weeks after commencing hormone therapy, dressing less flamboyantly, but androgynously, in baggy tops that hid my budding breasts, and baggy jeans that rendered my groin genderless. I was eventually awarded worker's compensation for the period of my reactive depression, but I was also criminally charged for not declaring my income (from the nightclub) when claiming sickness benefits at the time. I had not meant to gain by fraud, and indeed there was no overpayment of benefit, since it was all repaid by worker's compensation. To end the drama, I pleaded guilty. This gained me a fine and another attempt by the public service to sack me.

Again they were unsuccessful, and I returned to work with a less androgynous, more female presentation, armed with a letter from my doctor advising that I was undergoing treatment for transsexuality and was to use the women's toilets. However, I was threatened with disciplinary action if I did use these toilets. After losing an appeal against this directive, I went on sick leave again, suffering depression and feeling helpless.

During this next period of sick leave, I became romantically involved with a boy. He used my checkbooks to commit fraud, and I was charged with the crimes he committed. While awaiting trial, the public service had me examined by its doctor. He declared that the side effects I reported from the hormones (nausea, depression, poor concentration, and short attention span) were fictional, and declared me fit for duty. I was ordered to return to work, and duly did so. Less than one hour after I reported for duty, I was suspended without pay, on the basis of the charges I faced. The department's timing was utterly cruel and humiliating.

I was found guilty in the initial trial, and immediately launched an appeal. However, as soon as the first trial was over, the public service moved swiftly to dismiss me, although it was contrary to its own rules to do so pending an appeal. The day after my dismissal, I won my (self-represented) appeal. The court cases and appeal had put me on the front page of the city newspaper far too often, and I became paranoid in public, thinking people were talking about the transsexual freak. In retrospect, well, probably most often they were. But it was years before I realized that when men were staring at me on the street, this was just the normal behavior many men exhibit toward unescorted females.

While awaiting the result of the appeal, I was offered a part in a professional play, *Magpie's Nest,* in which I played a transsexual prisoner. My character was a manipulative murderess and the jail kingpin's lover. It was through this part I realized that a transsexual could be a strong protagonist, not just the poor victim I had become.

After the appeal, I was eventually reinstated to the public service. This time, I was directed to use only the disabled toilet at work. Finally, I was sensible enough to see that a battle wasn't always worth fighting, and, after lodging a claim for payment for the period I had been suspended, I resigned within a few weeks.

Finding Refuge

I couldn't stand the persecution and the whispering in Perth any longer. As soon as the play closed, I fled across the country, abandoning my flat and those possessions that didn't fit into two suitcases. I ended up finding a place to stay in the transsexual refuge in Sydney. It was like catching up on all the years of girls' school camps that I never had. The residents taught me how to wax my own face (I had been paying a fortune at beauty salons!) and how to be proud of what I was. "I'm a queen," said one older girl, although she had that ultimate transsexual status symbol: a sex change. "I'll always be a queen. Why should I be ashamed of that?"

While I was at the refuge, the public service paid up big, an ex-gratia payment for the final period I had been suspended. I used this to book a sex-change operation and paid in full. The psychiatrist who assessed me saw that I had been through enough trauma and, based on my presentation as a sane, attractive young woman, approved the surgery.

Ironically, Sydney gave me boys who liked preoperative transsexuals, and I even had a boyfriend who made me feel like a well-loved woman regardless of my genitals. In the month before the surgery, I finally realized how others could see my hermaphroditic body as beautiful. It wasn't less sexy for being both male and female, it was doubly sexy! But I had spent too many years as a victimized preoperative transsexual who was focused on the operation as my salvation. The psychiatric approval had been obtained, the payment had been made, and the momentum was unstoppable now. For old times' sake, I attempted to penetrate a boy the week before the operation, but the hormones had made erection impossible. But the morning before I went into hospital, I peed standing up one last time.

While I was safely unconscious, my testicles were removed, my urethra repositioned, the nerves at the end of my penis wound into a clitoris, and a vaginal cavity was created and lined with skin from my penis and a graft from my thigh. The only thing that hurt afterwards was my thigh.

I got work in a straight bar, which provided me with a steady stream of lovers. Those who were interested in more than a one night stand, however, broke off with me when I told them why I couldn't have children. It seemed that I had made myself unsuitable for the gay world, but the straight world wouldn't accept me either. Some of those straight boys became angry when they found out that, as they saw it, I wasn't a "real woman." What more could I do to be accepted, to gain love and respect? I had done everything I could to gain acceptance on other people's terms, yet this was ultimately impossible. The one night stands stole my video recorder; the affairs ended in near violence.

I had briefly tried sex work as a preoperative transsexual, but I was too uncomfortable with my genitals to cope with it. So many transsexuals "worked" that I was known in Perth as the one who didn't! However, after working in Sydney's Kings Cross providing services and supplies to sex workers, I really internalized a nonjudgmental attitude to their profession. I had a boyfriend who, unknown to me, had an expensive heroin habit, and he seized the opportunity to pimp for me when I expressed an interest in sex work.

I worked in the back streets of the Cross for a few weeks, got busted by the cops, and found employment in a female parlor in the suburbs. I really enjoyed working there, bonding with the other women. I also enjoyed the income, being able to furnish a home for my partner and me. Some clients, however, were angry when they suspected I wasn't the "real thing." The house was closed a few months later after a suspicious fire, and I don't know to this day if this was caused by an irate client of mine or some other business complication. Shortly after, my boyfriend left me for a social worker who was my confidante, and I was so devastated that I cut my wrists, cut half my hair off, and vowed never to "work" again.

But a few months later, when a lesbian friend who did sex work offered to pay my phone bill, I reasoned that I couldn't let her do something I wasn't willing to do myself, so I put on a wig and got out onto the street the transsexuals worked. I finally felt like an equal part of the transsexual community when I joined their sex-working culture. I saw it as a professional prerequisite to leave my inhibitions behind and prostrate myself over a car on the main street. It was very liberating! And finally, I had much more in common with the people I had always hung out with.

I enjoyed a lot of professional respect as a sex worker, much more than I had as an amateur taken advantage of by predatory males. As an amateur, they stole my video recorder and tortured me emotionally. As a professional, they paid me, and there were very safe boundaries around the transaction. I could devote myself totally to the pleasure of another, knowing that this would be limited by the agreed time frame and that I would be rewarded for my efforts. Working in the transsexual strip, I had a lot of customers who wanted to question and explore their own sexuality and gender. I was doing hands-on sex therapy and counseling, so it was quite appropriate that my hourly rate was the same as a psychiatrist's.

After attending some workshops on Tantric Taoist massage, I did these commercially in my flat. After a few months, however, I became frustrated with the men who couldn't keep their focus within and wanted to project their fantasies onto me, which was contrary to the Tantric Taoist principles I wanted to work with. I went back to "straight" street sex work, although it became harder to get out in the cold for diminishing returns when other employment became available to me.

Through a counselor loaning me a book about codependence, I began my recovery from other people's expectations. I reasoned that since I was now a woman, all my actions were those of a woman, and therefore I could stop policing myself on the basis of gender appropriateness. I explored feminist self-help books, and learned that it was good to be in touch, not only with the inner Aphrodite, the seductress, but also with the inner Artemis, the tomboy. I attended personal development seminars, and was freed from shame about my past as a male, shame about my preoperative transsexual past, and shame about my postoperative transsexual present.

Discovering Androgyny

Learning to trust myself and to depend on myself, I no longer wanted to be dependent on hormone pills to make me who I was. I tried jumping off them, but the withdrawal was unbearable. I told a transgendered friend, Aidy, about my desire to free my body, and she referred me to a doctor who would support my choices. With the advice of this doctor, I safely weaned myself off hormones, over a period of six months. And my brain started to work again as it had when I was an A-grade student.

Where previously I had seen my transsexuality as something to keep fairly hidden, I began creating a positive profile of my transgenderedness. *Naughty Sydney* became the first publication to pay me for writing a piece exploring how straight men viewed the sex identity of transsexuals. *Campaign* put me in the centerfold; well, perhaps not as such, but I was reclined across the center staples, while I waxed cosmic: "How others see me is a reflection of themselves."

Aidy lent me academic papers on gender and transgender. The book *Five Sexes* was particularly eye opening for me. I still had some sort of faith in the Creator of the universe, and to me, the natural occurrence of hermaphrodite or ambiguously gendered humans was the divine stamp of approval for androgyny. I began questioning the transsexual process I had been through.

I reached the conclusion that not enough options had been known to me when I chose surgery. Why couldn't my male genitals have coexisted with my feminine personality traits? Would any woman who woke up with a penis have it immediately removed? Wouldn't she try it out for a weekend at least? Why was it assumed that the only healthy option with gender was to be uniformly male or female? It seemed to me that intersex babies had their birthright destroyed for the same reason the doctors were so keen to support my surgery—to ensure we fit into the binary sex system they believed in.

Aidy talked me into submitting a proposal with her for a series of articles on gender and transgender to the city's major gay newspaper, the *Sydney Star Observer*. Aidy provided the academic discourse, and I focused this postmodern deconstructionism through my own experience. My first column of *Gender Agenda* was a firebrand attack on the "Great White Medicine Man" and the classic transsexual medical model. I later learned that one of the psychiatrists who assessed candidates for transsexual surgery gave copies of this to his patients.

The column changed how I experienced myself in terms of sex and gender. Shortly after the first one was published, I had a conversation with myself that went something like this:

"Do you wish you still had a dick?"

"Yes."

"Ah, but when you had a dick, you wanted rid of it. Do you just want what you don't have?"

"No, I want to be female . . . *and* male."

And so I gave myself permission to explore my maleness and my femaleness, and even to be comfortable with the idea of being not "she" or "he," but "it." I was a spiritual hermaphrodite and a physical neuter.

I felt the need to acknowledge and go through a grieving process for the maleness that I had lost. I collected photos of myself as a boy and as a young gay man, and put them up on my wall. It was so liberating to fly in the face of the standard transsexual practice of burning and denying the pre-female past! I dared to accept all that I was, and all that I had been. A year or so later, when I met a boy whose behind awakened a long-forgotten urge, I became adept with a strap-on dildo.

I acted on a strong, long-lasting urge to shave my hair off, only realizing in retrospect why I did it. I was shaving off the identities other people had given me. I was shaving off the perm my mother had suggested for me. I was shaving off the back-combed bouffant I used to attract boys. I was shaving off the biggest gender signifier I presented to the world. And my head was so smooth, so beautiful, so free to be itself without possibly being measured up against other hairstyles.

The shaved head made my gender appear neutral, allowing me to explore the identity of neuter. I started wearing harem pants, for the only image I knew of eunuchs was harem guards. Then I did some research and found that eunuchs had been the power behind the thrones of many empires. In imperial China, for example, castration was the key to a great career in the public service. I devoured Mary Renault's *The Persian Boy*, about the eunuch who became a lover to Alexander the Great.

I used to compare my body unfavorably to nontranssexual people. As a transsexual, I had no reproductive capacity at all. I sometimes thought this rendered my body of less value than others. Eventually, however, I realized that I have what is, for me, the best body in the whole world. After all, this is the only one with nerves connected to my brain.

I was drawn to tantra and yoga through a breath orgasm workshop, which interested me as a person whose physical sexual capacity had been compromised (the operation having cut a few nerves). I discovered the power of breath and mind focus, and have found a new spiritual grounding in yoga. Perhaps most important for me, unlike other traditions, it works with the yin (feminine) and yang (masculine) that are within every individual.

After the sex-change operation, I had pretty much abandoned the gay scene in favor of heterosexual pubs and clubs. I had reasoned that this was appropriate, because as an anatomical female attracted to males, I was heterosexual. Now, however, I embraced my difference from non-transsexual heterosexuals and immersed myself in the gay scene again. I was invited to join the organizing collective for the 1992 Stonewall rally in Sydney, and learned the history of the original Stonewall riots in New York, 1969, that were taken as marking the birth of the modern gay liberation movement.

This riot was known as the first time gay people fought back against police persecution, but the gays involved were not the niche-market white gay men of today. They were Latinos, queer prostitutes, transsexuals, obvious bull dykes, and screaming queens—the most marginalized of society and the people with nothing to lose. They were the ones who first fought back.

Yet their inheritors, the people who now shaped gay culture, had redefined gay to mean homosexual, and excluded the gender transgressors. One of the transsexuals who had led the 1969 riot was asked to lead the twentieth anniversary march in New York . . . providing she wore a man's suit. Gay men and lesbians were formally invited to partake in the Mardi Gras and the Gay Rights Lobby, while transsexuals were used to entertain at their fundraisers. Trannies were, I observed in my speech to the Sydney rally, "the niggers of the gay community," expected to serve but never formally invited.

Newly politicized in queer rights, I joined the board of the Gay and Lesbian Rights Lobby of New South Wales, but they were not ready for my agenda of including transsexuals and bisexuals, and I was rudely expelled. I later went on to attack nontranssexual control of the trans-sexual refuge, and succeeded. I was only partially successful in my bid to end sexuality-based discrimination by the Sydney Gay and Lesbian Mardi Gras. They now accept membership applications from transsexuals on an equal basis, but still demand extra of bisexual applicants. I am often credited with winning the inclusion of transgender people in the Anti-Discrimination Act of New South Wales, but in truth, I was only a support person for the real architect, my friend Aidy.

While I eventually let my hair grow back so as not to frighten people, I now live openly and comfortably as androgynous. I have a professional career in the community sector, an occasional film and TV career, and a sideline as an advocate for the rights of sex and gender diverse people. Other people's ideas of male and female are just that: other people's ideas, and I am at peace with myself.

BAD HAIR DAYS

THE STORY

Rebecca J. Dittman

I WAS BORN Alan David Dittman, in the early hours of June 7, 1946, at Chatham House Maternity Home, Balmoral Road, Gillingham, in the county of Kent, England, the second child and son of a teacher and Royal Navy gunnery officer. I am now in the latter part of my life, and although I am at ease with the idea that eventually all life ends, I do have that perverse human desire to be immortal. The reality of existence is that it refuses to accept that possibility, so perhaps through these words I can achieve my longing. I hope that they will inform, stimulate debate, lend support, create dissent, and generally get in among the minds of those who subsequently read them, for it is through the lives of others that we gain our immortality.

Gender and All That Jazz

It's 7:02 A.M. The news on the radio is not worth talking about, and I'm going through that daily ritual of trying to make myself look presentable for work. Bath first, deodorant, body spray (must smell good, as I work closely with the public). Dry my hair and set to styling it. I peer myopically at myself in the mirror. What a sight! My hair is in one of those uncooperative moods and seriously needs cutting. Although short in style, it has started to become wayward and straggly at the ends. I look again and recognize those feelings that occur regularly when my hair starts to rebel. I feel male.

Don't ask me why, but my hair has become a signifier of the way in which I sense my gender. Being transgendered, as opposed to a transvestite or a transsexual or any other permutation of the gender spectrum, my gender description floats around a point that very much depends on how I feel at a particular time or within a set of circumstances. It has not always been so and is just part of a whole lifetime of dealing with an identity that is at odds with the binary position that most of society happily adheres to.

Transgender is a term that I have only recently used to describe myself, and it has come as a blessed relief. Although not one to resort to labels, I, like everyone else, need some words to give my individuality a name. For most people in society, this of course is an easy task. They are "normal," and this allows them not to even think about their identities. But for those of us who would challenge the binary nature of society, words become problematic, not only for ourselves but for all of those around us.

For many years I had struggled to understand myself, largely because I did not have a language that adequately described me. My early diagnosis was that I must be a transvestite, as I desired to dress in the clothes of the opposite gender. However, that did not support my need to live full-time in that way, as it appeared to me that the essence of being a transvestite was about the comfort that a person gained by dressing as the opposite gender, but not actually living as the opposite gender. So did that mean I was a transsexual? Transsexuals, as we know, are those who have an unassailable belief that they inhabit the wrong body, and those feelings motivate them to seek permanent alterations to their bodies.

Again I was lost, as I had never considered that I was a woman trapped in a man's body. Yes, I recognized that there were strong aspects of my personality that could be seen as more feminine, and yes, I did have some desire to change my body so that it had a more feminine look and feel, but I was generally content with the sexed body that I inhabited. So what could I do to find the words that summed all this up neatly?

Apart from language, being transgendered is about choosing to live in the gender role of choice. When we are newborn infants, others surround us with love and comfort, and in exchange they impose a gender role, which most people can happily live with throughout their lives. But many of us are just not like that. Whatever it is that drives us (and I am not going to get into theories or current research on the formation of gender), we believe that this imposition, totally outside of our control, was wrong, and the veracity of this is demonstrated in the confusion and unhappiness that fractures our lives until we can overcome it.

Well, for me it came unexpectedly in my attending a lecture given by Dr. Tracie O'Keefe, associated with the publication of her book *Sex, Gender and Sexuality: Twenty-First Century Transformations* in 1999. In a lecture theater at Liverpool University in the north of England on a wet and windy November night, I sat transfixed as I watched and learned about the many people like myself who did not fit into or try to emulate the binary nature of my society. And with this revelation also came a term that was foreign to my ears: *transgendered*. How would I define myself now? Well, transgendered, of course, but also I have made my peace with the English language and its limitations, and accept the need to choose certain words to assist communications, even though perhaps they do not describe me accurately. Most important is the use of pronouns. My choices are *she* and *her*, as my sense of self is one of a person who is, on balance, more feminine than masculine.

On Being a Child

I was born a postwar baby boomer. My parents married during the Second World War and already had a daughter, my sister, five years before I came along. I came into this world like many children, with a set of expectations placed upon my tiny shoulders from the very moment I uttered my first cry. My father, a life-serving Royal Navy man, immediately signed me up for a navy training school, while my mother, a primary school teacher, had ambitions for me of an academic nature.

The first significant occurrence in my life that I suggest had an influence on the cultural development of my sense of gender was that my father, unable to get suitable engineering work in this country after the Second World War, took up a job in the Middle East as a petroleum engineer. He left when I was four, not to return permanently until I had reached the age of thirteen. During this period of my life I grew up in a family almost exclusively female: a mother and sister, and an extended family consisting of maternal grandmother, aunts, and female cousins. Male influences, although they were there, were small in number, and could not counter the weight of feminine inspiration. I cannot propose an unassailable thesis on what effect this had on my personal development, but it would seem logical within commonly accepted theories of child development (nature versus nurture and so on) that this imprinting of femininity was the starting point of all the confusion that led to much unhappiness in later life.

My first recollection of an expression of this confusion was my stating to my mother at the age of around five that I wanted to be a girl. I was choosing girls as my friends, and enjoyed the company of my female cousins much more than the male family members. It therefore seemed the most natural thing in the world to make such a statement. Of course it was met with a kindly but firm explanation that such ideas were not to be indulged, and such were the times then that I am sure my mother had no knowledge, even as a teacher, about the basis for my request. You were born and gendered by others, and that was that. Children were to be seen and not heard.

So, life went on as usual, but I have clear recollections of being envious of girls of my own age over their dress and appearance, which I wanted to emulate. I remember secretly trying on some of my sister's clothes and have a memory of playing at dressing-up at my grandmother's house with a few of my female cousins at the age of eight.

Growth to a Sexual Being

My sexuality, such as it was, showed an early indication that throughout my life I would be attracted to females. It is interesting to note, however, that in some of my early relationships with girls there was a kind of vicarious pleasure attached. I once wrote a letter of undying love to one girl at around the age of nine, which contained more comments about how much I liked a certain dress that she wore and the style of haircut that she had, than about her as a person. This was more than an attempt at trying to compliment her, but expressed some of my desire to be like her and wear the clothes she had. I made the error of putting this letter, undelivered, under the mattress of my bed, where it was discovered by my mother. Mortification followed, and I learned an early lesson about not disclosing certain things about myself.

My sexual relationships have never foundered on the rocks of technique, but have always been colored by my need to perform a role that would normally be seen as the province of a woman—that is, a more passive and accepting one. The enjoyment of sex, for me, has largely centered on the pleasure that I can give my partner, and I have always felt uneasy when it comes to acknowledging my own needs.

As in many people's adolescent development, masturbation came to be a way of escaping into a fantasy world where I could indulge in a view of myself that could not be fulfilled in the real world. Now this was a time when you were told in no uncertain terms in sex education class that masturbation was unhealthy, would make you blind, and all those

Victorian/Edwardian notions of sexual behavior that led to so much unhappiness in many people's lives. It was not surprising that this activity, therefore, became doubly tainted, not only with society's view but also with my feelings of guilt arising from the thoughts contained in my indulgences.

I, like many others with gender dysphoric tendencies, became fascinated by the signifiers of difference, especially in the area of dress. Therefore, female underwear became a symbol of femininity, a "must have," containing in it a potency that was out of all proportion to its actual function. Many years down the road from all that, I no longer have the same thoughts, but this obsession would in time damage all the intimate relationships I had as an adult. It would also feed into my growing burden of guilt.

In transition and beyond, my sexuality has never wavered, but it has been a common experience that people will assume that I must be attracted to males, and it quite unnerves some when I tell them that no, men have never been attractive to me. This is, again, of course, a reflection of the deeply bigendered nature of society, where in general men must be attracted to women, and women to men.

Of course, posttransition I am left in a rather curious position of wanting to find a female partner but living in a community where I am not viewed by women as a potential sexual partner because I still have my male genitalia. At the beginning of my transition, I found this extremely distressing, and I pined for a partner. I think this was mainly because I was seeking support at a difficult point in my life. But now that I feel like a whole person, my ability to support myself emotionally means I am free from those needy feelings, and anyway I have come to quite enjoy the freedom of being footloose and single!

Pretransition

At the age of twenty, I made the rash choice of marrying the young woman I believed I was in love with. She was the first person I spoke to about my mixed-up feelings. When we parted some two years later, I found that the problem with honesty is that those words can be used against you, and when you're down, some will go on kicking you. This period was the beginning of a lifelong dance with depression, self-loathing, and suicidal thoughts and actions. Even now, at a point where I would consider myself to be well grounded and living a life that is comfortable and satisfying, I am ever on guard against those negative thoughts and actions.

By the age of twenty-eight I had successfully completed training to become a registered nurse, and had remarried. This relationship lasted for seventeen years and produced a son. The early years were ones in which I disclosed my needs, and we both enjoyed the frisson of my desires to crossdress, but after a time my wife found this threatening and no longer indulged me. Back to the old unvirtuous circle of action-result-guilt. This was very damaging to both of us and, for me, over the length of the marriage, caused many internal resentments.

As is the experience of many trans people, I had to endure the roller-coaster ride of denial and the regular crests on the ride when I believed that I could overcome all this by just ignoring it and being "normal." These times resulted in the destruction of any clothing, makeup, jewelry, and so on in the belief that this was an external process; by removing all traces of this other person, I would be like everyone else, and my life and relationships would be successful. The reality was, of course, that this process was only of short duration, and before long the internal identity and associated confusion reasserted itself. The only ones to benefit from all of this over many years have been the retail outlets that have parted me from my money!

For more than twenty years I lived a closet existence, where the only opportunities for crossdressing were in total privacy when I was alone at home. Occasionally, as in all situations where a person is carrying out secretive actions, I made mistakes, such as not clearing things completely away, and my activities would be revealed to hostile gaze. More guilt, more resentment, more anger, more inertia.

Crossroads Always Come

In 1992 Queen Elizabeth II had what she described as her "Annus Horribilis" (bad year), following Princess Anne's divorce, the separation of Prince Andrew and Sarah Ferguson, the fire at Windsor Castle, and the Andrew Morton book about Princess Diana. My Annus Horribilis started the following year.

I had been in a long-term relationship, following the breakup of my second marriage, with a very understanding and positive woman, who from the early days had encouraged me to find help and come to understand my complexity. As a person with a deep understanding of the nature of change and its effects, she could only have done this in the clear knowledge that there were dangers in letting the genie out of the bottle. And so it turned out.

After three years of personal counseling, I had started to acknowledge that what I was seeking was not wrong, unrealistic, or impossible, but rested on my willingness (a) to make choices and (b) take responsibility for those choices. The first was exceedingly scary, and the second was something I had largely avoided most of my adult life, preferring to blame others for what I perceived to be the shortcomings of my life. This was a time in which I was like a child let into a sweet shop, surrounded by all the goodies that I could ever want, but unable to make the choices I needed to. So I did what most of us do in such situations—became greedy, and wanted it all.

Now I tell of a period of my life for which I will be forever ashamed. I was then working part-time as a registered nurse in a nursing home. I worked the night shift, and it was December 31, 1993. It was bad enough having to work that night, and my partner, a Scot, would have preferred for us to be celebrating Hogmanay. So what did I do, just on the point of leaving her to go to work? In my naive thoughts, I had come to the conclusion that the only way of resolving my gender dilemma was to vote for the other side and "become" a woman, so what could be better with the New Year starting the next day than to let my partner, the one who loved me most, know that this was my plan for 1994! And, to add insult to injury, I hadn't even considered that she might, in some small way, object.

Therefore, by the end of 1994 I had descended into a very black period in my life, seriously depressed, in hospital and grieving over the ashes of a relationship that I had done much to destroy. But, as the cliché goes: every cloud has a silver lining, and in my case the worst of all times became the best of all times. I had burned all my bridges and had nowhere else to go than toward the very things that I had kept away from for far too long. So after a long period, both as an in-patient and out-patient of a psychiatric unit, I came to the brave decision to adopt the lifestyle that I wished for.

From A to B: A Story of Transition

The path that led from this crossroads took me immediately into the uncertain territory of homelessness, unemployment, and ill health. Being placed by my social worker in a bed-and-breakfast hostel in one of the less salubrious areas of Liverpool was perhaps not the best start to this new life, but one thing that I have learned from those times is that being honest about who you are, especially to yourself, opens many more doors than it closes. It has never failed to surprise me the number of people who will unexpectedly give you their support and encouragement. And so it was, and hopefully always will be.

The transition to my present identity has been a long and, at times, painful one. When I look back at the early days, when I started to wear very androgynous clothing and a minimal amount of makeup, I smile with the recognition that these are really enormous barriers to overcome for someone who has existed in a society that is generally hostile to nonconformity. There were many moments of self-doubt and decisions about backtracking to "safer" climates, but once the first step had been taken, there was little I could do to prevent the inevitable—thank goodness.

Fear is a most powerfully limiting factor. For all of my adult life I had lived with the fear that becoming myself would be full of rejection, antipathy toward my needs, and hostility, both verbal and physical. There was plenty of anecdotal evidence in the press and media about the way in which trans people were treated in society. I clearly remember an incident in which my fear might have prevented me from moving forward.

Up to that point, venturing out in public had mainly taken place in the evenings when I was less likely to meet others on the street, and darkness was a comfortable cloak of invisibility. On this particular Saturday I had reached a positive decision to make my mark on the world in the full glare of daylight, and got ready to go out wearing clothes that I wanted to wear—hang convention! But could I get myself through the door? I then spent the next couple of hours changing my clothes back and forth, female to male, male to female, until I reached a point where the futility of my indecision became too much to bear without laughing at the idiocy of the situation. So I faced the world with my head high and the butterflies in my stomach in danger of beating me to death. But I survived, and like every step from there on, it became a way of learning about myself and my fears, and through experience, recognizing that the fantasy was not matched by reality.

Don't get me wrong, things have not been easy, and I have had to face derision, verbal abuse, and physical violence. None of this has been pleasant, but what it has done for me is to strengthen my resolve and reinforce my beliefs that what I am doing may transgress the norms of society, but it does others no harm and should not be apologized for.

Medical Support

My first encounter with the medical profession in regard to my gender dysphoria occurred when I was twenty-three. I talked to my then general practitioner, who happened to be the uncle of my partner at the time. He referred me to Charing Cross Hospital in London—a consultation that I shall never forget.

I was ushered into a gloomy, wood-paneled consulting room and talked to what seemed to me a very ancient consultant. I remember that there was a loud and slowly ticking clock in the room. After asking me questions about the nature of my problems, he turned to "treatment." What he was offering was aversion therapy. He wanted to photograph me dressed in women's clothing, and then his proposal was that he show me these photographs mixed in with other images, and whenever I looked at an image of myself, he would administer an electric shock! I was petrified. I ran from that hospital in fear of my life and never returned. Oh, those were the good old days, when beer was a shilling a pint, the 1960s were swinging, and the potent force of electricity was held to be a cure for every sort of deviation or perversion. It took me a long time to overcome my unwillingness to be honest with a doctor again.

I have also been the experiment of a number of generalist psychologists, had psychiatrists interested in "curing" me, and spent three years in personal counseling, but it was not until 1995, after twenty-six painful and unhappy years, that I was at last referred to a specialist gender unit in Liverpool and came under the care of a clinical consultant psychologist who specializes in this field. She has been my salvation, and I owe her a debt of gratitude for allowing me to explore my identity without setting any boundaries.

It is my understanding from other trans people that I am in contact with that many "specialists" in the field still hold to the view that in life we have only the choice of male and female, masculinity or femininity, and that trans people are as bound to that norm as anyone else. I have never felt those dichotomies were appropriate, and have been allowed to seek an outcome that will serve me well in my remaining life by achieving a good fit.

My body, as mentioned earlier, has never been congruent to my inner image, and so hormone therapy has helped me to go some way toward squaring the circle. I maintain my hormone regime under the care of my GP, who is part of an exceptional joint practice in Liverpool. I would encourage any trans person seeking such treatment to do so under the care of a physician. I know that many take the risk of obtaining hormones on the black market or through websites and so on, and although there is anecdotal evidence to say that many do so successfully, there are real risks to health, and it would seem sensible to monitor things like blood pressure, weight, cholesterol, and other factors in the blood on a regular basis.

Although I at one time considered reassignment surgery while in my "transsexual" phase, this has now passed me by. I had an orchidectomy (removal of the testes) in 2000, but only on the basis that in order to maintain my long-term female hormone treatment, I would have fewer problems and would no longer need to take damaging antiandrogens (male

hormone blockers). The only remaining goal that I now have of a medical
nature is breast augmentation. At the time of writing this in 2002, I am on
an approximately twelve-month waiting list for that. I have always seen
having breasts as being wholly appropriate, and not in the least unusual,
even though other parts of my body remain decidedly male! My view is
seen by many as perverse and, by some, as perverted. Who's right?

The other thing I will say about my medical support is that unlike
many, I have achieved it all through the National Health Service (NHS)
of the United Kingdom. Am I just lucky or more assertive, or do I know
the ropes better because of my nursing background (not that I have pulled
any strings)? I don't know. All I would say is that there is provision within
the NHS, and that any trans person in the United Kingdom should fight
hard to ensure that they take advantage of it. Unlike trans communities
in other countries, we have largely been very silent about the difficulties that surround us in society, be it prejudice and bigotry or the inertia
of services and governmental agencies in accepting that we have rights.
My concern as a transgendered individual is that for so long as we continue to believe that our security lies in our invisibility, we shall never
change these barriers to our happiness.

Friends, Relatives, and Partners

I think out of all things, the consequences to family, friends, and partners
seem to be the hardest things for trans people to have to deal with. Not
only does this hold true for me, but having come to know many others in
a similar position to myself over the past nine years, I would suggest for
most it is a truism.

But the reality for me at least is that the outcome has been a pleasant
surprise. From the belief that I would be excluded, marginalized, and
forced to live a twilight existence, I now find that I am surrounded by
truly supportive friends, that family members have had mixed reactions
to me, and none has completely disowned me. Why? My observation is
that we all respond much more positively to anyone who is true to themselves. We have all met people who, for one reason or another, are unwilling to expose themselves to our gaze. We understand this, but often
cannot respond to them, as they appear to have something to hide. I, on
the other hand, have nothing to hide. My life is an open book now, I do
not fear intrusion or curiosity, and on the whole, people respond to that
openness positively.

I regret the pain that I have caused the various partners in my life, but
accept that I was not able to do more than I did at the time, and after all

they also played a part in the game, so I don't beat myself up too much these days. I have had only two brief relationships since my transition, both foundering as I was still exploring my new identity and had some of my old hang-ups about it. Whether the future will bring me another close relationship with a woman, I can't tell, but I do know that my whole attitude to this area of life has changed and that my priorities are very different from my pretransition days. I believe that I am actually in a much better position to maintain a relationship, as I am at ease with myself and can therefore concentrate on the needs of the other person.

The only other relationship that I would like to acknowledge here is the one I have with my son. He has, in his short life, had to make major readjustments to the way in which he thinks about me, and it is a testament to his strength of character and the depth of the relationship that we had before my transition that out of a period in which he was confused and angry, we have arrived on a new plane where we can relate to each other more equally. He still calls me "Dad," but accepts that this label does not come with the same stereotyped image. The dilemma of trans people with children is a difficult one, and I can offer no easy solutions. Suffice to say that on the whole, if there is a strong foundation of love in existence before transition, then that is likely to offer the best possibility of relationships being forged again, given time.

The Trans Community and the Future

When I set out on my road of discovery, there was one thought clearly in the center of my consciousness: "I do not want to become part of a ghetto." I believe I have achieved that and live openly in a mixed community. I consider myself to be as normal as my neighbors, and hope that on the whole they see me in that way as well. This has resulted from a fierce belief in my rights and the willingness to confront antagonism along the way. Perhaps my chosen position on the gender spectrum has helped, as there are times when my maleness kicks in with a vengeance and helps me through difficult times, much to the surprise of any adversary.

My connections to the trans community have been very limited. Being an independent spirit and free thinker, I have not sought the support and safety in numbers that being part of a trans group brings for others. Interestingly, it is now that my transition is largely complete that I feel more at ease with the trans community and want to play a part in the support of others. My publishing of the Transgender UK website in 2000 was part of this. But I remain largely skeptical about the ability of the trans community in the United Kingdom to make significant inroads into the social and political issues that face them. I would put this down to (a) the dominance of the need for invisibility by many transsexuals in the debate while seeking public acceptance, (b) a few strong personalities who would prescribe to others how their journeys should be planned and executed, and (c) a refusal to recognize that gender diversity is a much wider concept than is accepted both within the trans community and society generally.

The trans community appears to remain enthralled with the male-female model of society, and until we can gain acceptance of gender rights in this country and allow each and every one of the population to choose where they sit on the gender spectrum, we will continue to meet with hostility. We must accept that we are part of the problem. *The International Bill of Gender Rights,* as first proposed by JoAnn Roberts, Ph.D., in 1990, is something that I support, espouse, and would offer as a way forward, as it sees gender diversity as "mainstream" and affecting each and every one of us, not just those with so-called gender dysphoria. Wouldn't it be a wonderful day if we didn't have that term to fall back on as an excuse!

And the future? Well, what I have learned is that it's not finished until it's finished. I have journeyed down a path that, when I first stepped onto it, I believed was finite and would have at its terminus the goal that I wanted to achieve. What has actually happened is that on my journey I have released a part of me which knows that the permutations are endless, and that if I choose, I can go off in a completely different direction, or even go back up the route I came down at any time. For many people this is an unsettling notion, certainty and security being their watchwords, but for me it means that the future is an ever-unfolding series of exciting possibilities, until that final day comes when the biggest mystery is where it might lead then. As any good child of the 1960s would say, "Roll on, Sister!"

○

ROBYN'S JOURNEY

Robyn Walters

THE FERRY CHURNED THE WATER BROWN as it began the trek to downtown Seattle, and I knew I was dead. They'll figure it out, and they'll throw me overboard, I thought. Oh, God, what have I let myself in for?

A few women stared, mostly at my hair. Some smiled and nodded. The men were oblivious. Somehow, I didn't panic, but my stomach felt the vibrations of a silent jackhammer known only to me. The anonymity of my car felt as refreshing as a cool washcloth on a hot summer day when I slipped behind the wheel again. My breathing returned to normal when cars began driving up the ramp to shore. Now all I had to do was to find an address and a parking place in a strange city.

Dr. Johnson was professionally pleasant. I was relieved that she would work to help understand my situation. The hour rushed by, and I was once again on the ferry. I had crossdressed my way across Puget Sound in broad daylight and survived to tell the tale. I had a gender counselor and an appointment for the next month. I was going to learn about this compulsion to wear women's clothes. Maybe it would be all right.

Gray and white gulls flew over as I sat alone, remembering another day, not quite two years earlier in Virginia. The kids were home from college and sleeping in that July Sunday morning. I had finished my morning meditation and had spent some time in the computer room, checking e-mail and chatting with friends.

The aroma of pancakes cooking slowly in melted butter was heavy in the air when I joined Nicky, my wife of twenty-two years, in the kitchen, the room in which our lives always seemed closest and most comfortable.

A pair of mourning doves cooed on the deck rail. Sunlight dappled tulip poplar leaves that moved slightly in a gentle morning breeze.

I had recently been attuned to the second level of Reiki healing, the level that works with mind and emotions. My teacher warned me: "You will drink a lot more water, and within three months you will experience a major emotional upheaval." Now, two months later, the volcano was about to erupt and change our lives forever. Nicky and I talked about spiritual things, about how quickly the world seemed to be changing.

"I can feel the acceleration," I told her. "I can feel changes in my life."

"Like what?" she asked, placing a golden pancake on a warming plate in the oven. I took a deep breath, and it all bubbled over.

"You know I like lingerie. But there's more to it than that. I want to be a crossdresser. I may want to take hormones. I don't know, but I want to get some counseling to understand what is going on."

Nicky turned back to the stove and poured more batter into the frying pan. "Oh," was all she said. She seemed calm. After all, she had chided me early in our marriage for being homophobic and uncomfortable around her gay and lesbian friends. Surely, I thought, she'll be fine with my wearing women's clothes now and then—maybe a nightgown to bed.

It's amazing how quickly a marriage can end. A matter of seconds and a few words are all it may take. We stayed together for over a year and waited almost four years to divorce, but our marriage ended that morning. I just didn't know it yet.

Later that day, we went for a walk along a favorite path by the reservoir where we had often laughed, held hands, and hugged trees. That day we were quiet and pensive. I tried to answer her insistent questions, but often said, "I don't know." I was in more inner turmoil than I could imagine. It was only the beginning. Before long, I was on the wrong end of her wrath. "How could you deceive me? How could you destroy my femininity? You must be homosexual. You must want to be loved like a woman."

"I didn't deceive you," I replied. "I didn't know. I always thought I just had a lingerie fetish. My wanting to explore femininity has nothing to do with your femininity. I am most decidedly not gay. I want to be your husband; I just want to be able to dress now and then."

She said she'd try, yet she wouldn't go to a gender counselor. "I won't see her unless she has a husband who's a crossdresser. How could she possibly understand what I'm going through if she hasn't been through it herself?"

I received a clean bill of health from the counselor. "You seem to be a perfectly normal crossdresser. It's not you I'm worried about; it's your abusive wife. She needs to learn to control her rage."

Nicky did try, and spent time with a therapist friend who thought cross-dressing was a terrible perversion. She helped my wife release anger through role playing. She was a pleasant seventy-one-year-old woman without a clue about transgender issues. The role playing must not have helped, because I found myself abused for the rest of our time together. I never knew when it would come or what would set it off. Sometimes it was verbal abuse, sometimes things were thrown. Too often it involved bloody nail marks and bruises on my throat or a threatening butcher's knife. "I might as well cut it off," she'd scream. "You don't need it anymore."

"No, no. Wait. It's just me. I'm still the same. I just want to dress some. Maybe go out now and then."

"No."

"Well, maybe just for Halloween?"

"No."

"OK then, how about just around the house?"

"No."

"What if I just give it up completely? Maybe I can do that. I'll throw everything away."

"Doesn't matter. I can't ever trust you again. When you move west—without me—you'll be living full-time in no time."

Just a Crossdresser

The moving van pulled away, and we drove to our temporary apartment. The house we owned for most of our children's lives was sold. Our remaining time together was numbered in weeks. On the Fourth of July, we watched fireworks together for the last time. In August, we went to our beach timeshare for the last time. In early October, we drove to the North Carolina beach for a Cherokee Full Circle. We had a nice time together and with the others who gathered for a weekend of spiritual healing. A different way home led us to Virginia Beach for a late dinner after a long ferry ride. It was very late when we arrived home.

Early the next morning, I flew to San Diego for a Navy meeting. When I returned, Nicky had left for a spiritual retreat in Findhorn, Scotland. By the time she returned, I was halfway across the country, thinking I'd never see her again. All because of the boxes of damned clothes that filled the trunk of my new car.

She was wrong though. I didn't live full-time as a woman. I was still the ancient-looking bald guy, and we did spend more time together. She invited me back for Christmas. One daughter stayed with us on

Christmas break. The other made excuses and visited her boyfriend's family in Texas. We laughed and cried, and parted again.

Six weeks later, I was on the ferry, going to see my new gender therapist. I heard about a big transgender conference west of Seattle, only some fifty miles from my home. I signed up for five days as Robyn. Esprit was an eye opener. So many pretty women, and a few who just weren't. I had a roommate about my age, a happily married crossdresser whose wife was very supportive of her husband's feminine forays. I learned a lot from Vicki and thought nothing strange about our shaving twice a day and primping before the mirror.

At the registration desk one day, a woman leaned over the table, and I thought, "Oh my God, she has breasts!" This was no crossdresser. This was a transsexual. I was both thrilled and disappointed. Where were my breasts? I took them off at night and inserted them in my bra the next morning. No way. I ached to have breasts.

One course offered late in the week was titled *Blue Monday*. The objective was to help us put away the feminine persona and to cope with returning to male mode on Monday. I didn't go to the class. Instead of attending *Blue Monday*, I went to see Dr. Toby Meltzer's presentation on sex reassignment surgery. Several people in the room were either Meltzer graduates or were scheduled for surgery. Brave people. Brave people with breasts and more. But I wasn't ever going to do that. After all, I was just a crossdresser. I was proud that I got through the talk and the slides without feeling squeamish.

I rode home en femme that Sunday afternoon and drove up my neighbor's drive to pick up my mail. "Hi," I said. "There is something you should know about me." I'm sure I didn't really have to point that out to them as I stood there in a blond wig, with false breasts under my blouse. The cat was out of the bag. News about the neighborhood crossdresser spread quite rapidly, and my local social life dried up immediately.

Not a Crossdresser

In June 1998, about three weeks after Esprit, I had the following conversation with my therapist:

"Robyn, I have good news and bad news."

"Um, what's the good news, Dr. Johnson?"

"You aren't a crossdresser."

"Hey, that is good news. Maybe I'll be able to save this marriage after all." I had airline tickets for another trip to spend time with my wife. "Uh, what's the bad news?"

"The bad news is that you're a transsexual. What are you going to do about it?"

Talk about being whapped alongside the head with a two-by-four. "Where did you ever get that idea?"

Crossing her legs and leaning forward, she looked at me intently and said, "You told me that you'd like to have a woman's body and that you could see yourself living full-time as a woman. Crossdressers don't do that. They don't want a woman's body. They are happy in a man's role. They just like to visit the other gender for a short time and then go home to their wives or girlfriends." I shook my head in denial, and then in amazement. It was suddenly so clear.

I went full-time around the neighborhood, at church, and with friends. But I went back to Virginia in male mode. One last chance to convince my wife to come live with me. We spent two weeks in our North Carolina oceanfront timeshare. One night, with the sound of the surf murmuring through an open window, I asked if she would please come out for a visit.

"What would I find if I came to see you in Washington?" she asked. I hung my head.

"I'm living full-time as Robyn," I replied in a soft voice. "But I'm not going to have surgery." She fell to the floor and sobbed for an hour. Sleep was hard to come by that night.

A week later, she dropped me at the airport. As she drove off, she looked back over her shoulder, and I could see tears streaming down her anguished face. That picture was burned into my soul. I knew that it was over for us. No divorce yet, but definitely no hope of saving our marriage.

The next day, back in Washington, I walked into a shop at the mall and said, "I'm sixty-one years old, and my mother finally said I could have my ears pierced."

A month later, I stood in front of our county judge, angered when he said, "Enjoy your new name, sir," but exhilarated that I was legally Robyn. My Real Life Experience could now begin, although I wasn't going to have surgery. Nope, I was a nonoperative transsexual. Living full-time as a woman was enough.

A daughter came to visit over Thanksgiving. She was great but made it clear I'd never be "Mom." The morning after taking my daughter to the airport, I stood in front of the mirror with a bottle of pills in my hand. The reflection of an older woman looked back at me without flinching. She shook out a purple pill shaped like a football and tossed it down. I was on feminizing hormones. Within a month, I turned over in bed and said, "Ouch." My breasts were tender and growing. My interest in nonexistent sexual opportunities diminished rapidly. I cried more readily. I cried over my losses. I was alone. A granddaughter died. My youngest child ignored me. I wondered if I had ruined my life and my chances for happiness in my older years. And then the coincidences began.

I joined a new group, the Transgender Aging Network (TAN). Within a month, the TAN founder started a news list for transgendered people age fifty and over. There was an even mix of MTFs and FTMs at the time. One of the women mentioned something that would have happened in school had she been a girl. Another member added a paragraph, as did a third person. I jumped in as a new girl in the school, and some of the boys did, too. We had an alternate reality story going, but some of the more serious members of the list complained. We formed another news list called TGPlay, but how to get some romance into the stories? Aha, I thought. A Sadie Hawkins dance.

This shy eighth grader asked a boy named Emery to go to the dance with me. He agreed, and before long, the kids were going steady. Emery was more interested in putting goldfish in the punchbowl than with romance, but he did love young Robyn. Soon the adult Emery and Robyn were exchanging e-mail, phone calls, pictures, and small gifts. Falling in love with someone two thousand miles away was scary, and we fought it. Eventually, we decided to meet.

I walked off the plane into the Detroit terminal looking for a familiar face. And there he was, leaning against a pillar with a bouquet of Tootsie Pops in his hand. While I was visiting Emery, he proposed. "Yes," I said. "If you can winter over in Western Washington, I will marry you."

Two months later, I picked Emery up at the airport in Seattle. We married on Valentine's Day, 2000—one biological male and one biological female. Despite the order of names on the marriage certificate, I was the bride, and he was the groom. In March, we had a formal church wedding. Emery wore a jacket and slacks. I wore a floor-length satin burgundy gown and walked down the aisle of our church to the song *Lady in Red*.

Three months later, on my sixty-third birthday, I slipped under warm covers on an Eastmoreland Hospital gurney, and heard the anesthesiologist say, "You won't remember much."

"Remind Dr. Meltzer that this is my birthday," I said, and woke up six hours later to see my husband walking in the door. Dr. Meltzer came in soon after.

"That was the easiest SRS I've ever performed," he said.

It was the next morning before I performed the time-honored act of raising the sheet, looking at the bandages and saying, "Yes!" Within a few days, the Demerol (morphine substitute) pump was removed. I liked the Percocet pain pills I was then given, but used only half what I was prescribed.

On the eighth day, the vaginal packing was removed, and I could walk instead of waddle. I was introduced to the four bachelors—stents, or vaginal dilators—each one an eighth of an inch larger in diameter than his smaller brother. Bachelor number four is sometimes called "Ohmygawd."

On day ten, we flew home to our own bed. An abdominal suture site became infected and I tried stronger antibiotics. No effect. Two days later, I went to our naval hospital and suffered the only bad medical experience I've ever had there. Our regular doctor was unavailable and his stand-in was quite rude. We left his office and walked to the emergency room where I was treated with utmost respect and urgency. Within thirty minutes, I was in general surgery, and the infection was excised. The faded scar is a reminder of that one minor problem. The SRS site healed without problem, and the four bachelors courted me one after another over the next few months.

Life was good, other than having two of my four daughters who wouldn't talk with me. Emery took a picture of me a month after surgery, and that remains one of the happiest pictures ever recorded. We were happy, and our friends were happy for us. Two of my daughters and all four of Emery's were happy for us.

Dilating four times a day during the first month was rather restrictive, but a small price to pay for being whole. Dropping to twice-daily dilations was freeing, and once a day was like a gift. Now it is a regular twice a week routine.

Four months later, I returned to Portland, Oregon, for the second surgery with Dr. Meltzer. Labiaplasty was a two-and-a-half-hour procedure under local anesthetic. I discovered that Dr. Meltzer is a great conversationalist and that they play lovely music in the operating room. No Demerol pump that time. Just Percocet. This surgery was a bit more irritating, probably due to two hundred or so stitches in a very sensitive area. I drove with a pillow for a couple of weeks, and then things were back to normal.

Sex reassignment surgery, gender reassignment surgery, gender confirmation surgery. By whatever name, I found it to be a piece of cake, albeit expensive cake. It was the paperwork that was a killer. Most paperwork changes were easily accomplished. But changing sex as a military retiree took almost eighteen months. Everyone in the Department of Defense (with the exception of that one doctor) was most understanding and sympathetic, and I had no problem receiving women's services, but the database can't be changed without proper military authorization, which is slow in coming.

Before the military officially recognized me as a female retired officer, my nonmilitary husband had his surgery. We went back to see Dr. Meltzer, who told us that we were the only couple for whom he had performed sex reassignment surgery on both spouses. Our fifteen minutes of fame!

Several months after Emery's surgery, we walked into the identification card office at the local Navy base and presented his SRS letter and my letter from the Navy recognizing me as female. The young enlisted man keyed in M for Emery and F for Robyn, and we were officially swapped in the military database. Then I had the change made to my retiree payroll records and the hospital computers. We were done, and the computers were happy.

Has it been easy? Not exactly, but it sure beats the alternative—severe unhappiness and perhaps suicide. For sure, I have had losses and pain: an ex-wife and two daughters who have little to do with me. But I have had gains and joys, too: a wonderful husband, two children and four stepchildren who are very supportive, a welcoming church, an accepting and supportive employer, and the peace that comes from being comfortable in my body.

I am who I was meant to be. When I look at my body, it matches what my brain tells me. When I wake up next to my husband, I feel a joy that was missing from other relationships. Was I gay? Did I always want a man? No and no. I was a heterosexual male and expected to transition to lesbian. I am still mostly attracted to women, but, after a year on estrogen, I suddenly looked at a man and felt that "oh my" sensation. It took another year for me to accept that I could be with a man after surgery. It was difficult, because I had a lot of homophobia to overcome. Finally, I realized that, as a female, being loved by a man would not be homosexual, it would be very normal. Once I accepted that, what did God send me but a female-to-male transsexual? So I now consider myself to be a bisexual in a faithful monogamous relationship. Polyandry doesn't appeal to us, but I can still feel and enjoy the sensations caused by seeing an attractive woman or older man.

Where Did It All Start?

So where did it start? I can trace it back to age nine, but it probably began in the womb with a heavier than usual estrogen concentration infusing the developing male embryo. My mother had more impact on me than my father. During my early years, she was nurturing, protective, and fun. She seemed not to mind that I was a quiet boy, not given to the boisterous actions of my peers. She never insisted that I go out into the rough-and-tumble life of the neighborhood toughies. I did at times, without a lot of success, and preferred reading and my imagination for companionship.

Baseball was OK. Sandlot baseball with school friends was fun. We played in a big lot across from the train station in Madison, New Jersey. I even hit a home run one bright summer day under a fleecy wool sky. The town turned that lot into paved commuter parking the next year, and my halcyon baseball days were over. Instead, it was summer programs at the YMCA—pure torture. I was the small one. I was the weak one. I was the one made fun of during the naked swim periods. Oh, how I hated to expose my underdeveloped body in the midst of the boys who were beginning to look and act like men. "Hey, kid, are you ever going to grow any hair?"

If swimming and diving off the three-meter tower were bad, the pommel horse and rope climb were worse. No coordination and no upper body strength left me stuck halfway over or halfway up and feeling very inadequate. Why couldn't I be a successful, sweaty boy like the others? The answer might have been apparent had I been caught at age nine. I wandered into my parents' closet after school one day and wiggled my way up into one of my mother's dresses. I forget what it looked like, but it had a silky lining and a wonderful fragrance. It fell off the hanger. Panicky, I hung it back up and ran out of the room, forgetting one detail. "Bobby," said my mother when she came home from work. "The light is on in my closet. Did you go in there for something?"

Lying was never my strong suit, but inspiration saved me that day. "Um, yes Mom. You said I could use your roller skates, and I was skating in the kitchen for a while." Phew. I had survived my first crossdressing experience but was so scared that I must have submerged it to the depths of the Marianas Trench.

I retreated into my world of books, acting out my fantasies of deep-sea diving and pet dinosaurs—fantasies that I could play out alone by a brook in the woods behind our house. And I had an imaginary friend. I forget her name, but she was a companion with whom I felt a strong bond of warmth and friendship. One day she disappeared, and I grieved her loss.

Years passed, and my body began to mature, sort of. At least, there were strange sensations and urgings that no one ever told me to expect. When I was twelve, I found a beautiful lace-trimmed rayon chemise beneath my mother's velvet wedding dress, stored in a bureau drawer in the guest room. Flesh colored and incredibly silky, that garment released many of the sensations that came to a pubescent lad. Soon it was mine, moved to a safe spot in my bedroom, the first in a collection of lingerie that spanned decades. I remember visiting backyard clotheslines at the age of thirteen or fourteen, while walking home at night, as well as poking through the laundry basket at a cousin's house. It wasn't long before I first wore a piece of lingerie.

In sophomore year, I walked uptown with a friend who had to give up his after-school job. My parents were surprised when I announced at dinner that I had a part-time job in our town's photo shop. I learned a lot from the owner of our store. Working with the public also gave me a lot of poise. Adults were easier to deal with than macho classmates or the girls I liked but with whom I didn't know how to behave. Some days I handled the store all by myself. All by myself and dressed under my outer clothes. The feel of a slip next to my skin was both comforting and exciting.

My high school days weren't without challenge. The academics weren't particularly difficult, and I was surprised to end up valedictorian of my class of about one hundred. There were some fun things, like being the lighting director for several plays and talent shows. Learning the 1950s state-of-the-art lighting system was fun, and I could mix and match colors to my heart's content. Lavender was my favorite. I could also watch the girls on stage in their pretty gowns.

I was still far from Joe Cool, far different from most of the boys in the class. They seemed interested only in cars, cigarettes, beer, and whose panties they could get into. I didn't know too much about any of those delights, although two of the nice girls became pregnant and two others had very bad reputations. If I had a reputation, it was probably as a nerd, although the term hadn't yet been coined.

I did have two buddies. Dave and I flew model airplanes together, and Bill and I just hung out, mostly at his house. Unfortunately, I lost track of both of them shortly after college. Girls were a disaster. I was attracted to some of the girls and to their clothes. I never learned how to relate to them and rarely had a date, never anything beyond an icky high school prom or an occasional movie. Icky because I didn't know how to dance—it was still years before the twist saved me—and because I had to wear a suit and tie. I still have some pictures of girls in braces and pretty gowns with this gawky kid in an ugly suit and bow tie. One was a white satiny scoop neck gown I would have given my eyeteeth for. Oh well, all I had was my lingerie stash. I learned well that a lingerie love life was always available and quite satisfying. Too inept to have a girlfriend, I still managed to keep the pubescent machinery well exercised.

In June 1956, a skinny kid from New Jersey rode south to Annapolis, Maryland. The sun was shining when we stopped at a lookout on the approach to the Severn River Bridge. The naval academy was just off to the left on the far side of the river, with Chesapeake Bay spreading out behind its seawall. Breathtaking, and it was to be my home for the next four years.

Gone was any thought of privacy. Gone—for a short time—was any doubt of masculinity. Hey, I was a midshipman, cream of the crop. I was going to be an admiral. But gee, most of the other guys were so macho and so much stronger than I. Some didn't care for the bookish, nonathletic kid from New Jersey. But I had a good roommate, Denny, for all four years.

Hours after the Naval Academy class of 1957—our senior mentors and tormentors—graduated and threw their hats in the air, half of my classmates and I were shuttled to an armada of ships standing in Chesapeake Bay. The other half went home for six weeks of summer leave. My first ship. And what a ship: the USS *Iowa*, BB-61, lead ship in the last and largest class of battleships in the U.S. Navy. Huge, massive, and with sixteen-inch guns that could hurl a projectile the weight of a Volkswagen beetle twenty miles. I learned how to holystone the teak fantail under the watchful eye of a first-class boson's mate. I was sickened by food poisoning following the failure of a refrigeration compressor, and I got laid in Rio de Janeiro. First time. Second and third time, too. I was a man. I proudly took my penicillin pill each night when I came back to the ship. An experience of a lifetime, but when it was my time to go home, I fell back into my old ways. No woman to seduce and no young Brazilian prostitute to pay. Not even a lingerie stash. I had thrown it all away when I left for the academy.

Back to Annapolis in late August, no longer a plebe. Now I was a youngster and had some privileges, among them the right to date. By the time that year was over, I had had several dating experiences and an honest-to-goodness girlfriend. Again, there was some fumbly foreplay but no intercourse until we married after graduation.

In June 1960, I was commissioned an ensign in the U.S. Navy; I married Ginny and settled into an apartment in Washington, D.C. I was a married man who soon had a baby on the way, and I was working five-and-a-half days a week designing nuclear submarine fluid systems for Admiral Rickover. Pretty good, except that I didn't have a clue how to be a husband or a father. I think I did better on the father side than on the husband side, and our marriage was soon on a downhill slide. I very soon had a lingerie stash that was kept in a paper bag atop a ventilation duct in the basement of the townhouse where our second daughter was conceived.

After four years with Rickover, I received orders to the guided missile cruiser *Little Rock* (CLG-4). We moved to Norfolk, but the lingerie stash stayed behind. There was little opportunity to replenish while there, although I did manage to secrete a few small things in the state room

I shared with another officer. Eventually, I threw them overboard in the Mediterranean Sea. Typical purging pattern.

Things began to gel following that sea tour when the Navy sent me to MIT for naval engineering graduate studies. We owned a house, and it had a perfect hidey-hole in the downstairs bathroom, which eventually held two bags of lingerie. These were visited every day, and I began to wear lingerie again whenever my family was away for visits to my wife's parents.

We were in the seventh year of our, by now, loveless marriage. One night, in my frustration, I took a beautiful nightgown from her dresser, one that she never wore. I fell asleep with the nightgown spread over the bed on top of me. Ginny never said a word, but the cat was sneaking out of the bag. I put the nightgown away when I awoke the next morning and stayed away from her things for some time.

When we divorced several years later, she stayed in the house until she married a priest from our parish. So far as I know, the house was sold with those two bags of lingerie still hidden in the bathroom ceiling. Of our two daughters, one is now nearly a stranger and the other, one of my biggest supporters.

That summer of 1972, I met a woman in an evening physics class I was teaching, after my daytime Navy job. I was waiting for my divorce to be final. Nicky was separated from her husband but hadn't yet bothered to file for divorce. By late fall, we were living together, and I was a man again. I knew I wasn't the man that some of my Navy colleagues were. They were macho and loved Navy trips where they could go trolling for sex after hours. Their exploits were legendary, and they were so masculine. I was my usually inadequate male self, full of doubt. But a year later, with orders in hand, Nicky and I married and were very quickly in a family way. Sixteen months apart, our two daughters—my third and fourth— were born in Brunswick, Maine.

Life settled into a comfortable pattern of Navy, work, family, and hobbies. I spent many hours improving my flying skills in Maine and later in Virginia. And I was able to put up some decent antennas for my amateur radio station. But always in the background was the lingerie and the occasional opportunity to try on a skirt and blouse from my wife's side of the closet.

The radio room was downstairs and held a desk, two computers, and several radios. Adjoining the room was a bathroom with shower. As a considerate husband, I shaved and showered there in the early morning hours so as not to disturb my wife. The morning routine involved changing from pajamas to a nightgown and then back again before returning upstairs to eat and dress for work. I'd lie on the floor doing stretching exercises and could almost feel the breasts that should have been there. Most mornings, there was a sexual tension that had to be released as well.

Eventually I yielded to the pressure from my wife and started an account with an Internet service provider. We were on the Internet! Well, I was. Nicky very quickly lost interest in e-mailing the girls at college. One day, shortly before the Reiki II attunement and the Sunday morning confession, I typed *crossdresser* into the search engine, and my world changed.

So, my father's son became a woman. I answered the challenge and finished an important part of my journey. I can now answer a question that stumped me for several years. Why did I transition? The answer turned out to be very simple. I transitioned to female to be true to myself. May each of you who read this find your truth, whatever it might be.

JAPAN: A SEXUALLY UNIQUE COUNTRY

Masae Torai

"JAPAN MUST BE FAR MORE CONSERVATIVE than almost any other country." This is the viewpoint of many Westerners. I, who was born and have been living in Tokyo for thirty-eight years, can honestly say that this statement is both true and untrue. Before telling you my story, I would like to tell you a little bit about Japanese culture. Japan is a very rigid but also free and unbelievably peculiar country. Yes, we may value society much more than the individual, so we hate the whole "me" thing. Also, compared to the people of many Western countries, we may be more polite, more formal, more humble. Yes, we may be just conservative in many aspects, but I am quite sure we were once sexually a very complicated people in a good sense.

We were also complicated religiously. Even now, this is the case. First of all, I would like to say that we don't have any special religion. Many Japanese people are purified at a Shinto shrine when they are babies and as children at the ages of three, five, and seven. In the old times, children often died at those ages. Shinto is one of the original Japanese religions. It has been around far longer than Buddhism and has never been practiced outside Japan. It has a lot of gods and goddesses of nature, just as Hinduism has, and they are deeply connected with agriculture because Japan has been cultivating rice since the beginning of time. Japanese people celebrate New Year's Day at Buddhist temples or Shinto shrines every year. Wedding ceremonies are also held at Shinto shrines or Christian churches (even if the person is not a Christian). Funeral services are usually conducted at Buddhist temples. So we go to shrines, temples, and churches every year to meet, but foreigners tend to see us generally as only Buddhists. It's true that Buddhism is quite important to us, but Shinto is our original religion.

Old Japan

I think old Japan resembles ancient Greece in some ways. Like the Greeks, we had many gods and goddesses. The holiest god is female—the goddess of the sun in our Shinto mythology. Buddhism came to Japan from China in the sixth century. I am not a Buddhist, but I went to Buddhist kindergarten when I was a child and held a Buddhist funeral when my father died, so I know a little about it. One of the important teachings of Buddhism is equality. Buddhists say, "Everyone can become Buddha, which means the awakened person." They also say, "Every living creature is equal. Even a human being and a bug are equal, because we are from the same sources." That is why people's attitudes in Buddhist countries tend to be kinder and more tolerant toward trans people.

However, even in this religion, the male is far superior to the female. It is said that every male can be spiritually awakened, depending on the length of his serving as a novice, but for a female it is very hard. And this is so interesting because some schools of Buddhism (there are so many) tell us, "Therefore, to be spiritually awakened like a male, the female may turn into a male. Then they can be spiritually awakened." Isn't it wonderful? Some aspects of Buddhism encourage female-to-male sex changes! I remember I used to stay for many hours in the huge Buddhist library to find the way to turn into a male when I was age eighteen or nineteen, but I couldn't find any specific ways. I wondered if ancient Japanese female monks could turn their female bodies into male ones with some Buddhist charm.

Shinto and Buddhism are, compared to Christianity, far more liberal. Personally I love Christianity, though I am not a Christian. (I am a kind of Shintoist and like to read New Age books—a typical complicated Japanese person!) My favorite place is a church, my favorite music is the pipe organ, and I used to play many hymns on my toy organ when I was four or five in the Buddhist kindergarten. I dreamed a lot about Jesus and heaven when I was in elementary school. But because I knew Buddhist countries were kinder toward trans people, my love for Christianity has been complicated since then. I even feel relieved that Japan is not a Christian country. But this makes me a little sad, as I know Jesus and God love us anyway, but so many nontrans Christians don't understand us.

In old Japan, like ancient Greece, homosexuality was natural to us, especially among men. Some Shoguns are well known to have been homosexual. I saw some drawings that were done about two hundred years ago of a woman who has her legs open and shows her private parts. The title is something like *Looks Like a Butterfly* and there is some explanation, which goes along the lines of, "This kind of vulva is very rare and quite precious. Both labia are long, and it looks as if the huge butterfly is opening its wings." In short, she was some kind of intersex person. So, intersex people must have been highly valued at that time. The traditional art of Kabuki, where male actors also take the female roles, was and still is really popular. We were truly sexually broad-minded until the opening of our country to Western culture.

When we did this, Western culture with Christianity rushed in, and Japan was Westernized quite rapidly. Of course this was a good thing, because if we had kept Japan isolated, the Samurai would be brandishing their swords even now. However, this new wave of Western influence washed away our sexual freedom. Men and women were strictly separated, and sexual minorities came to be seen as deformed people.

But we have remained free as far as religion goes, so there are several unique aspects to our culture. A dramatic troupe of all-female actors was started around the Second World War. The numbers of bars where trans people (both MTF and FTM) worked increased, and they are still popular. They are important places, especially for MTFs who cannot pass as female. Because of the existence of these bars, these people don't have to work as prostitutes and can save money for their treatments. So, in some ways, transgendered culture is welcome here in Japan.

But the cultural things are just cultural things. The trans people who tried to live ordinary lives became depressed, as they wanted to live as ordinary males and females with low profiles. However, they could not get proper treatment easily and were not able to change their gender on any identification documents. Japanese people could accept us only as special cultural people, not as their neighbors. They still can't accept us like this, even now. There is also a law that prohibits castration without any reason, so no sex reassignment surgery was done in Japan until recently. That is why I went to the United States to have all my female-to-male surgeries in the late 1980s.

"A Kind of Intersex Person"

So, let me tell you about myself now. My mother miscarried three times before me and twice after me. But she wanted to have a child, so she consulted a female doctor. The doctor gave her some medicine to prevent a miscarriage. It is some kind of hormone that has been prohibited in Western countries because it may masculinize a female embryo. But my mother used it, and I was born. I was a very masculine, hairy child, but my health was always bad. From the age of two or three, I believed I would have a male body as time went on, but it never happened, and my breasts started developing when I was nine. I was so depressed! But at almost the same time, I heard the news about a famous Japanese dancer who underwent SRS in Casablanca. As soon as I heard the news, I decided to have the same kind of operation.

Perhaps because of the medicine my mother took, I had almost no periods, and facial hair started growing when I was nineteen. As long as I didn't speak, everyone thought I was a boy. Several doctors said I was a kind of intersex person. But I thought my body was female and hated it so much. With tight bandages to conceal my breasts, I went to university and worked at the same time to save money for my treatments. Also, I was writing novels and sent them to many publishing companies, because being a writer was my dream from the age of three. Since I was a very weak child, I was always reading books and started to dream about being an author.

After I graduated from university, I flew to the United States to start all my FTM treatments. Almost all of my Japanese friends accepted my transition because they believed I was still the same person. But my parents, of course, tried to stop me because I am their only child, and they knew I was weak, but also they knew my nature. They knew they had to kill me to stop me. So they were resigned, after all.

I was aware that I might die during the surgeries because I was weak, but so what? I have looked forward to seeing the world after death, so I wasn't afraid of it. Also I would have had no regrets if I had died, since I had done my best in life until then. However, all surgeries were done successfully, I'm pleased to say. I visited the United States four times and spent more than $20,000. But the memories and friends I gained there were just priceless. I am proud of being a Japanese samurai in an American-made body!

Education

I know there are many more trans people living quietly with low profiles, even in the United States, but the action American FTMs were taking for themselves stimulated me a lot. So after getting my neo-penis constructed at Stanford University in the United States, I started writing a newsletter aimed at uniting FTMs all over Japan. I also started to lecture and to appear on television, radio programs, magazines, and newspapers to educate Japanese people. I have been doing this for fourteen years now. I also became a writer. I have written ten books so far, and one of them has been translated into Chinese. Come to think of it, I made two dreams come true—having a male body and becoming a writer. What a happy person I am! When I came out as an FTM writer, journalists at first asked me the same questions, again and again, such as, "How much money did you need to get a penis? Can you penetrate with your artificial phallus? Can you urinate standing up?" I was a very rare creature to them then!

As time went on, Japanese doctors stood up for trans people to help us get our treatments. In 1998, the first Japanese official SRS was carried out under the category of treating the condition of Gender Identity Disorder. This was because doctors had to find a reason to do the surgery, which included castration, to avoid being arrested.

Then everything changed! So many support groups started actions. Society started to treat us as patients, so they stopped asking rude questions, and expected the activists like me to do new actions so trans people can gain human and legal rights. It means nontrans people know we still don't have the same rights as they have.

So, as you can see, Japanese people are so simple, yet so extreme. Right after opening our country, we changed a lot very quickly, and right after the first official SRS, it happened again! Also, Japanese society wants to see us as special people. As long as they feel we are special, or something to pity, they are nice to us. Because of our religious freedom, people don't generally reproach us; they just feel we are like clowns. And who hates clowns? People just laugh at them, that's all.

That may be why we cannot change our gender on any legal papers. I have been legally female since I was born, even though I got a penis fourteen years ago, because all my papers state that I am female. Trans people in Japan can't get married of course, and it's very, very hard to find regular jobs, to rent rooms, to get bank accounts or credit cards, to buy insurance policies, to vote, or to see doctors, as we have to show our ID and have to carry our passports that show the opposite sex of how we currently look and live.

Taking It to Court

This can cause serious problems, sometimes, so I have been fighting in the courts to change this awful legal situation. I may lose, but I'll never give up. A group of six of us who have undergone SRS filed civil suits in 2001 to seek to have our new genders recorded on our family registration documents, as Japanese citizens are required by law to be entered on a family register. These are the first lawsuits of their kind since SRS officially began in Japan three years ago. Out of the six of us, four became men at Saitama Medical College in Saitama Prefecture, one became a woman in Singapore, and I became a man in the United States.

Every kind of identification document is based on what is written on the family register, so if we can change the gender on this, we can change it on all our papers. And if we can't, we can't change it on anything. All or nothing. Because Japan treasures the family system, they made this stupid law. I know of only Japan, China, and Korea to have this law. It was brought in by the Japanese when we, or old Japan, occupied these countries a long time ago. However, in these other countries they can change the gender on their identification documents, although they need to go through the courts, but not Japan. So now we are suffering from the negative heritage of our ancestors.

In Japan, intersex people can change the gender on their documents if they want to because the law recognizes their conditions as physical and congenital. So if they see us as some kind of intersex, we may be able to win our case.

A couple of years ago, Dr. Milton Diamond came to Japan and gave a lecture titled *Transsexual May Be a Sub-Type of Intersex*. Also, the other day I was moved to find the phrase written by Dr. Tracie O'Keefe in the "Press For Change" newsletter of April 2000: "Transsexualism is a form of intersex condition and the legal community needs to treat it as such, with all the rights and privileges afforded to the intersex to change their documents." She can say that again! When this idea becomes accepted here in Japan, it will be much easier to change the gender on our documents.

There is also a move to create a special law to allow the recording of our change of gender on our legal papers. It is, however, tougher than people expected, because there are many different types of sex and gender diverse people, such as transvestites, transgenders, and transsexuals. Some people insist they cannot live without the genital surgeries, and others don't need them. But if the law is created, it will require all of us to have the lower surgeries to be admitted as ordinary males or females (though we have to doubt the concept of "ordinary" male and female). It bothers the trans people who say they don't need the treatments such as surgeries but want to change their gender on their papers. These kinds of trans people are campaigning against the creation of this law. They insist the law should protect all kinds of trans people at once. It is truly an ideal law, and it may happen in the near future since Japan is such a sexually unique country.

United We Stand

But, to my sorrow, it's not happening now and probably won't in the next ten years. But I think it is easier to make a tiny hole for the trans people who have had the surgeries and then widen it for the ones who don't want them. To unite all kinds of sex and gender diverse people may not be so hard, either. I have seen Western trans communities and ours, and found a big difference. We are even more complicated here! To me, Western trans communities (though I may be misunderstanding a little bit) are more divided and separate from each other than we are here in Japan. Because we were given the concepts of what a TV, TG, and TS are from Western studies, our meetings are always full of all kinds of trans people together. Transvestites learn about the lower surgeries and transsexuals learn about cosmetic things together. Also MTFs and FTMs are there together almost all the time, so we have the basis to communicate with each other from the beginning. We can discuss anything together and find the best way for all of us.

In this way, I feel we may be able to build trans solidarity rather easily, but sometimes I feel that hate crime by nontrans people may happen when we get the same rights as them. It is nothing to do with religion, but because people may hate to see us as the same ordinary citizens they are. Now they see us as second-class citizens, so they may have been overlooking us.

However, such an awful situation may never happen. I am not sure, but I have a fear and a hope at the same time. Remember our good old sexual broad-mindedness! Even now, in some supermodern city near Tokyo, an old peculiar festival has continued. People carry a huge penis as the portable shrine! I think it is a symbol of fertility, but the holy festival permits male-to-female trans people to carry the portable shrine, which looks like a huge pinkish penis. And nontrans people, male or female, young or old, enjoy seeing it and licking the candies, which look just like a penis and a vagina. All the people have fun together and enjoy the bright, healthy eroticism there.

This scene brings me hope. Old Japanese nature may die hard. At the moment, only two medical organizations are performing SRS, so only four to five people per year can have surgery, despite about seven hundred people waiting. But once the situation is changed and we can change our documents to reflect our true sex and gender identity, Japan could be a heavenly place for trans people. Until then, I will continue fighting.

I am delighted that, year by year, I have opportunities to express what we hope in front of more and more people than ever before. This fall, I will be a part-time teacher at a national university. There have been several MTF transsexual teachers at universities, but this is the first time an FTM transsexual teacher has such a job officially. I do feel that Japan, this complicated yet at the same time simple country, is changing for the better. May it become a sexually broad-minded place as it was in the old times. No one should bother anyone who is doing the right things. If this simple idea were really understood by everyone, this world would be easier for us all to live in.

SO, WHICH ONE IS THE OPPOSITE SEX?

THE SOMETIMES SPIRITUAL JOURNEY
OF A METAGENDER

Phillip Andrew Bernhardt-House

MY MODERN IDENTITY as a metagendered person has only crystallized fully in the past few years. I define *metagendered* as someone who identifies as neither male nor female, neither woman nor man, neither neuter nor feminine nor masculine. However, a metagendered person may have characteristics that others might label as any or all of these things, yet the metagendered person is not defined by any of them. A metagender is less of a "both/and" combination, "all of the above," or androgyne, and more of a "wholly other" third/fourth/eighty-seventh category, or "none of the above." Metagenders can have any body type, genital configuration, or chromosome type. Finally, as with many such categories in non-European cultures, there is a spiritual dimension to being a metagender as well, a dimension that may be innate from birth and yet definitely develops and demonstrates itself in the evolution of a person's life.

I was born in Oak Harbor, on Whidbey Island in the San Juan Islands of North Puget Sound, in Washington State. Between my mother, father, and step-parents, I am the second oldest, at twenty-six, of seven children, with three brothers and three sisters. I am currently living in Cork, Ireland, pursuing a Ph.D. at the Department of Early and Medieval Irish at University College Cork. I have been involved in college and academia ever since high school and plan to be a professor so that I might prolong my studenthood perpetually. It is within this environment of study, both scholarly and personal, that I have come to be what I am now. I did not become a metagender suddenly or out of the blue, just from some spur-of-the-moment decision or realization; there has been a discernible progression from some of my earliest childhood experiences and memories, tied up with my sexual orientation and body image as well. Some of these progressions are chronological, but others are not, since they are only sensible in self-reference to earlier experiences, and it is with a series of these that I will begin.

Witches, Sailors, and Dress Codes

At about age six, I was told, along with my older brother, that my father—whom my mother divorced when I was three or four—went through a transvestite stage, though my mother did not use the term, which contributed to their divorce. When I revealed to my mother at age twenty-two that I am bisexual, she responded quite well, but added, "With your father being who he is, I'm not totally surprised." And yet I remembered as she said this, though I made no comment, about something from a few years before. We were watching some old slides that I had seen many times before of baby pictures, and we got to one that Mom didn't seem too happy about and asked us to advance past. My curiosity was piqued, and I grabbed the controller, switched back to the slide, and asked what the problem was—I knew that this baby in the photo was me, less than a month old. She told me, with reluctance but without emotion or fuss, that she didn't like the photo because it reminded her of something. She then commented that the baby clothes I was wearing were for girls, and that after having my older brother just over a year before me, she was really hoping for a girl. So, a couple of times she dressed me thus (honestly, I don't recall thinking that the outfit was particularly girly) and pretended, but she realized this was wrong and stopped doing it, and yet this one photo remained. Can it have started for me so early?

I was very much a part of my mother's world throughout my earliest memories, which my older brother never was. I lived in a kind of idyllic, goddess-centered state (because I thought my mom had generated not only myself and my brother but also my father) of not really knowing or understanding, much less caring about the fact that there are differences between boys and girls. At my parents' work, I would use the men's bathroom as frequently as the women's (and my mom said it was OK to do so); there was no real difference between them anyway, besides the signs on the doors. A girl my own age gave me a lecture on this one time after I had walked in on her and her sister in the bathroom earlier that day. At the day-care place I went to, the girls and I often stood around the toilet together, and while I never saw them pissing, as I recall, they certainly saw me do it. And it was in this same day-care place that I fell out of that goddess-centered state, because of two incidents that I remember very clearly.

The first was when one day we were taught to make hats out of newspaper for a parade we were going to have around the parking lot the next day. The girls got to make tall witches' hats, and the boys, by doing one further fold, would make sailors' hats. I made a witch's hat and was well pleased with its neat triangular height, having no interest in the shorter sailors' hats that the boys were all now wearing. I wore my hat proudly, happy to be a witch, and our overseers (I have never thought of these often abusive people fondly) smiled and laughed for a while uncomfortably, and then they took my hat, made the further fold, and returned it to me. I cried. On another occasion, an overseer woman (whom I especially loathed) was speaking to me during outside playtime, and when I had her leave to go, I walked away in an odd gait, which I knew was odd, but I wanted to do it. She called after me, "Phillip, don't walk that way, you look like a girl." I turned to look over my shoulder, understanding that something was different, and somehow things have not been the same since. I was sometimes reprimanded for having my "hands in my pants" (I was usually not even doing anything in terms of genital touching, I just liked having my hands in my pants), and this eventually stopped when my mother told me, "If you play with it too much, we're just going to put a box over it." A great amount of fear, loathing, and repression came as a result of her saying this to me only once. I know that recollections of childhood can be overly romantic or idealized, but this is how I remember it.

At age five I was diagnosed with asthma and multiple allergies, which severely limited my physical activities and even made going outside on a sunny day difficult, due to grass pollen. Swinging on the swing set or climbing on the play structures was OK, but anything involving running or going after a ball was out of the question. One thing that was very popular was boys literally chasing girls and girls chasing boys, which I could not do at all. Instead I developed an even more active imagination, devising elaborate scenarios of make-believe in which I was Spiderman, but seriously ill and in need of outlandish help, and sometimes (with the help of fellow superheroes, whether other kids or imaginary) I got it.

Things took a turn for the worse, and I was diagnosed type I (insulin-dependent) diabetic at age eight. Now I could not do much physical activity at all, and had to sit and watch while the other kids did physical education. My health was awful, with both diseases and their medications antagonizing one another. I turned inward to a much greater extent. Though always intelligent before this, I really accelerated at this point, especially with reading and writing. But this had other effects—I missed school frequently, and on the day in fifth grade when the class was divided into boys and girls for the "New You" body changes video and lesson on puberty, I was absent; there was no make-up lesson, and I did not even get a copy of the literature given out on the day. Very often subtle desexualization of people who are disabled or seriously ill occurs. Who wants to be confronted with the possibility of pain and the reminders of mortality when engaged in talk or activity having to do with sex, the ultimate pleasure? And lack of appeal becomes lack of entitlement eventually in many people's minds. I remember this happening quite early after becoming diabetic.

My peers kept me in the dark when I inquired about sexual matters, and then made fun of me for asking. One time, a friend asked me at age ten if I wanted to get married, and when I said yes, a particularly boorish boy said, "That's just what this town needs, another diabetic." Whether he meant diabetic children or misunderstood diabetes as a sexually transmitted disease, the point is the same. Accusations about me being a "fag" began then—accusations that I could refute, because contrary to belief, I didn't hold hands with other boys. While I had not acknowledged fully my budding sexual feelings for males, I knew that I liked girls, so how could I be a fag? At the end of fifth grade, my very permissive teacher allowed the class to do "talent acts" (most of which were improvised on the spot) on the last day to pass the final hour, and a few of the more popular boys got up and said, "Can we have all the guys up here?" Every boy in class, even the class nerd, went up there and did a very bad rendition of a Beastie Boys song, but I was voluntarily not up there and was glad of it. Oddly, I don't remember getting any flak about it afterwards.

Coming Out in More Ways Than One

I was brought up as a Catholic. My stepfather's mother (the Catholicism coming from him and his family) once tried to help me through my illnesses by sending me a prayer card for Saint Jude, patron saint of lost causes. My mother, sometimes subtly and sometimes bluntly, suggested that I enter the priesthood. I sometimes daydreamed on this notion as a child, imagining being a great liturgist in a parish of my own with no congregation—just me, an organist, and a lot of books to read—but this faded eventually as I realized more and more that getting married (which I thought was necessary for kissing, much less having sex) was high on my list of things to do in the future. Because of my health difficulties, I did not have physical education classes at all after elementary school, which was a bit of a blessing, as I think my attraction to males would have been harder to hide in a locker room, but it was also a loss that further desexualized me in the eyes of my peers.

It was only at church youth group that, as God created male and female, we youths were sorted into groups by sex at various times. White dresses and veils versus white shirts and blue ties at first communion years became separate groups as early teens, hearing from the celibate virginal priest about the male and female sexual facts of life, masturbation and menstruation, respectively. Here I was in a room with boys my age and older, including my older brother in whose shadow I constantly lived, hearing that everyone masturbates (everyone male, that is), that it's normal and unavoidable but nonetheless a grave sin, and I didn't even understand what it was and remained afraid to ask. The human sexuality courses in public school where I lived were given after grade seven as a part of physical education, so I missed out again. I was shy and reserved enough, but on top of this, everyone (even those few girls who thought I was cute for a smart guy) assumed that I had no interest in dating.

After I experienced a brief interlude as an uninformed Catholic fundamentalist at age thirteen, and a particularly bad series of health complications at fifteen, a very inspirational high school teacher of mine got me into the writings of the mythologist Joseph Campbell, which not only led me deep into the Arthurian legends, Celtic myth, shamanism, modern paganism, and comparative religion but also finally showed me that my faith in Catholicism and Christianity generally was nonexistent. I heard about holy mythical androgynous figures, but did not yet know that there were human spiritual persons who took this role on themselves. However, these were not revelations that I could share easily, and after great pain, guilt, and self-doubt, with some encouragement from a highly insightful female friend, I had my first coming out experience in August of 1993—coming out as non-Catholic to my mother and refusing to begin classes in preparation for the sacrament of confirmation. When I came out to her again five years later, this time about my being bisexual, she said, "I could handle you not being Catholic, I think I can handle this."

Because of my thinness, I was called an "anorexic fag" occasionally at school, even by those who were supposed to be my friends. One time my stepdad's best friend from the Navy said that men who wear pleated trousers (and I happened to be wearing some at the time) were "gay hippie faggots"; I could not talk back to him and expect to go unpunished, so I went in another room and sobbed. In my hometown, I knew of only three nonstraight people (apart from all those kids who were rumored or slandered to be at school) and an old friend of my mom and dad's, who years before had divorced her husband and "became" a lesbian (and even appeared on television), who was sometimes mentioned as a joke. There was one supposed bisexual at my school, a boy with whom I came into direct opposition with publicly one time, but apart from the film *Basic Instinct* and a TV show on the spread of AIDS, this was the only familiarity with the term *bisexual* I had.

Despite the lack of any (much less positive) role models, I made a late-night determination during the few months before leaving for college that I was bisexual and would attempt to present myself as such. I had the luck and pleasure of having a gay roommate in my first year, and I received an interesting letter from him. My mother asked to see his letter. I told her no, and (though the thought had not really crossed my mind and he had said nothing of it in the letter, apart from liking the lesbian group the Indigo Girls) she automatically assumed I said no because I didn't want her to know he was gay. She reassured me by saying, "Just because you have gay friends doesn't mean you are," and I knew that an uphill battle would be on the way.

The Ways of Man

At college, for the first time in my life, not only was I taken seriously and assumed to be a sexual being, but I was also "sexed" for the first time and called a man on a regular basis. Sometimes I was called a man in a way that highlighted my unknowing complicity in the heterosexual, patriarchal, male-privileged world (a common reaction from feminists and/or lesbians due to my very presence), while at other times it was a term of respect and an acknowledgment of maturity (as opposed to being called a boy or a guy, the word *man* was somehow positive), and still other times it was used as a neutral term that was considered a default recognition of the obvious. No matter which it was, I was sensitive to it, and it was very difficult to get my head around it.

Men were creatures that I was meant to aspire to become—a highly prized ideal to reach one day, and yet I was never allowed to play that part, ridiculed when I tried, and generally excluded, and thus I developed an ambivalence for the idea of everything male alongside the growth of my intense physical lust for the male sex, which remained as much a mystery to me as the female sex. But with the recognition of my "maleness" also came an assumption of my heterosexuality, and since I was completely unaccustomed to characterizing myself in any sexual sense, I rarely affirmed or denied this accusation. I felt even more alienated that some good bisexual friends of mine did not recognize inherently that I was one of them! If anything, this pushed me further into the closet.

My hair and beard grew that year, and an older woman approached me in the guise of common spiritual interests—she was a pagan high priestess looking for a high priest. In a few short months a number of awakenings occurred: a powerful spiritual one, but also sex itself, which opened a floodgate that has never since shut. It was hard to hide my bisexuality, or my interest in bondage, domination, and sadomasochism, but the gender matter seemed quite clear to everyone but me. Most mainstream neopaganist thought places great emphasis on male and female gods and goddesses, with human sacred functionary equivalents, but (in this woman's educating me on this), unlike the "evil patriarchal" monotheists, the Goddess is eternal and supreme whereas gods are consorts that come and go. I researched the "male mysteries" and found this spirituality, which was based on having a dick, vapid and quite uninteresting.

What Kinds of Clothes Do Metagenders Wear?

A great transformation happened during my second year of college, when for the annual Coming Out Week dance, unbeknownst to everyone but a good female friend who helped me with makeup, I went to the dance in full drag—not typical "drag queen" drag, but convincingly female yet risqué drag. Hours before this, my beard was huge, and few people remembered what I looked like without facial hair. One of the first reactions to this, and my favorite, was when two people I didn't know very well saw me and began staring in fascination, and when I approached them and they realized who I was, they said, "Oh my god, Phil, it's you? We saw you, and thought: 'Who is that really tall girl? We should tell Phil about her!'" I walked the walk that made my day-care overseer correct me, I wore an outfit that would have killed my mother to see, I watched the looks of surprise from acquaintances, joy from queer friends, and disappointment from straight men as they realized I wasn't all girl, and I loved every minute of it.

However fruitful and liberating this time of redefinition was for me, there were also problems that persisted. Though somehow I got the reputation for being the best drag queen around by senior year, I did not fit the typical profile or acceptable behavior of a drag queen (I was often mistaken as the "straight friend" at gay events and clubs), and wanted to go to all the trouble of getting dressed and doing the hair and makeup only on very rare occasions. As I came to shed the label of man in favor of male, then male in favor of androgyne, and androgyne in favor of metagender, I have felt more and more at home and true to myself, but it has not made relating to others easier. What kinds of clothes do metagenders wear, and why don't we have a section in the department stores? I'm left to wear men's clothes because they're the only ones made big enough, and look with disappointment at the women's fashions, which do not appeal to my own sense of style (nor do I have the body to pull most of them off).

My friend Rook coined the term *metagender,* and the way Rook often characterizes it is by declaring, "In the war of the sexes, I'm a conscientious objector." As I began learning about alternately gendered spiritual functionaries around the world, I felt that being metagendered in my own case fit the picture: childhood illness, social difference, subverted gender expectations, and a proclivity for religious experiences and thoughts, all interlinked with one another, reinforcing each other toward an identity, but one that my own culture lacked. In a way, it is funny, because my mother got her wish in terms of my becoming a priest, but it was simply not a Catholic priest!

I began meeting transsexual and transgendered people at queer conferences and in life, including Kate Bornstein, who speaks of *transgendered* as being "transgressively gendered," which is an idea that I love. I found great kinship with transfolk, but often a shared sense of community developed between us merely in opposition to the cute gay contingent and the womyn-born/womyn-loving lesbian cliques at such events. The people with whom I have felt the greatest ease in the past few years are those at the nexus of a number of subcultures, including bisexuality, polyandry, bondage/domination/sadomasochism (BDSM), goth, pagan, and sci-fi. However, even with these, there have been problems, the main ones being sexual.

I often wonder if "biological sex" is as cut-and-dried as we often think, since the fixedness of gender is an illusion of which far too many have been overly convinced, and also because we know that there are various types of intersexed people. I know someone whose brother is outwardly and inwardly a fully functioning male but has cells that are about half XY and half XX. How many of us know for sure what our genotype is? I certainly don't! I wonder about some of my own internal hardwiring in terms of sexual response: while I have all the apparent "male" equipment, my normal reaction to sexual arousal is not becoming erect, it is "getting wet." I sometimes experience orgasmic feelings without ejaculation or from stimulation of a nongenital sort, and I am known to ejaculate without being erect as well. Because of this, my ideas on sexual interactions are not typical, even for queer people, and as a result people quite often don't know how to react or deal with me, and explanations are seen to kill passion. Confusion is often the result of sex with me.

But on top of all that, if I feel true to myself, I can't simply say, "I'm metagendered," leave it at that, and expect anyone to know what this means. How would a bisexual male or female, a straight woman, or a gay man be interested in someone who refuses to identify as male or a man? How would a bisexual female or male, a lesbian, or a straight man be interested in someone not female or a woman? While in theory many bisexuals would be less attached or attracted to gender and sexual characteristics and more interested in "people," in reality this is rarely the case.

I am happy with my genital configuration as it is (and it has only been with great effort and struggle that I am somewhat comfortable now with being in this body at all), but I do get clit/vagina/tit envy on occasion, and castration anxiety is to me more a situation of "what would it be like?" The anima/animus (male/female energy) theory among Jungians is interesting to me, but for those of us who aren't Native American and can't therefore be classed as "two-spirited," how can we understand ourselves? A year or so back, I had a lucid dream in which I became a female archangelic form of myself that had sex during flight with a male twin archangelic image of myself, an intensely sensate experience that I remember exquisitely. Although this dream has great significance on a number of levels for me, it does highlight the problem well: which one *is* the opposite sex? I feel about as opposite as one can be from both—alien to both the macho ideals of manhood and maleness as well as the mores of feminine sensibility and taste—and yet this illusion of gender has enthralled me most of all because I am in love with both men and women, males and females, masculine and feminine.

In certain cultures where more than two gender options are presented as viable, the only real prohibition in terms of partner choice for nonmale/nonfemale people is other alternately gendered people. Since metagenders are a new phenomenon in this culture (and hopefully there are more than two of us out there!), these rules do not need to apply or be set down, and thankfully so. The people who turn my head most quickly are those who are not clearly distinguishable as male or female. Women and men are lovely equally, but androgynes are rare jewels. Our union may be one of opposites or likes (or more likely both).

What to Call Me

I speak of this metagender identity as a spiritual path, and this is the way I take it in my own case. But oddly enough, it is among many open-minded and "spiritual" people that my identity is most opposed and resisted. Less than a year ago, when attending a spiritual retreat, I dressed in full metagendered/androgyne drag: an outfit of half-trousers and half-skirt, half barechested and half covered, half bearded and half makeup, in which I felt most like myself and most happy, but the looks of the people at the retreat varied from acceptance to laughter (both positive and negative) to confusion and outright hostility, and I knew that I would not be able to do this on the streets in most places without serious danger of harassment and injury.

While combining masculine and feminine is often a religious ideal or iconic image in these circles, someone who attempts to embody this physically can be heretical, blasphemous, or simply reacted to with difficulty. I have had certain spiritual assholes critique me on my presentation, saying I should change my name to something more androgynous like Pat or Chris, but apart from liking my own name, whether Phillip or the more common and familiar Phil (the latter of which can be short for Phyllis, Phillipa, or Philomena, to name a few), who is to say what a nongendered or differently gendered name really is, lest I change it to something totally unrecognizable like Tsviirtschdt (which I once suggested, jokingly, as the name of my first child, no matter what sex it would be)?

Because this thing that I am, which I have worked hard to create for myself, is not easily or simply explained, I feel less than authentic on a daily basis for not explaining it to every passer-by or challenging others on their pigeonholing. I have yet to come out in terms of gender to my family, and feel that this would be more difficult than any other coming out before; at least with being non-Catholic or nonheterosexual there were definite areas I could "come in" to, whereas with this coming out, it would be to come out into a void, and in the other cases of coming out, the unliked is at least not unknown.

When I have left the sex or gender box blank on applications or various forms, I'm thought absentminded or careless and it is filled in for me, and yet again the extra folds are enforced on my witch's hat. In Ireland, where I now live, the common currency of courtesy in shops and on the street is the use of terms like "good man," and it feels annoying, at best, to hear this as praise for giving the correct change at a cash register. Worse so are the occasions when I explain my identity and am dismissed as purposefully difficult, living in a theoretical mental fantasy, out of touch with reality, or simply stupid. I see small victories when someone asks me for the male viewpoint and I answer, "Why are you asking me?" or "I really wouldn't know," and they are perplexed enough to be on their guard in the future without further explanation. The only ones who have heard the full story from me, and accepted it (though not without exception), are those who are trans or some other nontypical gender identity themselves.

However, most disturbing to me is the fact that I cannot fully assume my gender identity publicly within my working environment until I have my Ph.D. and am published. Celtic studies as a field is stuck, in more ways than one, back in the eighteenth century, and it will take them a while to get to the twentieth century, much less the twenty-first. In my previous collegiate experience, I have found that a certain level of effeminacy is allowed and even acceptable in hard-core academic males, especially in medieval studies. In my own field, I am writing and researching about notions of sex and gender in ancient cultures and in literature, and if it were known that I am bisexual, never mind metagendered, my work would be suspect, deemed "agenda-driven," and I would lose all academic credibility before I could even begin my teaching career.

I can write this freely and without fear, though, because I am reasonably certain that no one who is already working in my field would ever encounter it! I do not fear being thrown out of my university for this (indeed, I think my adviser would have to be quite oblivious to see that I'm not a typical person in many respects), as there are statutes in place protecting people from discrimination based on gender and sexual orientation. I fear being dismissed as a crazed, self-centered, self-interested person who is looking to justify a minority interpretation of material that has been ignored or underplayed up until now. It is always the privilege of the majority culture to appear logical and objective.

Meanwhile, I struggle in terms of what I would like to be called. I hate "sir" and "mister" and cringe when others refer to a group of people as "guys" or "lads" regardless of their sexes. The transgender pronouns "sie" and "hir," in addition to feeling not quite right to me, are confusing to pronounce! Part of me, for so many reasons, looks forward to the day when I will have my Ph.D. conferred, because then, no matter what, I will be "Doctor"; I am already "Reverend" because of my spiritual ordination, but since most people would be equally confused about the Universal Life Church as about metagenderism, I don't often tell this to people either. I recently was asked for a biography for a queer studies seminar at which I will be presenting, and I asked not to have any gender-specific pronouns attached to my name. Though it is somewhat awkward, I generally just like being called and referred to as Phil. The gender closet, for me, is very deep, but unfortunately there are not too many outfits in it yet that I would like to wear outside of it.

In our very heteropatriarchal culture, it is easy to see why looks askance would be the typical reaction to anyone who has a penis but does not run the axis of their identity through it. I am simply one who is saying that someone can have a penis without having it tied around a whole set of matching baggage of biological sex, gender, and manliness. In my case, it is as hard to imagine as the idea that someone's penis could be big enough to tie around such a large load of baggage.

BEING HUMAN

A PERSONAL TRANSSEXUAL PERSPECTIVE
OF TRANSITION

Sarah J. Rutherford

THERE IS NOTHING HARDER than trying to write something informative, of educational value, dealing with a subject many people can't or won't understand, or have a whole swathe of views about, negative or otherwise. There is nothing harder, except when that piece or subject drags a gut-wrenching need to run for the nearest mountain and hide away . . . forever. Emotion is probably the biggest enemy of rationality and sensibility, so to write about yourself, transition, and all the associated problems, and somehow disassociate yourself from that is like asking God (any god) to step down from heaven, or wherever, and argue your case personally. Imagine the torment of being transsexual, and ask yourself: if every time, every day, you looked in a mirror, the body that you saw was not right, was in persistent conflict with the brain and mind and with the spirit within, how would you feel?

Most people believe that transition is a matter of choice—most non-transsexuals, that is. In truth, transition is a need often driven and equally inhibited by fear. I have never thought of myself as anything other than a woman inside, so in essence I am a woman going through transition to achieve mind and body unity. My name is Sarah, which, ironically, was also the name of my paternal grandmother, whom I knew only briefly before she died, and until I transitioned and had taken my new name, I could never recall hers. In the first twenty-five years of my life, she was the only person I recall ever hugging me, the only person who ever showed me any affection or what could be taken for love.

I was born in Hull, East Yorkshire, England, but migrated to Australia in 1973 when I was twenty-two. Familywise, I had three sisters; the eldest died aged thirty-six, the second eldest died at thirty-four. My surviving sister was delighted with my transition, as she says she now has another sister again. After thirty years away, I naturally miss my sister, and now would be a good time to have her around. We talk regularly on the phone, but it's not the same, and I can't cuddle her on the phone, and I want so much just to hug her and tell her how much I love her.

My eldest sister was also TS, but it was impossible in the 1950s and 1960s for her to deal with any form of transition, and too dangerous in those times. I often ask myself: Why us? Why were we TS? The answer is simple—no one knows for sure—yet how much I need to know the answer, need to understand the reason for the torment I have suffered, the losses I have endured. I guess I want some sort of justice . . . I can only wish.

I have lived in Adelaide for the past twenty-seven years, though I have never felt anywhere to be my real home, physically or spiritually, although Adelaide is a pretty place to be. For several years I was a nurse, a karate instructor, as well as a soccer player, coach, and referee, so I guess when my partner came along, I had every reason not to keep moving on. Unfortunately, while I thought and believed that I had a firm control over my transsexuality, it got the better of me eventually.

My transition began four years ago in 1998, but not by choice. For myself and my partner, it was the best year in the twenty-one that we had had; there were no money worries, no major concerns, and our sons were in their teenage years and, more important, happy and healthy. In this environment of no concern, I let my guard down, and before I could retract or correct myself, I had unintentionally blurted out my deepest desire, a secret I had kept to myself for forty-six years: to be me. Yet even then I kept denying it to myself, even as the changes were happening automatically: body language, speech, and behavior. I kept telling myself I could "put it back"—that I wasn't TS, it was just some sort of emotional angst that came and went, all under my control.

My partner saw me in a different light; she saw a new me that she liked far more than the previous one. It was, she said, just a shame that I had to be female with this new, more likeable persona. I had abandoned my former macho image, that of karate instructor, football player, tough guy, 110 kilo (240 pound) facade. Yet in those first few months fear drove me, and because of this fear and stress, my weight dropped to a mere 67 kilos

(148 pounds). I doubt that I stopped crying in the first six months, for I knew what was happening—I was losing my world, and everything in it. The freedom I had always dreamed of was happening, but like a hungry dragon released from prison, it was devouring everything else in its path, and my comfortable if not absolutely perfect world was disappearing before my eyes, and at such a speed I could not comprehend or cope with.

My partner and I separated within four months—again not a choice, but a necessity to protect the boys and my partner from the ridicule that would come if people found out. It was also, my beautiful partner knew, the only way I would stay alive in the long term, by pushing me into a transition I was fighting against yet wanted so much. Contradictions . . . life is full of them.

I unhesitatingly signed everything over to my partner, as I wanted no disruption for her or the boys, and to protect them from any upheaval, other than what they had already gone through. I was in truth more afraid for them than for myself. Telling the boys we were breaking up was gut wrenching, and we just cried. It was the worst time of my life, and I really wished I could just die there and then and put an end to my misery, and alleviate theirs. We couldn't tell the boys that I was transsexual—it was just too difficult to find the words, and too terrible a thought to destroy their image of the hero figure, their big macho dad. Not telling them the truth made the pain worse for all of us, but worse was yet to come.

It was in pure frustration and fear that some weeks later I sort of blurted it out. My eldest son immediately turned against me for a while, but then a few days later we talked about it and he came back to me. Unfortunately, several months later the church destroyed that rebuilding. He had lost his hero, and the church told him I was sick and possessed by the devil.

My youngest son, on the other hand, was amazing; he took it all in his stride, became the mediator between us, and promised his absolute support. He never broke that promise. He grew up rapidly, and he is way ahead in maturity, understanding, and acceptance. He is not afraid to talk about me to his friends, and he has been a tower of support for me and his mum; his love and tolerance are awe inspiring, which are qualities I thought him incapable of possessing. If anyone was going to reject me, I would have said for sure it would have been him, not my oldest son who I was far closer to. These days I see him regularly—he still calls me Pops, and is more than a son to me—he is the very best friend anyone could wish for. He is my greatest hope for a reunion with my partner and older son, for I still love my former partner with all my heart, and as I told her before leaving, when she suggested that I was free to look for someone else: "I have only one heart, and I gave it to you; I have nothing left to give, nor will I ever want to. You were more than a wife, a friend, or a lover; you are my spiritual twin, and no matter what happens, or what changes come, I love you, have always loved you, and always will, no matter what."

My partner did what she could to help me adjust, corrected my mistakes, helped me become me, helped me unlearn everything I had learned as a male, and for the first time in my life, despite the pain and fear, I felt as if I was waking up at last. We went shopping together, bought clothes, she taught me how to use makeup, and all those small nuances that most girls learn from their mothers that I had never had a chance to discover. It was the calm before the storm, though.

On the Attack

After four months, and having had my local doctor and friend order me out of his surgery, my partner and I separated, and I had a breakdown. I remember the fear; I remember the terror of losing everything: my family, home, the only love I had ever had in my life, and it all became too much. I fell apart in my new doctor's rooms, and she sent me to the local mental health authority hospital. There, I was interviewed by a "doctor" whose attitude was, when he had finished writing his notes: "So you think you want to be a woman, eh?" I was a mess, and all I could answer was a humbled "Yes," even though I wanted to rip off his face for being such a callous and indifferent bastard.

There is a stubborn side to me, and we had a family saying: "This bastard won't beat me," and it was all I could hear in my head after my breakdown. Once out of hospital I found a flat, got set up, then hibernated for several weeks. I was still scared shitless, despite my stubborn resolve to fight my fear. It was a beautiful friend who broke the deadlock for me and took me out into the sunshine for the first time, as me. We walked around the block at her insistence, and the world suddenly opened up, and a little fear dissolved. It was the push that I needed. Over the next few weeks I went walking during the day dressed as I wanted to dress, and though scared, I was determined not to give up. I had paid such a heavy price for my freedom, it had to be justified.

It was after only nine weeks that the attacks started, and along with them the death threats. Unbeknownst to me, I had chosen the worst street in the small town, in which lived the original neo-neanderthals, hell-bent on destroying this "faggot" in their midst. It is notable that they wore their ignorance like a badge, for they referred to me always as a transvestite or faggot. Ignorance and aggression are synonymous with each other. Yet despite the attacks and violence, I saw the fear in their eyes and wondered what they were afraid of: girl germs? Did they ever consider that their closed, egotistical, exclusively macho male camaraderie could easily be misconstrued as their being gay?

For a week the attacks happened day and night; the fear was awful—I couldn't leave the flat, go shopping, drive, or anything. The police refused to intervene unless, they told me, the villains were inside the property and beating the life out of me. So I moved. Staying with a good TS friend back in the city, I searched for another place to live, but I was badly depressed and extremely self-destructive in outlook. Suicide is not a new concept to me—I have lived with the idea since I was eight, when I first truly understood I was not physically a girl. I had always known that something was wrong before then, but the reality was too shocking to bear. I tried to kill myself the first time when I was just eight. It was quite comical, though I didn't think so at the time. I sat chewing on my pencil, and the teacher demanded to know why. I told her I wanted lead poisoning so I would die. Her reaction was a swift and painful backhanded smack across the ear and an order to stop being so stupid and get on with my work. There was no social counseling in the fifties; if you had a problem you fixed it yourself, because no one else was interested. How times have changed. These days, kids are battered on all sides to talk about every aspect of their lives, their every move and action is queried, as is every action of their parents. Society has gone from complete indifference to complete intrusion and paranoia.

Eventually another flat came up, not too far from where my family lived in the suburbs, and I took it. It was small, really small, a bit like a dog kennel with a window, but the view from the front window was across a marshland, and along a river, long and winding; it was beautiful, if not just a little smelly during hot summer days. The place had at least fifty units, and unfortunately the nasty side of life lived there also. I found myself living with a born-again Christian on one side of me, a drug dealer on the other side, and a drunk at the end of the building, who spent his entire time playing with and raucously abusing his Nintendo game and consuming his income in beer. As a side distraction, his young son would stay over on odd weekends, and I would listen in abject horror as he abused him repeatedly, physically, mentally, and verbally.

This merely served to remind me of my abused past at the hands of my violent and alcoholic father, as well several foster homes. My car was sabotaged three times, my flat broken into, and, as per normal, the threats against my health and well-being were plentiful. If I wasn't being abused, I was the butt of the communal joke—the weirdo, faggot, or queer bloke who dressed like a woman. Understanding in such environments is minuscule, and intelligence even lower. I reconciled myself with the fact that I was going to regain my life and better myself, which was far more than any of my neighbors allowed themselves to consider.

It was eleven months in this hostile place before I managed to move again, only this time into a place far more civilized, far quieter, and with neighbors who approve or disapprove but otherwise don't bother me. In my new city abode I felt the safety I had not had before in other places. At last I had a garden again, room to move, I could have pets, at least have some small semblance of a home, as well as some sense of safety. It was, for me, a neutral area with a chance to start afresh, where no one would know my previous self. I was three-quarters of an hour away from my family now, which seemed a long way. Even though I couldn't see them anyway, I wanted so much to at least be close by. Reconciling myself to the distance and the separation was not easy. I felt that I may as well be on the furthest side of the universe.

A Time for Study

While in my second home, I had resolved not to hibernate but to study; however, as I am introverted by nature, this idea was never going to be easy. My real desire was to go to university, but the fear of so many people forced me to try something a little less taxing. I found myself back at adult high school studying English, history, and art and design, surrounded by a thousand people, some of whom were less than accepting, and not unwilling to let me know about it.

Despite abuse from some students and some members of staff, I survived the year, got straight-A grades, and, more important, proved to myself that given a good dose of a bloody-minded "up yours, I'm here" attitude, I could deal with the world in my new life. That year I sat the entrance exam for university, nervous as hell, but passed, though not with the score I desired to get the course I wanted, which was, of all things, psychology, with professional writing and communications as my sub-major. Instead I had to settle for my second choice, Australian studies, but I was encouraged by the idea that after the first year, if I wanted, I could transfer across to my original chosen course. By the end of the first year, I had done well, worked hard, given it my all. The end result was an 83 percent average, a vice chancellor's commendation, membership in the Golden Key Society, and a feeling that was better than climbing any mountain. At the same time, I had made a few new friends, both at the university and outside, especially in my support group. I adopted professional writing and communications as my submajor. As for the Golden Key Society, it is primarily an American university organization with chapters in other countries. Its motivation is to keep a list of the top 15 percent of students and eventually connect them to many different corporations and companies around the world—a sort of fancy employment referral agency, I suppose.

It had always been my personal understanding that if I could survive the first year, the second would be easier. Rubbish! The second was as hard as the first in many ways, but it felt easier because of my determination to rebuild my life. Financially, studying is hard. I live on A$250 a week, which comes from a bank loan and a payment from the government. No room for saving, new clothes, or luxuries. Being a student is more than being clever at school, it is having to be a financial wizard at home. Where surgery is concerned, the only way to pay for it is to get a loan; unfortunately I am a full-time student and don't qualify for a loan from any institution. Oh well, maybe I'll win the lottery! I know for sure that I have no rich and generous relatives.

A friend once said that when I got into university, I would meet a better class of people, less quick to abuse or judge. To be honest, I think she was wrong. Oh, I met a more educated class of people, but their discriminatory behavior was no different from anyone else's, nor was their ignorance or intolerance. If there was one lesson I had to learn fast, it was how to deal with abuse on all levels, and from all sources. I was able to use my fists and feet, but in truth, I was more afraid of hurting someone badly than defending myself, so I chose to be totally passive, unless of course I had no choice. Thus I adopted my favorite teaching: "The best form of self-defense is not to be there," and I was unavoidably "there"; ignoring abuse was by far the easier option. Oh I know, it is far harder to walk away or ignore abuse than to respond to it, but responding only makes things worse for the most part, and serves only to encourage the attacker or abuser to do more. Yes, there are and were times when I wanted so much to lash out and set an example. In truth, I knew that no matter what the justification, I would always be the villain, and my attacker would always be the victim, both legally and in the eyes of the general public. I learned very quickly that in this world, to males I was a traitor, whereas to women I was a mere intruder, a usurper. Transition means straddling both genders, and not being welcome in either.

To be passive, though, you have to develop a very thick skin, a lot of patience, and a first-rate sense of humor, and somehow I manage just that

. . . for the most part. Not that there were not times when I felt I would be justified in battering some people to a pulp for their abuse and ignorance. Unfortunately, the law was neither on my side nor interested in defending me or allowing me to defend myself. Our laws are far from adequate; indeed they are ill informed, ill constructed, and even worse, hardly ever enforced. Prejudice in our community runs deep and, one could also add, in all directions. It did not take long to discover that discrimination runs through the entire gamut of our community: straight, gay, lesbian, or whatever; people are people, and even those who have been abused are equally abusive, probably believing they have the right because they also have suffered. Having been abused does not, however, entitle anyone to abuse others. In my view, it can never be justified or rational.

In all fairness, I have discovered that it is far easier to walk away from potential abuse or conflict, rather than give the aggressors another bite at the cherry. One must also take into account the idea that responding in kind to every attack or abuse would take up most of the day and night, so is hardly worth the effort. I am also a great believer that if you fight fire with fire, all that results is more ashes.

Into my second year of university, I worked hard, got good results, took an awful lot of crap, but came out with an 80 percent score for the year. I was well pleased and wondered just how much better I could do if I didn't have such an abusive and discriminatory environment to work in. By now I was well settled in my new abode, which I will never truly, with any heart, call home—I lost my only true home when I began transition. Despite my academic achievements, things had deteriorated on a personal level in my second year, as my partner became involved in an evangelical church, with some not-so-Christian ideas and ideals. People I have never met or spoken to, who know absolutely nothing about me or transsexuality, have judged me, found me guilty, and condemned me out of hand, without a word from me, or the decency of any defense. Now I am the incarnation of evil, possessed by the devil, need baptizing to save me . . . oh, and to cure me.

Obviously such people have never read the Bible properly, nor taken into heart Christ's charitable teachings. It seems to be a case of doing unto others . . . preferably without their knowing what's being done. The hypocrisy of religion is alive and well, and still happily destroying people and communities with fear, ignorance, deliberate division, pulpit intolerance, and downright stupidity. If God exists, I feel sure that she wouldn't approve. I am not religious; I could never condone piety and bigotry, which seem fair bedfellows where such "Christians" are concerned, whereas you could also safely say that organized religion and true spirituality parted company about two thousand years ago.

In my third year of university, I had a slight disadvantage. Just prior to start of the semester I fell ill with a deep vein thrombosis in my right leg, which, a few days later, led to clots in my lungs and a heck of a lot of chest pain. The hospital physician told me I had to stop my hormone replacement therapy. I informed him in no uncertain terms, and perhaps in a less than ladylike manner, as to what he could do with that idea. We had a dispute, and he went away to get reinforcements.

Next I was told to take the year off university, and again I informed the doctors that this was another idea I was not too happy about . . . or words close to that effect. If anything, I am not, nor ever have been, subtle. I may be shy and introverted, but when necessary, I am blunt and always to the point. It was, I observed to the wonder specialists with no imagination and only textbooks for brains, just as easy for me to sit on my arse at university as it was at home; they went away shaking their heads in dismay.

Six months down the track I have had to cancel sex reassignment surgery, am still in pain, still taking tablets I hate taking, still struggling to get my work done. My grades have dropped to a miserable 70 percent average, but I am still going, determined not to back off. Indeed, I have already begun work on my Ph.D. thesis, for if I get a first next year in my honors year, I intend to push forward.

It seemed at first that time would drag on forever; that time would be forever my enemy, going too fast when I wanted it to go slow, and too slow when I needed it to speed up. In truth, the past four years seemed to have flown by, and unlike my first belief that life would end, it has gone on and, to some degree, improved.

Post Boxes Are Not All Red

I firmly believe that transition begins at birth, when those who should know better see the genitalia, or lack thereof, and designate the child for life, locking them into a specified sex and gender role. If nature enjoys diversity, then why not humans? Why must we think in such absolutes, such as we teach kids in preschool: the sky is blue, the grass is green, and post boxes are all red; that there is but one gender dichotomy; that black and white exist, and no one mentions the gray scale and multiple colors between. The sky is not always blue, the grass is more than just green, and post boxes reflect the colors around them, other than their base red layer. There are rainbows between the black and the white in tones and shades, and on a scale we can barely imagine; we just have to stop looking and start seeing. We have to see because we want to, not because we have to.

These days, apart from studying, I also run a support group for TS people, their families, friends, and others. I give talks and forums on TS issues, present papers at conferences, talk to politicians and a thousand others, anything to get the simple message across: we are still human! I have been writing for about thirty years, but write a hell of a lot more now than I ever did, for I believe, absolutely, that there is not enough information about the human aspect of transsexuality, that so much more should be said, that for those who want to understand, this information should be available.

I write from experience about the human side of being TS, and how to deal with the issues, large and small, how to cope with abuse, and how to laugh, because everyone has to stop crying at some time. On top of all that, I also run a twenty-four-hour hotline for emergencies, or during working hours for information and help. I'm not a counselor, never profess to be—I'm more in the way of a traffic cop, directing traffic to where it needs to be, to get the help best suited and needed.

If you ask me if transition and gender freedom is worth all the pain, trauma, loss . . . hell no, I wouldn't wish it upon my worst enemy; it has been a nightmare. Yet, I am me now; I am free to be myself and live my life accordingly, so transition has some small compensation, and if I can get to surgery, well, all the better. If you ask me, though, if I would swap it for my previous life, the answer is and always would be "yes," for in the world of sad reality, I wanted both: my gender freedom and my previous life, family, and so on. The harsh and brutal truth is, though, that this was never going to be possible without causing people I love so much pain, and was never going to be worth it.

So, here I am then, four years down the transition track, in my third year of a degree, making plans for my honors degree and Ph.D., writing like mad, ignoring (where possible) health problems and other likely distractions and nuisances. I mentioned before that I have a slightly stubborn nature, and nothing has changed. My determination is primary and singular: to make transition for those coming after me as easy and natural as I can, so that all the shit that I and others have suffered and still suffer will one day, through education and example, be a thing of the past.

PETER'S STORY

Peter Häberle

I WAS BORN IN 1969 and given the name Petra, in what was then the country of Czechoslovakia. My birth mother gave me away for adoption right after she gave birth to me at the age of nineteen, and did not say why she did this. Her name is Blanca and she is Jewish. Her family died in a concentration camp during the Second World War. I am told I have a brother whom I have never seen.

As I was underweight, I started life in an incubator. After that I was taken to a local orphanage where a nurse who worked there took a liking to me and took me home one weekend. I was about one or two at the time and quite behind in my development—I could not walk, and I did not speak or respond to anything. The doctors at the orphanage were certain I was deaf.

I think the nurse who took me home hoped that I would start hearing, talking, and interacting, but this did not happen and I remained nonresponsive. The nurse's mother, who would later on become my stepmother and whom I will call mother from now on, also started taking care of me. I began to improve, and when the doctors at the orphanage saw this, they took me to a psychiatric clinic in Plzen to examine me. As soon as my mother heard about this, she came straight to the clinic, where she found me in despair, neglected, with no diapers and covered with blood because of the infections I had. She took me home again, and after that life got somewhat better.

My situation stabilized, and one day when my uncle played the harmonica, I turned my head and proved I was not deaf at all! After that I slowly learned how to walk and talk, and grew and developed in a normal way, except I was about two years behind in my schooling.

I could not connect very well with the other children at school. I didn't play with them, instead spending most of the time on my own. Dolls did not interest me as a child—I liked cars, marbles, or a ball. I did not feel like a girl, but more like a boy, and I kept wondering, "Why do I look like a girl?" This question always bothered me and I wanted to ask my mother, "Am I a boy or what?" But somehow I could not get the question out of my mouth and was just hoping for the best that things would turn out right by themselves eventually. When I was eleven or twelve years old, I got into trouble with my mother as she wanted to dress me in skirts and dresses and I did not want to wear them. I wanted pants and a shirt—no girly things.

After I finished school I went to college to train to become a chef. This was 1985, I was sixteen and starting puberty: my breasts were growing, and I also developed a small penis. I thought this was normal, but when I saw other girls in the shower, I knew differently. Why do I have that? Why do I look like a girl? Why do I feel like a boy? These questions became so dominant in my mind that I became isolated. The girls would discuss dresses and perfume, and the boys would discuss the girls. I guess I was just jealous and felt left out. Also I did not want to hear what they talked about; life was like a cinema—I could watch it but not participate in it.

I wanted to be alone, and I did not long for contact with the boys. Before, I had been in love with a girl but did not dare express it, although I never had any sexual feelings. All I wanted was some peace of mind. I could not trust myself, and I did not know if I was a girl or a boy or something in between. I did not know anything about gay, lesbian, transgendered, or intersex people. I felt alone and believed one day I would be cured and everything would turn out right.

I decided to hide behind my books and started learning Russian and Japanese, which got my mind away from my problems. I particularly enjoyed the latter because I feel related to Japanese culture and traditions. It's like I have lived there, it is so familiar to me. I did not participate in any sport, and often I was alone except for when I was at the language school; I never spoke about what was bothering me and how I felt, and I never went to see a doctor. My mother became suspicious because I never dated any boys or showed any interest in them. She believed I was a lesbian. She couldn't understand why I was behaving so "badly" either. She asked me, "Couldn't you learn to walk in a different way?" Well, no I couldn't because I was actually a boy in girls' clothing.

During this time I felt consumed with rage—toward my mother and everyone around me. I did not love anyone, and I certainly did not love myself. All I wanted was some rest.

After finishing at chef school, I worked as a cook for a year and saved my money so I could leave the country, and in 1989 I took off for the West. While I was in Austria I asked for asylum but did not get it, so every year I had to extend my visa. I worked as a cleaner in restaurants and joined the peace and environmental movements, as well as antiracist and antifascist organizations. I spent a lot of time there and joined in many demonstrations. During this time I did some drawing. By keeping busy like that, I was able to push away my problems to the back of my mind to some extent, but they continued to reappear.

I lived in Austria for four years and became involved with a man who worked with me. I started the relationship because I believed it would help me define myself more clearly, but having sex as he wanted was not very successful. Because of this, I tried to avoid sex as much as possible, as there were so many other aspects of our relationship where we connected and had a lot of common ground, and I liked living with him.

When he became a teacher in Germany I moved with him, and as I did not have the right papers to live there, we got married. I spent another four years in Germany working for the peace and environmental movements and also as a cook in a hospital. But the issues of gender kept coming back into my mind, and I started wondering about my life, living it with this man and so on. We began to argue a lot and I withdrew into myself again. I became very depressed, and when it all became too much I decided to leave, as I could not cope with the situation anymore.

I had been on holiday three times in the past to Holland and felt more at ease there than in Germany, where I felt like a stranger. So the moment I got my German passport I took off for Holland. I found a place to stay and got a job in a meat factory, where I continue to work today.

Resolution

All the time I continued to think about my gender situation and tried to get things clear in my mind. Then the anger that had been so prevalent earlier in my life came back. This time, when confronted with these explosions of rage, I decided to pay a visit to a doctor and ask for help. He advised me to go to a hospital in Amsterdam and see Dr. Louis Gooren, a clinician who runs a gender identity clinic in Amsterdam. After various examinations, I was told my condition: intersex, or both male and female gendered, with neither fully developed. I was also told I would never be able to give birth to a child, nor create one, as I had a vagina, breasts, a penis but no testicles, a womb the size of a hazelnut but no ovaries, and my hormone level was way out of balance. So I was ready for treatment!

By this time I was thirty, and for three months I visited a psychologist, because this is a requirement for treatment, but it felt good to be able to tell someone everything and ask questions. It gave me peace of mind at last. Right after that, I started hormone therapy. Immediately after the first shot of the masculinizing hormone testosterone, I felt a huge release, and never again did I have the attacks of rage. I was very happy to see my muscles growing, and I enjoyed experiencing a second puberty. I think I needed it somehow and liked it. I also got sexual feelings for the first time, and it felt wonderful. After one year I had a mastectomy and felt even better after that. I have also had my womb removed and a scrotum made, whereby the surgeon was able to pull my little penis out so it became larger. The result is more than satisfying, and I am looking forward to the final operation, which is the filling of the scrotum with prosthetic testicles.

Now I can urinate standing, I can have an orgasm, I can get a hard-on. And my penis is not really so small. Anyway, there are other men with large, medium, and small penises. I have a smaller one—so what? After all, people also have small, medium, or big noses. I feel sorry I wasted ten years of my life going around like a zombie because I did not dare talk about what was really bothering me.

But I also feel very good, especially because I am no longer floating between two genders like I was before. I feel as one gender. Some people, including those I work with, act weird toward me, but not everybody is like that, and most of them accept me and call me Peter. There will always be people who do not understand, so I get disrespect as well as respect. The world will not change in this aspect: there are nice people and there are assholes. I am more concerned right now with finding out what I want from life and how I will continue. I wonder if I will be happy. I wonder what is written in the stars for me. Big plans are not my thing, but I know I want to get more education and another job in the long run.

I divorced my husband, and we parted amicably. We had a coffee afterwards and never saw each other again. Recently I heard he has a girl-friend, and I'm really happy for him. My mother was not surprised when she found out about me. She said she knew it all along. She always supports me when I'm in the hospital, and so does my uncle, who is like a father to me. At the moment I feel happy and I look forward to each new day. Whereas friendship used to be difficult, I now like the company of others and attend the trans men's support group Humanitas. Because of all the operations, I had to take it easy, but except for the paperwork to enable me to stay here in Holland, the end is in sight. Once I get naturalization I will be a male citizen.

I would like to talk to my brother, and also to my birth mother, who both live in the Czech Republic, because I am so curious to know about their lives. What kind of life did my mother have? Easy? Difficult? I have no bad feelings toward her; I guess she had a reason why she could not take care of me. She was only nineteen, after all. In 1992 I tried to contact her through the Czech embassy, but she did not respond. I know she lives in the city of Volyne, and although I want to meet her, I do not want to make her angry. My adoptive mother is having difficulties with this though, so I guess one day I will visit my birth mother and won't tell her about it.

I do not know how things would have been different for me or how it is for people like me in what are now the Czech Republic and Slovakia. Maybe other eastern European people who are sex and gender diverse are less accepted, but I do not think it makes a difference whether you are from Eastern Europe, the United States, China, or wherever. The Czech Republic is not so different from Holland. The former communism that has not existed since 1989 was quite all right actually, although we had no right to free travel. Health care and education were free, nobody was hungry, and everyone had a job. Of course, you had to be loyal to the communists, otherwise it meant trouble. I spoke to someone who was operated on in the 1970s who has been living as a man since then, and my uncle also told me about a man in the village who was born female. I believe you can be treated for free in Czech hospitals, but I don't know for sure. Although the Czech Republic is the country of my youth, and my family lives there, society is more mixed in Holland, and I like that. I feel connected here.

○

THE HEADACHE IS
IN YOUR HEAD

Tucker Lieberman

Part I: Migraines and Resilience

Two days after graduating from college, I had another migraine. They always follow the same pattern: fifteen minutes of blurred vision, followed by two hours of splitting pain and nausea, followed by eight hours of exhaustion. I had always attributed the headaches to stress, and I assumed that once I left Brown University, that would be the end of them. So, when one of the beasts hit me just after graduation, I was at first disillusioned, but after some thought, it was a relief to know that school doesn't give me migraines. Wayne Dyer, a self-help guru, reminds me on an audiotape: "Traffic doesn't make anyone anxious. Traffic just is." School doesn't make me get migraines; I get migraines because my head is stressing out over school. And if you can appreciate the difference, we'll get along just fine.

I grew up just outside of Boston and applied to Brown University in the city of Providence, Rhode Island, one hour south of my home. I entered Brown in the fall of 1998 as an eighteen-year-old male with acne-inflamed cheeks and barely enough hair for a ponytail—an unremarkable fresh-man, except for the fact that three months earlier at my high school grad-uation I had been legally female. I had been an ordinary girl until hitting puberty at the age of nine, at which point a nameless dissatisfaction, depression, and self-hatred began to ferment. By age fourteen, I had five years of blood under my belt while other girls were just starting to men-struate, and after these years of opportunity for self-reflection, I suddenly

found a name for my unhappy condition: I was a female-to-male transsexual.

This self-diagnosis surprised even myself, yet it was so obviously correct. The only other transsexual I'd ever heard of was a male-to-female
named Christine Jorgensen; I'd never knowingly met any type of queer
individual in person. I thought I was the only female-to-male in the world
until I got an Internet connection to prove otherwise. It wasn't until my
junior year of high school that I was able to come out to a couple friends
and teachers. I had hoped to survive high school as an invisible person
and to transition immediately after graduation, but transition can take a
long time, and as my senior year started, I realized that I would have to
get moving if I wanted to be a boy in time for college. This deadline was
coupled with the fact that I was cracking under the pressure of enduring
an incorrect gender assignment. I didn't have the strength to survive a
fourth year of being called by a girl's name and being completely isolated
in my misery. So I came out to my teachers at the beginning of my senior
year and asked them to call me by my chosen name.

My mental state before and during transition was an angst-ridden, self-
centered roller-coaster ride that is not completely atypical among
teenagers. I thought I was the unhappiest person in the world, but I survived, and people were basically good and wanted to be helpful, even
those who were patronizing and weren't ready to accept me as a man. I
had the good fortune never to be beaten or threatened at school, and to
be raised in a Reform Jewish temple that embraced gay families and had
no trouble accepting the fact of my transition. My parents helped me
begin testosterone injections in January of my senior year, and they helped
me get male chest reconstructive surgery three weeks after graduation.
They were surprised to learn of my identity, since I was never butch, was
never a lesbian, and had never enjoyed stereotypical boys' activities.

At first they thought it was only a phase and worried that I was rush-
ing into a decision that I would later regret. It helped when I introduced
them to other happy, successful transsexuals who confirmed that transition is physically safe and psychologically necessary for those who need
it. It gave them an idea of what my body could some day look like and
the transgendered community I could be part of. They needed a few
months to get used to the idea of me being a boy, but although I'd never
been butch, I hadn't exactly been a model girl, either. I'd always seemed
awkward and miserable, and they were willing to help me accomplish
whatever it took to feel comfortable in my own skin.

When I showed up at college for freshman orientation, I was still scratching my scars from the chest surgery and felt disoriented. On one hand, being

called "he" without having the pronoun be a loaded term—being an unsus-
picious, unqualified guy—was the most welcome normalcy I had ever experienced in my life. On the other hand, I was used to thinking of myself as a
transsexual with a personal mission of self-transformation, and now that
the process was suddenly over, I didn't know who I was or what made me
special. I no longer had a chip on my shoulder about being a girl, and this
freed up untold amounts of energy to use—for what? I had assumed that
after transition I would just date other gay men, and that would be the end
of the miserable chapter of my life. I hadn't thought much about the details
of "happily ever after." Was I just going to be a regular guy? How could I,
when that meant forgetting my past, lying about my body, and denying
myself future lessons about what it means to be a transsexual?

As soon as I realized that going stealth (concealing my history,
thoughts, and feelings to disguise the fact that I was formerly female) took
effort, and transsexuality still remained an inseparable part of my identity and my human experience, I started to come out. The transition
between genders and between schools had been exhausting enough. I had
no energy left for false pretenses. After all, hadn't I transitioned so that I
could be truer to myself?

There was no single bombshell that outed me. I published a memoir on
the English department website, consented to half a dozen interviews,
walked shirtless around the dormitory with my prominent double scars,
left my books and magazines lying on my desk, and listed myself as the
contact person for Brown University's transgender support group. I just
kept putting the information out there. None of it was with the intention
of showing off—I just treated my transsexuality like any other part of my
life, body, and history, and didn't see any reason to hide it or, for that matter, to unduly emphasize it. Transgenderism was a topic that I gave a lot
of attention to, and I was not ashamed of that.

It wasn't until my senior year that my friends began to let me know that
they knew. I almost never discussed my transsexuality directly with anyone. No one ever introduced me as "my friend Tucker who used to be a
girl," or made jokes about my lack of a dick over the dinner table at our
vegetarian cooperative. I don't suppose I would have minded if they did—
at least I would have quickly gotten over my insecurity. I can laugh at
myself when that's the only option left. But it's hard to speculate about
what my life would have been like if I had volunteered to share more of
my story. I didn't self-promote or actively solicit conversation about my
gender. That's just not the way it was.

Overall I was content with being "out to anyone who asks," and if I
had to do college over again, I'd take the same approach. The only glitch

in this policy is that no one will ask—ever. People might ask questions that are difficult to answer coherently without outing yourself as female-bodied, such as questions about your sex life, your childhood, your body image, your bathroom habits, your friends from before you transitioned. But even if you answer these questions honestly, these people will only furrow their brows and worry that you are being sarcastic with them. They will never, ever guess that you are a female-to-male transsexual, not even if you show them your chest scars or testosterone vials. The majority of people don't know that FTMs exist and have never considered that they might exist. Even if they have met other FTMs, they're just not used to putting the pieces of the puzzle together. You can't wait for them to ask if you want to be out. They need to be hit over the head with an explicit tell-all phrase. If you take a passive approach to outing yourself, the most you can hope to induce is confusion.

It is impossible to engage in normal conversation and not make confusing, self-incriminating statements. Everyone wants to know how many kids you have, where you're spending the holiday, what your favorite magazine is, who gave you the necklace. Barney Frank, an openly gay congressman in my home state of Massachusetts, quips, "When straight people do it, it's called talking." That's the gap between the expectations of mainstream straight conversation and the gay person in its midst; a similar disjuncture exists between mainstream gay conversation and the transsexual in its midst. Gay people make small talk by asking each other, "So when did you first realize you were gay?" or "When did you come out?" If you changed sex, this simple question is impossible to answer without launching into a story that outs you as a transsexual. "Well, I realized I liked boys when I was twelve, but I was a girl then, so . . ." You can be out as transsexual or you can be closeted, but there's not much of a viable in-between.

Outing myself to reporters was comfortable, but only because I vowed to be resilient. The interviewer necessarily represents you as he or she sees you, not as you really are. The language of the report is going to sound funny because it's not coming directly from you. You have to be ready to read something strange, something familiar placed in a new context, like your own voice on tape.

I did establish at least one boundary for these publications: I will share just about any detail of my transition, except for my girl name. There is a reason for this. Naming something invests it with power and makes it real. Naming myself "Tucker" made me a man, while burying my girl name symbolically keeps that chapter of my life deep underground. I want to be one whole person. That means having only one name. Although I'm fine with people knowing that I'm FTM, I don't want anyone to try to imagine me as a girl—which was a wretched existence—in vivid detail. Denying people access to a girl name makes it impossible for them to generate that image. There is, indeed, something magical and creative about names.

But sometimes boundaries are violated, and that's where the need for resilience comes in. I was interviewed as one of the "Five Seniors to Watch Out For" in the commencement issue of the *Brown Daily Herald*. Overall it was a fair and decent article; however, after refusing to tell the student reporter my girl name, she invented one and presented it as a fact. Through four years of interviews I had successfully kept my girlhood anonymous. On graduation day, that one last sacred privacy was violated, and a fictitious girl name was printed in the first line of my profile that was passed out to thousands of graduates and their families. It wasn't as bad as being, say, outed against my will; it was more on the level of an erroneous report that I was dating my best friend or that I had a hobby that required me to wear a funny suit. It was offensive at first sight.

I wanted to march around announcing that there was a serious misprint, but it's a strange sort of conversation to make, especially on graduation day when everyone is saying farewell forever and clutching the paper to read on the plane home and save in their scrapbooks. There was nothing I could do about it, so I let it go. Hopefully, those to whom it matters will ask, and my future biographers (one never knows, but I could be famous some day) won't reproduce the error. It was ironic and therefore almost funny. Resilience is the key to survival.

Trying to breathe evenly as the university president addressed us, hiking up my gown and adjusting my mortarboard, I sought a more detached perspective. A misprint in an article, even on such a sensitive subject, is hardly a great injustice on the scale of things. The more I thought about it, I realized that if I considered this unfair, it was because life had shown me nothing but good fortune, and that if this was all I had to worry about on graduation day, I was blessed with confidence about my future.

Whenever I feel that my identity is threatened—whether I have been outed in a way that I did not want to be, my crush is not attracted to me, or I meet another person who challenges my stereotypes or ideologies—I will pretend I'm standing in the middle of a college quad on graduation day. My friends, family, and classmates are packed in tight around me. Everyone is using abstract, cosmic terms to talk about the future, counting themselves grateful for their many role models and support systems, and wearing funny hats. From this spacey, surreal perspective, I might start to feel better. We all need a shift in perspective now and then.

It is liberating to know that migraines are not caused by homework and that anxiety is not caused by being outed. My headache is in my head. Now that I have pinpointed the source of my problems, I don't have to waste time believing that anyone else has the power to "make" me feel a certain way.

Part II: Men, Women, Sex, and Data Entry in Rhode Island

I've always felt more comfortable around men than women, in every role conceivable: as friends, lovers, coworkers, teachers, helping professionals. Much of my anger toward women is just a projection of my anger at my own gender dysphoria. There is no vocabulary that expresses gender dysphoria, and my frustration builds and spills over until I begin to resent women in general.

After graduation I worked for an eighty-two-year-old professor, handling his personal tasks as much as his professional ones. Before he decided he liked me, the job was insufferable. He needed his spam e-mail printed out, the staples inserted at a forty-five-degree angle, notes taken on particular size piece of paper, the office staffed eight hours a day in case his wife were to call, and computer systems administrator services, even though my degree was in philosophy and I was being paid little more than minimum wage. It took me a while to learn his habits and his boundaries; until that point, he accused me of being lazy, incompetent, and deliberately ineffective. For some reason, men just don't bother me. They can annoy me, but I manage their nonsense more naturally than I manage women's.

I subverted my boss's reign by practicing feminism on his database. You see, his business involved keeping records of university professors, who were mostly male; the "gender" box was filled in usually only if the professor was female. Many feminists have complained that this sort of practice implies that maleness is the basic condition of humanity. Men have no gender; only women are seen as gendered beings. As someone who consciously genders himself as a man, I took it as my personal mission to enter an M for every masculine name in the database. It may not have accomplished anything, but it made me feel better.

Of course women and men—as long as I'm going to stereotype into these hopelessly broad categories, and I am, because I am a mere mortal and my mind hasn't yet been entirely liberated—both have their problems. It's not that I think that women's neuroses, addictions, and violence are worse than men's. In fact, as I see it, men's violence is usually much worse than women's, as it tends to be directed outward instead of inward. My discomfort with women has nothing to do with an objective assessment of their crimes. It has to do with the fact that I'm uncomfortable with the stereotype that I have of women. If I were to meet a world leader ranting about who he's going to blow up, where, and when, I'd want to put my arms around him, talk him down, and tell him his penis is a perfect size just the way it is. But if I saw a woman having a premenstrual fit about her frizzy hair in the restaurant bathroom, I'd have the urge to skewer her with a butter knife. Neither of these reactions is rational.

This is a visceral fact about how I relate to people. I feel compassion for perpetrators of masculine hostility and I feel frustration at sufferers of feminine self-hate. I'm glad to say that my anger at women, and my stereotyping of them, has been progressively decreasing. The more years I spend without hearing the pronoun "she" in reference to myself, the more my anger and unrest dissipates, and the less I feel the need to discharge my anger on the group from which I'm dissociating myself. I no longer find women as threatening, now that they no longer expect me to be one of them.

I've tried to address the matter with four therapists, pleading with them to teach me to be less sexist. None of these relationships worked out; they couldn't understand my problem and didn't know what to do with me. I suspect it's my fault for not having a vocabulary to convey my feelings. There are so many facets of transgendered life that I wish we could develop a common vocabulary to discuss. The distinction between physical sex and gender identity is immeasurably useful, but I wish we had more. Probably the common language hasn't appeared because everyone's gender experience is unique.

Look at testosterone, for instance. As politically incorrect as it sounds, the fact is that testosterone has allowed me to think. I used to be hysterical, self-absorbed, unable to focus on a project without lapsing into depression; once testosterone kicked in, I switched my creative interest from poetry to prose and my academic interest from a vague environmentalism to analytic philosophy. Testosterone keeps me placid and rational. But it has not amplified my sex drive, contrary to the experience of every FTM I have ever talked to. In fact, while I was in high school and not enjoying my natural female hormones, I considered myself to have an average or somewhat above average female sex drive; since testosterone, my sex drive has dropped to zero. This is probably not the fault of the testosterone, but something that has happened despite it.

There was one day when I felt an increased libido. It was one month after my first testosterone shot. I suddenly felt consumed by a nameless hunger and restlessness. I ate a pound of chocolate and then lifted some heavy furniture, which came close to satisfying the hunger, but wasn't quite right. I felt like the zombie in *Return of the Living Dead: Part III* who doesn't yet understand that she craves live brains, so she binges on cupcakes instead. Finally I happened to catch a glimpse of the Backstreet Boys on television and I suddenly knew what I wanted. I went straight to my bedroom, unzipped my pants, and remembered in horror that I had no penis and therefore no way to scratch the itch. That was the first and last time I ever had a powerful, male sex drive. My nonexistent libido probably isn't the fault of the testosterone (which is supposed to increase sex drive in females), so much as the fault of my anxiety that I will have no way to release sexual tension once I allow myself to experience it.

The physical problem in men used to be called impotence; the emotional problem in women used to be called frigidity. I get the worst of both worlds. I'm not complaining merely of unsatisfying orgasms, but of the complete absence of any sex drive, arousal, or physical gratification of any degree. There's this ugly thing that hangs between my legs, which I'd call a clit if it served any sexual function, but it does not. It's a little robotic appendage programmed in binary: it is either in pain or not in pain. Pleasure is outside the realm of its experience. Sexual activity tends to induce pain, while celibacy does not, hence my asexual preference.

I hope to get a metaoidioplasty (surgical enhancement of the clitoris) within the next few years when I can afford it, but I'm not in a rush. A metaoidioplasty isn't going to give me the interest in sex that I already don't have. I remember the man who asked, "Doctor, will I be able to play the violin after surgery?" and the doctor said, "Yes," and the man sighed, "That's fantastic, because I've never been able to play before." Genital surgery can cure a lot of sexual anxiety, but it won't be a total brain transplant. I try to keep my expectations realistic.

My endocrinologist and gynecologist couldn't find anything wrong with my anatomy, so I finally screwed up the guts to see a urologist. I fantasized that he would perform various neurological and blood-flow tests, and show me a glossy blue-and-white print of the nerves in my lower abdomen, and tell me I have an obvious problem, which would be a wonderful thing, because then I could blame my sexual dysfunction on something other than my own incompetence.

In reality, this is not what happened. The urologist told me that neurological and blood-flow problems are not localized, so if I suffered from dead nerves in my clit, I would also have urinary or bowel incontinence or numbness in my thighs. When I told him I couldn't feel any sexual pleasure, his eyes popped out and he breathed, "Not even with oral sex?" He wanted to help me but said that my problem could not be organic and could only be psychological. (It feels strange, from an earth-worshipper's perspective, how these words are placed in opposition: I am not "biological" when I am transsexual, not "organic" when I am psychological.) When a European male in a white lab coat flips open the telephone book and gives you the number for a hypnotist, you know he thinks you're a strange duck. Ironically, I'd already had advice from alternative healers telling me to seek the benefits of Western medicine. So I'll back off my demands: I don't need my sex problems fixed, but I'd like to at least believe that someone can understand me and relate a little bit. Being an asexual freak who is capable of surprising a urologist is a lonely place to be.

Again, the problem is the lack of vocabulary to describe the transgender experience. My experience is unique, even among other transgendered people, and I can't find the words to make myself understood. That's why I often feel frustrated at "women," the group to whom I feel the least able to relate.

Donning the funny hat and trying to see it from the graduation day perspective, sexlessness is not such a terrible thing. I've certainly had my bouts of depression with it, but you can get depressed about anything, even things that are good for you. When I reflect on it, both my sexual experiences and my celibate periods have helped me mature into the person I am today. For a while, I searched for a celibate ideology—perhaps Buddhism, Christianity, or yogic practice—that would give meaning to my loneliness and separate me from those who pursued sex for its own sake. I no longer feel the need to separate my sexuality from my celibacy. Most people experience both in their lifetimes, and the combination makes us who we are. I'm also more tolerant of other people's interest in sex. All I ever wanted was to fall in love with a nice man, but I can accept that other people may have complicated sexual identities, swing with their best friends' lovers, and own enough toys to keep a military base in training for a week. I don't have to feel pressured to behave the same way. We are all finding our own paths. Celibacy can be just as feminist and liberating as rampant sexuality is advertised to be.

I try to think of my sexuality and gender identity as something I've chosen, even though it is frequently a source of inhibition and unhappiness. If I were to say it is involuntary to boot, that would reduce it to the level of a curse. But when I see these challenges as features of my chosen path, they are more like the trials of a quest, and can be looked forward to and embraced. I try not to pity myself as the dickless man, whining that I want to get laid as other men do. The fact is, I could have their sexuality if I had their lives, but I've chosen a different life for myself. Life is a package deal; I want to keep the one I've got, and I'll take the challenges and inconveniences that come with it.

Being frigid and impotent isn't so bad when I consider the range of things that could be wrong with me. There are lots of things about myself that I love, am thankful for, and wouldn't trade for a lifetime's supply of orgasms. I have a strong back and knees; I am relaxed; I remember my dreams; I am making the world a better place; I am a talented writer; I feel connected to nature; I have nice hair; I have a clean criminal record; I have a reliable reputation; I have the best friends in the world; I have a bachelor's degree; I have a free spirit; I see the glass as half full, not half empty; and I find a way to make my life work out the way I want it to.

Part III: The Poetics of Getting Born

One of the traditional Jewish morning prayers involves the male worshipper giving thanks to God for *not* having made him a woman, *not* having made him a slave, *not* having made him a non-Jew. Women are supposed to thank God for having made them according to His will. During my search for a daily prayer, I was excited by the idea of giving thanks for my gender, but wanted to do so in nonsexist, nontheist language that acknowledged both the value of the body I was born with and the value of my spiritual quest to alter my body. I finally settled on the words *this man* to refer to my gender, since my gratitude is not for being just any man, but specifically for the man that I am.

After some practice, my prayer, offered at my altar every morning since graduation, evolved to this: "For these things I am grateful: that I have become this man; that this body is free of pain; that this mind is awakening; that the path of peace is ever more desired; that a grand imagination leads me on." Referring to my mind and body as "this mind" and "this body" helps keep me in a detached perspective. I also pay homage to the elements of water, fire, air, and earth. I am heartbroken that I haven't been able to incorporate Judaism into my spiritual path, but I can't practice what I don't believe. And, while a religious affiliation makes me feel part of a community, it also makes me feel cut off from people who aren't part of the religion, and we already have too much that separates us. I have come to think it is best to be secular. From a secular perspective, I can better embrace all people as equals and freely exchange ideas. Honoring the beauty, power, and necessity of nature doesn't seem so much a matter of faith as a matter of a common humanity.

The months surrounding my college graduation were an intensely fertile time for me. Before my senior year, I had written a personal essay about the removal of my ovaries and about what fertility could mean to a gay, sterile man. I forgot that I had submitted it to a gay men's magazine until a copy of the magazine, with my essay inside, showed up in my mailbox on the first of April. That same day, I was notified that I had won a literary award for nonfiction and that my first novel had just become available for sale. The serendipitous message was strong and clear: my fertility centered on creative writing. As I contemplated all this, it occurred to me that my novel had taken exactly nine months to write.

Two months later, I dreamed that I was about to give birth, a highly unusual dream for me, especially in the years since testosterone stopped the menstrual cycle. When I woke up, I calculated that it had been 292 days since I'd had my ovaries removed, which is a normal human gestation period. In the days that followed, I lost ten pounds and I puttered in the garden feeling like I was giving birth to the world. Not that I want my ovaries back, mind you. I don't really want to be stuffed full of blood clots and progesterone and see my pectorals swell up. I just like the idea of being full of spirit-babies and feeling comfortable in my gay, fertile body.

Dream analysis might identify the desire to have babies with the desire to get laid. The thought has, in fact, crossed my mind. I started flirting with a female classmate who was chronically depressed and needed company. On a few occasions we shared a bed and talked each other to sleep. She thought the scars on my chest were from heart surgery; I told her they were not, but never gave her any indication of what they were from, so she persisted in believing that my life was a miracle saved from the edge of the dark side. I had good reasons not to pursue a romance with her: I'm not attracted to women, and she was planning on going to med school in California. Another reason I could not date her was that she was straight and perceived me as a gay male. This was, of course, just an excuse.

I also flirted with a male classmate who came to a presentation by FTM photographer Loren Cameron and may have been more savvy in his interpretation of my scars. His antics were reported to my friends under the junior high–code name of "Straight Boy." His real name is Gabriel. We had lots of exciting dates, like the time he invited me to the mall to help him choose a blender, as though he expected me to have innate home furnishing skills. I had good reasons not to pursue a romance with him. For instance, his ex-girlfriend's name was Brynelle, and while "Gabriel and Brynelle" has a elegant ring, like "Griffin and Sabine," whose passionate, tragic correspondence sells on the fiction shelves of our college bookstore, "Gabriel and Tucker" sounds like a bumbling wannabe Mafia duo fated for the bottom of the lake before act three. Another reason I could not date him was that he was straight and perceived me as a gay male. This was, of course, just another excuse.

Just when it was becoming clear that I was a hopeless case and would never get a date that didn't involve wearing clothes to bed or buying blenders, I went to a personal growth workshop and was asked out by a gay man a little older than me. We turned out not to have much in common, so the relationship never grew past its infancy, and I never had to reveal what part of my body is missing. However, I hinted about my transsexuality, and he affirmed that he was interested in me as a person and that I should trust him not to be shallow. Who knows, but if a gay man can find me attractive, maybe my case isn't so hopeless after all. Even more important is the realization that dating isn't as romantic and essential as it's cracked up to be. I'm having more fun being single, celibate, flirting with straight friends, and otherwise enjoying the summer before I have to get a real job.

I've had the good fortune not to have had any negative repercussions from my transition or my identity. What has made transsexuality difficult is not intentional, hateful discrimination, but my unique perspective on the world and my awareness of my inability to communicate it. Sometimes I think I'm upset about being different. It usually turns out that I can feel better by reaching out and coming out, because it's the isolation that hurts more than the differences.

Sometimes, through magical, artistic means, I think I can project a glimpse of my experience to others. In my high school poet days, before testosterone and the university encouraged me to think in full sentences, I produced some good poems that still speak eloquently of my true self.

Poetry doesn't dissolve all barriers, but if I can trust my ability to express at least some of my feelings, that's a start. Pure communication happens when we catch a glimpse of ourselves in someone else and remember that we are all one being. There are many ways to provide others with the opportunity to see themselves in us. Many people have commented on my altar, at which I pray every morning: they recognize something in the arrangement of nests, hair clippings, feathers, drawings, rocks, and amulets, and although neither of us can explain what it means, we know our souls are touching. Creative writing and nature worship have always been ways in which I express my fertility. If I can only remember this, I will always be in touch with my unique powers.

When I can communicate, I no longer feel so alone. I feel calmer and safer knowing that someone understands a part of my life. As a transsexual, I may be unusual, but I'm still 100 percent human. This man, this body, this mind, this life is not deformed; it only sometimes feels unhappy and behaves anxiously. The negative attitude can be stopped if I choose to stop it. Often I think I'm in pain, but it's only my head that hurts.

GALLAE, OR REFLECTIONS OF A PAGAN HEART

Laura Anne Seabrook

IT'S THE MID-1960S, and I'm still at primary school in Perth, Australia. I'm in the playground and crying. The other children crowd around. "What's the matter?" asks one girl. "Don't know," I say between sobs. "Cheer up," says someone else. "It's OK, it's OK," says still another. But it isn't OK. After ten minutes, all the sobbing and crying has gone from me. I sit there looking at the other children in the playground, not able to understand their happiness. I look at the girls playing, and long to join them. Something is wrong, but I don't know what.

A few years later and our school's attending a sports carnival at Perry Lakes, and I'm bored. I hate sports—probably because I'm short-sighted, epileptic, and sickly—but I hate them nonetheless. For me it's a long and dull day, even with the book and comic I've brought with me. I'm keen to get back to school, to go home, anywhere but be here. It grows late in the day, and I decide to queue early next to the gates we came through that morning so I'll be the first back on the bus.

Somehow I miss that fact that everyone else has queued at a different set of gates. The buses leave and everyone else is on them, while I'm left there waiting. By chance some transport officials spot me and kindly give me a lift home. Not back to the school, but straight home to my family. Something better than I expected. That night I have a strange dream.

In the dream I'm dressed as a schoolboy like the day before. I'm lost on a deserted country road; it's dark and I'm worried about finding my way. Then a car approaches down the road. It's a Vanguard, just like my father has. It pulls over and the woman who's driving it (who for some reason is also "the Lady") asks me if I'm lost. I'm scared of being lost, but I'm not scared of her. I say yes and she offers me a lift. I accept and get in.

We talk as she drives. She tells me that it's OK to be me, and if sometimes I feel lost or confused, that's OK too; and that if I ever felt really, really confused, or so lost that I'd never find my way home, that She'd be there for me. The Lady reminds me of my mother. There were two large cats in the back of the car, but in this dream that seemed normal, and they seemed cute. One of them licks me on the face and I feel its rough tongue. I'm not afraid of them because She's there too. Finally we arrive home. The Lady gives me a kiss, I get out, and then she drives off. The only thing is, when I look down at myself I'm dressed as a schoolgirl. In the dream it doesn't feel strange or odd; it feels just right.

Predicting the Future

It's the early 1970s, and I'm looking into the mirror. I feel safe while the rest of the family's out, and here I'm alone in my parents' bedroom. The figure that looks back at me from the mirror is a girl, a pretty girl. I don't dare use any lipstick, so I've smeared my lips with mulberry fruit from the tree out the front. The erection I've been struggling to contain threatens to erupt in an orgasmic flurry.

Then, I hear the sound of a car coming up the driveway. I race through the house to the bathroom and the shower. Quickly I pull the women's clothes off and wipe the mulberry juice from my lips. I'd put a cache of male clothes there, just in case, and it's just as well. "We're home," comes my mother's voice from another room. "Where are you?" "Just in the shower," I say, as I turn the water on. Saved in the nick of time.

Years later and the dream's long forgotten, though the issues around it are still with me. I'm crossdressing off and on, and always in secret. Sometimes I purge the clothes I collect, but I always seem to collect more. But for now, there are three of us in the car: Bernie, Shamus, and me. We're returning from the World Science Fiction Convention in Melbourne in Bernie's car. Bernie is the only one who can drive, whereas Shamus and I act as support. It's been an eventful trip, full of unexpected events and memorable happenings. Bernie, who models himself on James Bond, has been quite happy with the mix of events and fun he's had on the trip. Even Shamus has had a lot of fun. But I'm miserable as hell. Nothing has seemed to go right exactly, and I have no confidence in myself or where I'm going. We are all tired and stressed. I offer to do a quick tarot reading for people—just one card each and I'll predict where we'll be in ten years.

I'd been studying tarot for a while, but had only just started to do readings. The card for Bernie is the Four of Wands: domestic happiness. I say he'll be happily married with kids. Shamus's card is The Fool: making his way through the world with the trust of a child. I tell him that in ten years he'll be doing the same as he is now. My card is a blank—a spare that I forgot to remove from the pack. No future perhaps?

Ten years later, Bernie is married with kids; Shamus is working at the same place; and I've begun my gender transition. Still, in the future, that transition seems a world away. Only two years later, though, and I'm in Albany, having moved here for a job. I've finally moved out from home, even if I am thirty. Back in Perth I have a girlfriend of sorts, who I met just before moving here.

Cynthia

Right now I'm knocking on a door. If I'm right, Ralph, who produces the homegrown comic *SCAM* (which I've admired from afar), lives here. A woman opens the door—his wife. "He's just having a shower," she says, and I wait. Ralph and I become good friends, sharing a love of comics, science fiction, and humor. The following year Ralph is no longer Ralph, but Cynthia. I stick by her in her transition because to me she's still the same person. Deep down, I know that some day I must transition too.

But today I'm leaving for Perth. My girlfriend there wants me to return and live with her, and I have a new job that will take me back to the city. I say my goodbyes to Cynthia, the wife, and the kids. Sometime later I hear that shortly after I leave, Cynthia attempts suicide.

Over a year later and I'm driving a hire car and giving Cynthia a lift home. "It must have taken guts to leave your wife and kids, and to start a new life like that," I say.

"Well, it was either that or commit suicide," she replies. "I just couldn't be Ralph any longer."

"Yeah, but it still takes guts. I admire you for that," I say.

"Hmph," she says. "I sometimes wonder what life would have been like under different circumstances, like if I'd been a genetic woman."

"Or never married—stuff like that?" I ask.

"Yes, still it's pointless exercise," she says.

"Oh, I don't know . . ." I pause. "In another universe, under different circumstances, who knows, we might have been lovers." We both laugh nervously.

It's four years later, and I'm in a hospital in Sydney. I'm visiting Cynthia, who's recovering from sex realignment surgery. After breaking up with my first girlfriend, I get together with Cynthia. I love and support her, and my family doesn't know that she was never born female. She lies in the bed, weak, but happy. I have the camera ready as she holds up the container. Barely the size of her hand, it contains a couple of chickpeas in water. At a casual glance though, they look like something else, something that she's been glad to be rid of. The grin on her face as I take the photo confirms that fact.

Another eight months and things are different. I'm visiting Cynthia in hospital again, but this time things are not so happy. She's been suicidal (again), and her friend Jemima had taken her down to the psychiatric ward, where she can be watched. I've been visiting her almost every day ever since. I think of the problems she's had since surgery: the complications and the pain, and the run-around the hospital gave her in trying to get corrective surgery later. And no one to blame or say, "It's OK, that can be corrected," with conviction. I think of the loss of faith she's had, and the drugs she's started to take.

All I can do is just be there, to catch her when she falls. Today I take her outside to see a film. The stress and paranoia in her almost seem like palpable entities. I try to be there for her, though somewhere deep down I know that it won't be enough. The film is good, she enjoys it, but later I have to take her back to the ward. It's evening, and I'm sitting on the bed with my head in my hands. A thought comes to me. One day I might wake up in bed next to a corpse, and I might end up a bitter, old man. I'm still unsure what I am, but know I'm not a man.

Cynthia has a new friend, Sonia, someone who she knew long ago. When they meet again, Sonia's living in Cynthia's parents' old house, in Cynthia's old room when she was still Ralph. An odd coincidence. I encourage the friendship, and they grow closer.

Months later and Cynthia's back at our house, the one that we moved to because it has more rooms and a bathtub. "I can't go on, I can't do it any more!" Cynthia shouts as she holds the kitchen knife.

"No you don't!" I shout back. We wrestle over the knife. I'm still the bigger and stronger of the two. After the struggle Cynthia is on the floor, and the knife is on the other side of the room, thrown there by myself.

"Let me die, let me die!" she cries.

"Like hell," I say. She moves toward the knife, and I knock her back to the floor near the phone. She struggles to get up.

"No!" I push her down and then sit on her, preventing her from moving. I dial a number carefully. "Sonia? Yeah, it's me. Look, she's tried it again. Can you get over here? Thanks." As I hang up, I wonder how long I can wait for Sonia to arrive.

A few weeks later and Cynthia and I are peering at each other over the table. "I've had it!" I say.

"Yeah, well so have I!" Cynthia replies. Jemima's staying out of this domestic scene, sitting quietly in the next room. "I've had it up to here with you. Christ, anyone'd think I was a piece of furniture around here, the way you treat me!" It hurts me to hear her say this, and other things.

"So what's your problem?" I ask, demanding an answer.

She pauses, and looks me square in the eyes. "I think I'm a lesbian. I'm in love with Sonia." Oddly enough, I feel relieved to hear this. "Well guess what? I think I'm transsexual!" I say in triumph.

"Oh shit, I hope you're not . . . anything but that," she replies. All of a sudden, everything's different. She goes off with Sonia, and I go off with a future.

Looking for Wisdom

Two years later and things haven't been that simple. After attempting to transition at work, things have been more stressful than I'd anticipated. With management denying me access to the women's toilets (I'm forced to use the disabled ones instead), I feel a lack of support. A week ago I had an anonymous internal phone call. It was probably a joke, but a death threat is something I don't consider funny.

Jemima and I are walking back home from the Star Trek club. I live in the inner city and my flat is only two blocks away. On our way back, someone in a four-wheel drive cuts us off at the corner, driving up on the pavement to do so. He shouts, "Transvestites, transsexuals—I'll kill you all!" Jemima isn't disturbed and walks on. The car drives off, and then comes back for a second round. We get to the flat safely, but for me it's the last straw. The idea that I was safe where I worked and lived was all an illusion.

Two months later and I'm in Sydney staying at a "trannie" hostel. All last year I'd been thinking of Sydney, that for some reason I needed to visit it. I hadn't been there since the trip with my ex, and yet something drew me to it. And here I am doing a "geographical," taking all the long service leave I'd accumulated and letting things fall where they may.

Before I leave Perth, I visit Melissa and Royd. I'd known them for over a decade, and we were all mad Trek fans. But they were pagan too. And before I leave, I go to a summer solstice ritual that they're involved in. I'm not pagan, not yet, but still, something draws me to the ceremony. I look up at the night sky and vow to look for Wisdom (which they call Hecate) while in the east. I take my tarot deck and rune stones with me on the trip.

Looking and finding are two different things. The hostel is not a good environment. Too many people with too many fragile egos. The tension is ever present, and some people are always trying to get others to leave. It's like the TV show *Big Brother* (which won't be broadcast for another six years yet) only without the cameras. A hothouse situation. I wilt rather than blossom.

Then, after a particularly upsetting incident, I hit rock bottom. Absolutely miserable, I decide to go to a meditation center and seek guidance through prayer and meditation. I get a "wrong number." What I got was an internal voice of shame that shouted at me: "Kill yourself!" It wasn't the only internal voice I heard; there was another whispering, "Persistence pays off." But that second voice was overwhelmed by the first. Hallucinations are nothing new to me—I used to get them when I was epileptic—business as usual.

The next day I try to go about my business, but the voice of shame and guilt keeps shouting, "Kill yourself." I feel like I'm filled only with a huge void that echoes these words. Finally, I find myself at a clifftop at Manly Heads (and later the irony of where I go isn't lost on me), deciding whether or not to kill myself. After four hours (and still indecision) I leave and go to a group therapy meeting. It seems that half the people there have been thinking about suicide. There was something in the air that day, and I realized that I wasn't nuts, I wasn't crazy, and I wasn't the only one.

On the way back to the hostel I keep hearing an old Pretender's song in my mind, *I'll Stand by You*. Somehow, that seems reassuring and meaningful. A week later, after being notified that all the counselors who work with the hostel will be away for a week, I decide to visit Newcastle rather than endure the place. It's a good move. Newcastle reminds me of Albany where I lived when I first moved out from home. I could live in Newcastle, if not in Sydney.

One thing remains to be done, however. I'd been thinking that maybe I should go back to school, go to university and finally get to do the visual arts degree that I'd wanted to do in my late teens. Lismore has a university and so does Newcastle. Just to be sure, I decide to visit friends in Lismore. I'm in town for only three days. In the early morning of the second I say a prayer to the Goddess and do a tarot reading for myself. Then I pull a rune stone for further clarification. Both say the same thing: trust your inner processes.

The university is sufficient, but I know that I'd go nuts in the town. At the prompting of my friends I spend two days in Byron Bay, a well-known spiritual retreat. It brings to a head something that's been growing in me over the past four years—a sense of connection to something greater than myself. The lodge I'm staying at runs dawn tours of the local lighthouse. It's supposed to be the easternmost point of mainland Australia.

Next morning I go with a group of eight. We have a champagne breakfast while we wait for the sun to come up. Just as it does, I venture out to a forward observation deck and begin my dedication. I greet the sun, and with it, the Goddess too. There and then, I dedicate myself to Her, as a willing and loyal follower and daughter, and I dedicate myself to living a fulfilled and joyous life in Her honor. I feel relieved and exhilarated. I know that nothing would stop me from this point on, provided that I remain loyal and sincere.

The Big Decision

Five years later and I have to make the big decision. So much has changed. I've quit my public service job and with the redundancy money relocated to Newcastle. I have a house and car, and am studying for a bachelor of visual arts at Newcastle University. The big decision is which surgeon to choose for reassignment surgery. Over the past year there's been so much stress. I've collapsed physically, had to start taking antidepressants, and ended up on a disability allowance. So much change, in so short a time.

But I'm getting things done. Despite the stress (or maybe because of it?), I feel I've blossomed. I've started expressing myself not just in my art, but in my clothing. I come out as a goth, though connections with other goths seem hard to make. And I've made other connections too. I now have an Internet connection, and through this come to know that there are other people in the world who are both transgendered and pagan. Some of them, including myself, call ourselves *gallae,* after the ancient followers of the cult of Cybele. Cybele is a goddess of the cities, but also of the wild fields and deep earth (and, oddly enough, epilepsy).

I go to the university library and read books about the gallae. The ancient gallae in Roman times were males who castrated themselves ritually and thereafter dressed and behaved as women. I read about the hijra in India, who seem so much like the gallae. I have a heritage that I never knew of before. Cybele, the Magna Mater, becomes my adopted Mother; Hecate is Grandmother. I make a connection in a big way. Somehow it all falls into place.

And now I have to make the big decision. Over the past year there's been this growing feeling in me that I'm "overdue" for my surgery. I feel ripe for the moment. It almost seems too important to make. I've taken a year off university, just for the surgery. My intuition tells me to go overseas, go to a surgeon in Thailand. I'm confused, and asking other "girls" about their surgical results only confuses me more. Either they can't praise the surgeon enough or they damn them to hell. No middle ground. Then, I have a dream.

In the dream I'm back in Perth. Not the real Perth, but one that seems to exist in my dreams. I'm in East Perth, where I used to live and work, and I'm the me that I was pretransition. I'm walking along Adelaide Terrace, and I meet someone I've known since high school—another transsexual—only she's pretransition too. We greet each other and compare notes about things and times. I see the block of flats where I lived in its heyday. Some of the buildings are no different, as modern as they were when I left Perth.

I enter one and go into a lift up to the ninth floor. The door opens and inside is a woman. She's the same Lady I met in that dream so long ago. She's wearing an orange caftan covered with mythological scenes. I feel drawn to talk to her. I mention that I'm upset and nervous, and she asks me why. I tell her that I'm so uncertain and unsure of myself, about the impending surgery and the complications in financing it and so on. She looks at me with a gaze that is both authoritarian and compassionate at the same time and says, "Listen child, no matter who you go to, things will be all right, and you will have a good outcome. Trust in yourself and your intuition." And on hearing these words, all my fears and doubts fall away like old rags off a beggar and I know, though how I don't know, that I'm talking to Cybele.

I get out at the ground floor again. I walk over to a building and sit down on the ground. That friend walks up with an acquaintance and also sits down with me. We talk about the ruins across the road and look at the old cannons and other features that litter it. Cybele walks by as we talk, with several orange-robed figures following close by in attendance. "Remember child," She says. "Trust in yourself." She drops a bright yellow rose to me as She passes. I catch it, drawing blood, but the aroma is sweet, and I feel fresh and clean and full of an ice-cold energy.

Then I say goodbye to my friend and walk past the ruins. I get to Hay Street and walk in the carnival that seems to be there. There are jugglers, fire-eaters, and other performers out in the street. Bright and gaudy lights are all around. I come to an office tucked away on one side. I know that a surgeon awaits me on the other side of the door. I smile and walk in. When I awoke, I knew that for me the right thing to do was to go to Thailand.

It's October of the same year. Robyn has arrived from Taree. She's a good friend, a devout Christian, and though I'm openly pagan, we connect where it counts. She's also had her surgery (while accompanied by a documentary film crew, no less) a year ago, with the same surgeon, almost to the day when mine is scheduled. I'm organizing a combined "surgery and birthday" party. The party is all I could have wanted and more. About a dozen friends turn up. A pagan friend from Sydney brings up a cake. It's made in the shape of stylized male genitalia. The highlight of the party is me cutting the cake with a meat cleaver.

A week later and I'm in Thailand with Robyn. Although she wasn't my first choice, she was the best choice for a companion for this trip. I needed someone to "hold my hand" while I went for my "day of blood" (as the ancient gallae would call it). Joe, my boarder, is at home looking after the house and the pets. The telephone system seems utterly alien, so I'm unable to "phone home" even if I wanted to. We do a bit of sightseeing before I go to hospital, as this is my first time overseas. We take in the sights, including a bar where the transgender Kathoey (show girls) perform. It reminds me of King's Cross.

I bring a makeshift altar with me made from a T-shirt I've screen printed with a rainbow pentagram, a figurine of a comic book goddess called *Dawn*, some candles, and a tambourine and cymbals. Once the nurses and cleaners realize that it's a shrine, they respect it. As I go off to surgery I light the candles and say a prayer to Her. There is a minor upset before surgery when a problem is discovered with my credit card, but that is resolved, and the next thing I know I'm under the anesthetic and lost to the world.

I regain consciousness five hours later, and the first thing I hear is Robyn's voice saying, "It's OK, Laura, it's all right—the surgery's all over now." There was a tone in her voice that was at once happy, concerned, and relieved. I am those things too, but am too far out of things to really know one way or another how I feel. They take me back to my room, where I drift in and out of sleep all night. Sometimes I watch the MTV channel on the room's video recorder. It always seems to be either U2's *Beautiful Day* or Blur's *Music Is My Radar* that's playing. Sometimes, I just lie in silence, or talk to Robyn and have her hold my hand.

It's some days later, and I'm still in the same bed, and Robyn, who was staying with me, has been moved to another room. The surgeon performed further surgery on her (a "free upgrade" as he put it) because he wanted to improve her results. But there were complications resulting in a hematoma. She was rushed off for further corrective surgery and is recovering in another room. I feel so washed out and lost. There is the usual morning routine of checking blood pressure, sponge bath, and breakfast, but it all seems so perfunctory. I miss Robyn.

I feel so tired, sad, frustrated, lonely, and frightened, and all these emotions rolled into one. I lie sideways, facing the window with the light off, shaking and crying. I think to myself that I ought to be tougher, better, stronger, more able to hold it together—and because I'm not, things are the worse for that. I feel like shit. I may have been forgetting to take my antidepressants again. Then in my mind I hear a song that I've heard before: *I'll Stand by You* by the Pretenders—a song that I now associate with Hecate. They've been playing it on MTV as the score to a Wildlife Fund advertisement. But the TV's not on right now. And I rally.

I buzz the nurse, get disconnected from the catheters, and get up. I compose myself and light a candle, both for Robyn and me. I visit Robyn. She seems to be in good spirits and much less pain. I also visit Portia, another of the "girls" here who's pagan. We are all tired and sore, recovering from that which we desired so much. But we are all happy too, because for each of us it seems the right thing to do.

Beautiful Days

And now it's two years later, and I'm fully recovered from surgery, finished the bachelor of visual arts course, and thinking about what to do next. I still keep in contact with Robyn (who's now become a Buddhist and also had a successful "upgrade"), though my boarder's long since moved on. Jemima is looking to sell her house in Western Australia and maybe move in. I'd welcome the company.

It's been tough. Surgery didn't fix my financial problems, or problems of loneliness, though it did relieve one important cause of stress. I've been in severe depression, and suicidal too, but not over gender issues, not ever again. Things have been better since then. I'm off the antidepressants, and maybe with the help of the Commonwealth Rehabilitation Service I might get retrained, or at least earn some extra money. I have a vision of myself writing, cartooning, of doing my art, of reading tarot at the markets, and selling homemade clothes and my own artwork. I have a vision of being creative, as being myself and being creative and thriving. Maybe.

The car doesn't work at the moment, but I know what's wrong with it. It can be fixed, eventually. My sewing machine needs a tune-up. It keeps breaking needles, but that too can be fixed. I feel the constraints of poverty but know that this too will pass. And maybe I used to feel broken too, and in some ways still do. But this too can be fixed, this too will pass. It wasn't something I felt right away, but since the surgery I've been feeling more and more confident in and of myself. The depression—well maybe that was a reaction to all the physical and social changes I've had in the past seven years. So much change, in so short a time.

But for now it's a beautiful day, like U2 sang back when I was still in Thailand. The damp ground and blue skies outside are strangely inviting. It's time for me to take my dog Pegasus for a walk. We'll go down the bush tracks and take in the sights and smells of spring. Both Peggy and I are good at finding trails as well, ones that barely seem to be there but exist nonetheless. Sometimes I slack off, stay at home, and watch TV instead. But normally when I make the effort, the walk is well worth it.

Maybe my life is like those bush tracks and trails. Sometimes the track twists and turns, is rough and occasionally strewn with junk. And maybe I don't always know what it leads to, but I know that in the end I'll be coming home. And sometimes, when I take a detour that barely seems to be there, I get a little scared of getting lost. If I do, it's only temporary; even if I don't know where I'm going, somehow I always find my way home.

So maybe I don't know where this path is taking me, but it seems right, and at the end of the day I'm happier in myself. Maybe the destination's not the point, in any case. Maybe all the enjoyment's in the trip itself. It's worth making the effort, and fun finding out.

TIME FOR A GOOD
TRANSGENDER STORY

Kam Wai Kui

THE PHILOSOPHER NIETZSCHE ARGUES that people will only become conscious of themselves when injuries are inflicted on them, because in being able to prove what's done to you, you have to give an account of yourself.

I cannot help but agree with these words, for I have been writing countless journals that reflect my struggles to come to terms with my inner turmoil. Long descriptions have been given to my first encounters with transsexuality and the endless negotiations that followed: the search for a way to make transsexuality an acceptable concept against my Chinese background, heated discussions with siblings about whether or not to come out yet, big questions about whether I can find someone who would care for me as I am, with all its complications. But there were also gaps, huge gaps between those journal entries. The gaps, or the unwritten, reflect the happy times, when things were normal or simply very pleasurable.

I wonder sometimes what would have become of my ability to reflect, articulate, educate, and explain if transsexuality hadn't come into my life and asked me to live my life this way, to feel the pain, but also learn to forgive. What if, to paraphrase Nietzsche, I have no emotional injuries that need to be addressed? What would have influenced my consciousness of gender and my search for other possibilities to make my life enjoyable and acceptable? What would happen to my consciousness of the flaws within contemporary Chinese society toward people who are considered to be outsiders?

Nowadays I find myself in those days of unwritten gaps, but I'm still aware of all those negotiations with pain, and the anxieties I had felt before I came to terms with who I was and who I am now. To achieve anything in life, a quest needs to be endured first. The painful negotiations are still present, but they occupy a peaceful place in my life, like a book sitting on my shelf. I now focus on sharing our stories on screen with a wider audience through organizing transgender film festivals, so that people can contemplate the myths and meanings of trans narratives and understand our struggles better. My own life is a transgender story that came out of a classic transsexual narrative.

A long time ago when I was still very little, I was put in a position in which I needed to choose between being good and being special. Without hesitating, I chose the more difficult option.

The Conformist

Nothing could prevent me from being a good child, but in my young consciousness it was somehow clear that one thing was more important than my gender, which was to be a good Chinese person. I was born in Hong Kong in the late 1960s and moved to the Netherlands in the 1970s. So I spent my first eight years living in the city that has shaped many aspects of my life. I had a short but effective and tough education in Hong Kong. I can still remember the nuns who ran the school. They wore long black dresses that came down to the ground and seemed to glide through the alleys because no one could see their feet while they walked. These strict and supernatural creatures made a huge impression on me as figures of authority. Discipline was necessary according to the adults, for I had no sense of fear: I hung my head out of the window from the eleventh floor to imitate prison scenes that I had seen on TV; I crossed the streets without looking out for traffic; I let my classmates read my answers while doing an exam. It was a time when I had to learn to listen and obey.

Hassle about my gender started even before I was born. I grew up in a middle-class family with three kids. I am the youngest and originally wasn't part of the family planning. My grandparents from my father's side were very unhappy about my mother bearing another child. They would not approve unless it turned out to be a boy—as if my mum could have any active influence in this matter! However, my mother decided to keep me, even though the pressure on her was huge. To the dismay of my grandparents, I was born a girl. Still, I was greeted with joy by my two older siblings. I was a smiling baby.

My father was hardly around, as his job required him to travel nine months out of the year. It was the only way for him to support both his own family and his birth family. For the kids it was just fine. Somehow we found a harmony in the family, even though it was hard for my mother to bring up three kids on her own. We stayed in Hong Kong until the mid-1970s. Despite the rather complicated living situation, I had a good time in those days. I did have problems attending the elementary school in a girl's uniform: it was a great drama every day to get me dressed on time for school. When I was outside of school, my mother actually let me dress as a boy because I was very determined about it, and the family managed to deal with my particular behavior with humor. At that time, my behavior as a-girl-acting-like-a-boy did not cause too much shame. It was just another addition to the collection of fun family moments. Complications came much later on in life.

It's a virtue for a Chinese person to know how to behave according to their position. For some people, this knowledge serves them too well. I knew how men were supposed to behave, and I was certain that I could become the best model of such behavior. I was convinced that my grandfather's model sucked, and I hardly knew my father's. He was the man of exotic postcards and foreign currency. Most of all, my father was the man who was never at home. Instead of him, I would be the responsible, loving gentleman who would provide his mother with the happiness she had missed in her life. I would fill the gap. I took on this task as a secret mission. Was I trying to act like the man of the house because I missed my dad's presence? I guess I was. At least it distracted me from my own negotiations with my gender.

Perceptions of Gender

The first memory of my trans behavior was a story that my sister remembered very well, and my mother would always eagerly confirm it with a smile. Apparently when I was four, I tried to pee while standing up, but all I could achieve was to dirty the toilet. When mum confronted me with my funny behavior, I told her that boys don't sit when they pee. Mum was quite embarrassed but at the same time very amused to have that discussion with her four-year-old but already quite stubborn kid. This is still a great family joke.

Not unlike the rest of the world, my early perception of gender was that there were only two. I was just unlucky enough to have been in the wrong category. As a kid, I thought that being a man meant to drive a car, to wear a three-piece suit, to have a secretary and lots of meetings. This strange perception of manhood was projected from Hong Kong's popular culture, which preached no other ideology except the dream to get rich. The major themes in television soap operas were all variations on this dream to climb up the social ladder. Being a real man meant looking sharp in a three-piece suit. That was also how you would get a girl too!

The other popular genre in Hong Kong during the 1970s that shaped my early perception of manhood was that of the martial arts stories adapted for television. In the world of martial arts, or *mo lum,* the hero is a man who can conquer all other fighters but remain untouched by the power struggles around him. My favorite characters were those who were powerful but chose to live outside the rules of power. Their character was pure. These heroes had their own codes of honor that remained outside of the complex hierarchies of Chinese society.

A hero is a man of virtue, a man of honor and honesty, a man of discipline and responsibility. However, a hero is not independent. To look for independence is a selfish act. This was my cultural baggage. Heroes sacrifice their lives as an act of honor, for they are good men; but the rules of society are golden, and mortals cannot overrule them. But what is the path of the contemporary man of virtue? What is the realistic substitute for the trope of honorable death? The portrayal of the guy in a three-piece suit with money and power was the only option represented. It may sound absurd now, but it did influence my determination to be a good student at school, to get a good job that pays well, and to gain respect. Born as a girl, I was supposed to find a good husband who could take care of me financially, but that option never occurred to me at all. No one takes care of me; it has to be me who takes care of others.

When we emigrated to the Netherlands to reunite with my father, we moved to a small town in the north of Holland. It was a weird experience for us because we were the only Chinese family in town. Yet moving to the Netherlands had also provided me with many positive changes: I was no longer obliged to wear girls' dresses to school, because the Dutch system didn't require uniforms. Unisex clothing was a big trend at the time, which made me suddenly less strange than other kids. Being a rebel and a dreamer in Hong Kong, I got lousy school grades, but once I had left the strictness of Hong Kong's system, I flourished in school and became one of the best pupils in my class. Even more important, I was able to create spaces where I could stay true to myself.

Although categorized as a girl, I was popular with boys as well because we shared many interests. I found out that I would be accepted as a boy if I did boyish things at their best: I learned to become cool and competitive and to stay well informed on the latest gadgets, games, and especially pop music. The head of the school once asked me whether I wanted to change my Chinese name into a Westernized name, but I refused. I enjoyed my ungendered name, which initially caused confusion for my classmates because my appearance did not help them differentiate my gender either. That served me perfectly, as each time I met someone new, I could prolong the perception that I wasn't a girl.

In the relatively safe and closed space of the elementary school, I had learned how to flourish and to be popular. However, it was a different matter in college. Negotiations for gender-free spaces became a difficult business. The college world was incredibly competitive. Class, money, and good looks would provide you with status, but inventiveness and good grades would not. Dating became a hot issue. However hard I tried, it wasn't possible anymore to escape gender division at that age, and a relationship with a girl was not immediately within my reach. It thus became impossible for me to escape the stigma of being unloved.

Have the Chinese Never Learned to Enjoy?

Taking up responsibilities early in life is not uncommon for a Chinese child. There is a constant pressure on you not to fail your family. To change your gender more or less means carrying the burden of shame for your whole family. Even if you decide to go your own way, the family is still judged as a whole; the absence of a family member is seen as a crack in the mirror. Many young Chinese people that I encounter nowadays still live under such expectations. I was no exception, despite my optimism and will to change the situation.

Nonetheless, I kept on doing what I knew was right for me, despite the knowledge that pursuing boyhood was an unusual mission for a girl. I would dress as boyishly as possible, and I distanced myself from any sort of girlish habits or behavior. My mother was not unfamiliar with these gender expressions. Sometimes she let me have my own way. Other times, she would make me feel ashamed of my behavior. However, we never sat down to talk about it. We lived above the restaurant, which opened seven days a week. We spent most of the time together during business hours in the restaurant. Apart from that, there were always other people around, as there were often relatives and employees staying at our place. Due to this lack of time and privacy, my mother and I became very bad at communicating with each other. We never talked about our feelings. We just made sure that we moved on without apparent problems.

For many years, two boys were my best childhood friends. We often pretended that we were detectives from television soaps, or warriors from ancient China and masters in martial arts. We even shared our childish boy fantasies of making out with a girl. We spent hours and hours at night trying to reach the highest level of computer games on my Commodore.

Those were great times. The boys' attitude toward me changed only when we got older, when our parents and siblings told them that it was uncool for a boy to hang around a girl. The fact that we had a genuine friendship seemed unimportant to our parents. These young men were shamed for their association with a girl as their playmate. What an effective social tool; it made us fragile, and our social status became dependent on the approval of this network of adults. The three of us shied away from each other in silence because of shame.

During my adolescent years, it became harder not to acknowledge that my gender identity had become a real issue. The incompatibility of my outer appearance and my inner gender expression was starting to cause serious problems. The growth of my female breasts especially was killing me, turning me into this monster with all the wrong body parts. The obvious solution to this problem also scared the hell out of me: the only option was for me to break away from this complex system of rules and obligations. Like many people who had to break hearts to break free, I discovered that my heart was that of a conformist. The conformist found himself on a lonely path toward his freedom and destiny, and somehow that pursuit of independence felt extremely lonely to him. It just didn't occur to me that the Chinese were not brought up to be independent and provocative. It didn't occur to me that we were simply taught to conform.

Active Negotiations

The concept of transsexuality took a long time to come into my life. I was fourteen when I first ran into a depressing autobiography of a transsexual woman. Reading that account really scared me off from thinking about the issue. Later, when I was seventeen, I saw a program on TV about the transitioning of two older transsexual women. There were still no representations of female-to-male transsexuals. Acknowledging that I was one of them did not fill me up with pride. The result was another two years being wasted on this refusal to accept my condition. I knew the concept of homosexuality by then, but unlike transsexuality, it didn't provide me with any identification at all. I struggled to understand how I could identify as a transsexual without making myself ridiculous. It was almost impossible to take a middle path because transsexuality' would put me in the spotlight and give me a nasty reputation among my huge extended family.

Our family situation wasn't very helpful either; my father was not capable enough of succeeding in the businesses he started, and his incompetence eroded my mum's spirit. The tension in the family was high. The only way to support my parents was to behave well, knowing that at the same time we could never ask for any emotional support from them at all. We all turned to a hobby or something that we could control. My brother turned to upgrading his car with the latest gadgets; my sister devoted her time to setting trends at school. I tried to use my artistic expressions in drawings, but they got stuck in my anger. So instead, I approached my problems intellectually by turning to the arts and literature. It was a time of insomnia. Midnight radio shows kept me company in the hours when there was no pressure.

My years studying at the university finally offered a change in my environment. I left my parents' place to live nearer to the university, and without the immediate pressure of my parents' judgment on my behavior and clothing, I became more at ease with who I was. I even started hesitantly to identify more openly with transsexuality, but it wasn't until I discovered the difference between having crushes and falling in love that I made the final step to the gender clinic, because being in love created other urgencies. I believed that in the state that I was—a nonoperative transsexual—I could not have any relationships, so something needed to be done about it. But there were conflicts too. Even though I may have considered myself to be a true transsexual for a long time, somehow in the back of my mind, I never wanted to pursue the medical solution entirely. To be dependent on hormones for a lifetime was an unacceptable condition for me; I don't want my body to be chemicalized to that extent. To be a transgender person was an unknown option at that time: "in-betweenness" was and is still considered to be too frightening. You either choose to go all the way as a transsexual, or you stay in your "original" gender role. The gender clinic wasn't helpful for those who looked for other options.

Fortunately for me, around the same time, four FTMs founded Het Jongensuur (the Boys' Hour), a support group for FTMs and those who are questioning, with more emphasis on creating a space for the latter. I benefited a lot from these meetings. Meeting new people made me realize that I wasn't playing madman all by myself. We laughed a lot about our different approaches to dealing with transsexuality. All kinds of life stories and lifestyles appeared in front of me; I took them in thankfully as future possibilities. All of a sudden, it created so much mental space. Also, I was tired of being angry all the time, so instead I became more tolerant toward transsexuality and started to talk about it more in depth. All my friends were supportive, whether they understood the condition fully or not. Even my decision to wait to find out what sort of medical help I needed was greeted with understanding. For my part, I've taught my friends to talk about my transsexual condition without treating it like a disease.

I remember there was one time when I could bring a family member with me to a session with the psychologist at the gender clinic. My sister came with me because she was my closest ally. I was twenty-two by then. When my sister and I sat there in front of my psychologist, all we did was explain to her how we wanted to change Chinese thinking about outsiders and outlaws. Looking back at our attempt, we thought it was impossible for me to receive acceptance from our Chinese family, and their acceptance was needed first before I could continue with any treatment. We were in pure fear of unpleasant reactions from our family and relatives. We have a huge extended family, and my sister and I just couldn't foresee the consequences of dealing with them.

Living among foreign people brings your own cultural identity to the surface. Where are you from? Do you like it here? Negotiating and adjusting started early on. I was constantly in a process of comparing, analyzing, and negotiating these apparently separate worlds that I lived in. To add a third one—the world of an outlaw—was simply too much. To unite the apparently conflicting worlds of my parents' and mine was already a process that tore me apart too often. It turned my body muscles to stone.

Reconnecting Body and Spirit

By the time I was writing my master's degree thesis, I suffered from all kinds of complaints. I was eating badly and suffering from panic attacks and hyperventilation. My therapist told me many times that I treated my body only as the bearer of my mind. As long as my body was still bearing features of the female gender, it was simply untouchable, even after the woman I loved told me how much she appreciated me for how I was (read: not operated on). The decision was my way of remaining pure to my trans self. I had an infinite trust that my intellectual mind would help me resolve my problems, but without any physical intimacy, my body collapsed from exhaustion and neglect.

A friend decided to send me to a hapto therapist, a person who practices therapy through the sense of touch. It was the right thing at the right time. Experiencing my hidden and problematic feelings through simply feeling the touch on my skin was a powerful and at the same time scary revelation. Every word that I said, I realized now, was connected with parts of my body. Intellectual solutions were useless. I learned in this process that I had been looking for answers to deal with my problems all my life, and those endless negotiations without a break had worn me out completely. It had put too much responsibility on my head, which had begun to feel heavier than my whole body. So my body bent forward, my whole bearing was forced in the wrong position, and it became too painful. What I always regarded as an act of purity, sacrificing my own needs in favor of saving my parents' honor, was, in the end, pure destruction to my true self. I had to learn again to let go of my tears and to walk straight. When that moment finally came, I could hear my crying coming from deep inside, like a caged animal that was finally released after sitting there for ages.

The physical breakdown brought back what was most important—the care of the body. It took me another year to restore my sense of intimacy by letting go of all those obstacles that I had put down for myself a long time ago. I realized that it wasn't my transsexuality that prevented me from starting a relationship. Chances and opportunities were there, but I used to let them go; it was the intense feeling of shame that was projected on me by my overly modest mother, limited as her view was, like many of her generation.

Is There a Chinese Way?

Although I pretended I didn't need my parents to help me in my own process of coping with transsexuality, emotionally I was very angry with them for their lack of support. Deep down I was unforgiving. It was love from my side that kept them away from the negativity around my transsexual condition, but why couldn't I receive love from them in return? I could easily accept the argument that free Westernized society is better in its tolerance for outsiders, while Chinese society should be blamed for being backward in this matter. But why was such an argument unacceptable to me? Because despite everything, there is love from all parties. Certain forms of love just served my condition better than others.

Within Chinese culture, the self-sufficiency of its network has been able to work in such effective ways that it does not need new influences, so revising old habits is never an issue. My parents' behavior was correct according to the rules of that social structure, despite the fact that the rules were and are no longer adequate for the younger generation. My parents did what was required: they devoted all their time to providing financial security for the kids, but showing intimacy and support wasn't particularly important in their job description as parents. Most of the Chinese parents that I know are too modest to show pride in their kids or encourage their efforts. I would like to see that kind of communication more, so that a visible space can be created for intimacy among family members. Love is there, but it needs to be communicated to be understood.

I have devoted quite some time to figuring out how to change this common fear of new thoughts and lifestyles, but that aim was too far out of reach for me alone. Now I'm excited to find increasing numbers of young Chinese scholars emerging all over the world who explore contemporary Chinese society and search for new critical frameworks. I find the development hopeful and encouraging. Besides, why not let myself be part of something new?

A New Condition

To accept my body, my being, is an unbelievably powerful experience. It cured me of my adolescent melancholia about lost chances. I began to enjoy losing bad habits, outdated concepts, and idle expectations. I decided not to take male hormones, for I hate the idea of a lifelong dependence on the distribution of chemicals from outside my body. Despite the fact that taking hormones is almost considered to be a must in the whole process of being trans, I'm happy with my principal decision. Not taking male hormones means I need to keep my reproductive organs that produce my hormones and also my monthly periods. However, these monthly painless "interruptions" are too short to cause me any real identity crisis. So apart from the mastectomy that restored my male torso, I have no wish to pursue further medical intervention of my body. The classic transsexual narrative, once my framework, starts to lose significance for my current situation. I used to believe that complete transition would cure me from all my insecurities; it may make a man out of me in appearance, but it certainly won't make a man out of me in essence. Since I pass easily as a man, an entire transition was not urgent to me. The current possibilities of medical intervention are far reaching, but they cannot provide any FTMs with the ultimate masculine body, especially that important organ for men. I don't mind waiting for the next great invention, but as far as I am concerned, I won't wait any longer to live my life in my version of manhood.

I find the discussions that I have with my dear female friends on gender, femininity and masculinity, and especially on the fear of staying in between the two genders, tremendously helpful. Being transgendered actually creates opportunities for new forms of manhood and masculinity. I find it interesting and exciting to explore the possibilities to engage in a form of new masculinity without the actual biological male body. This could be called transgender masculinity.

When I applied for a mastectomy operation at the gender clinic, it was difficult to get treatment from them because of their fear of creating "monsters" or "in-betweens." I was warned that I would face great opposition from some doctors, but my wish was granted after all, due to the strong influence of my psychologist, who backed my decision, and a few doctors who were sympathetic. The provision of care for transgendered people is still an open secret in the gender clinic. In some cases requests for surgery are granted only after records are falsified to meet with the classic transsexual narrative. This attitude still worries me.

I didn't dream of becoming a transgendered FTM because it's a trendy thing to do. Being a transgendered person still requires a lot of courage and especially a healthy sense of yourself. You need to be able to sustain the constant questioning of people around you. But now, since my sense of my body has become strong and healthy, I have learned to read the auras of people around me and to distinguish the positive from the negative. It taught me a lot of boundaries and about kindness at the same time. Here, I would love to say something about kindness.

I have read and seen many classic transsexual narratives, and most of them are goal- and appearance-oriented in their search for happiness. I seldom read or see an approach of the issue where the trans person is kind to, and not so hard on, themselves in their journey to self-acceptance. However sympathetic these narratives are, they also feel too restricting for me now. Society tells us that in-between genders or gender confusion is something frightening, so in return, I want to create friendly spaces for all of us, so that it's OK to feel confusion. Nowadays I'm using the same kindness that I needed to accept myself to explain to people about my transgendered condition. I liberated myself from harshness and strictness with kindness, so why can't I give the same to people that I encounter?

Now

In the early 1990s I gave several interviews on transsexual issues, in which I confirmed the distress a person has to go through as a transsexual. I don't think I could have imagined then my openness now. Moreover, I never imagined that the good boy and student, the conformist and the loyal son, would rebel and even become politically active for transgendered people by organizing transgender film festivals. Yet sharing the goodies with others is so rewarding! Once upon a time, love and relationships were foreign to me. Now, love is a gratifying and sweet thing. I can listen to and watch my love, who enjoys life in so many different aspects. The fact that she is Chinese as well is very special to me—we have both fought for ways to deal with our alternative lifestyles (queer and trans), but now it's an enjoyment to find each other on the path that we walk together. Funny, once I was taught to hold back, and now I cannot be happier than being in this position—holding hands with my love—to give people a good transgender story.

MELANIE: MY STORY

Melanie McMullan

FOR ALL BUT THE EARLIEST YEARS of my life, I have struggled with my gender and self-identity. I have followed a path that has much in common with other trans people, although mine has its differences from many others. My dilemma has always been: Who am I? Followed by: Who will accept me as I am?

I came into the world in 1960 and was born in Scotland. My childhood was a happy one and relatively unremarkable. I went to a private primary school, which had more girls than boys, and many girls were my friends. I had a good family and had friends at both home and school. My greatest testament to my childhood is the fact that I am still in contact with some of the friends of my childhood to this day.

Being brought up in Scotland, though, did show me that there was religious discrimination in that most men had to identify with either the Celtic or the Rangers football team. I did not want to identify with this religious identity. I also did not like football, and so even at a young age I had already set myself apart.

In my adolescence, my family moved to Devon. Even though I made friends here, the fact that I came from Scotland made me stick out from other people, and I was bullied. It was during this period, as I grew up and went through puberty, that I began to realize I was not like other boys at all. Puberty is a time of great adjustment for many people, but for me the advent of puberty came with my growing breasts just like a girl, coupled with mood changes. At the age of thirteen I was drinking water heavily and was investigated for diabetes. I did not understand myself at all, and I had begun dressing in my mother's or sister's clothes at the age of eleven, for reasons I have never understood, other than that it felt right and comfortable.

The fact that I was developing into a girl was alarming, as I thought I was a boy, even though I never felt comfortable doing boy things like playing or watching football. My mood swings and my diabetes led to my eventually being admitted to hospital for investigation. My diabetes was, in fact, caused by hormonal imbalances and by an increase in the production of human growth hormone, which substitutes for testosterone. It was suspected that the hormonal imbalance was due to mixed chromosomes, a condition known as Klinefelter's syndrome (XXY chromosomes). This meant very little to me, as I was too young to understand what it meant, and indeed I was never counseled or told what it might mean to me, either physically or psychologically. I was monitored in the diabetic clinic and was under the care of an endocrinologist until I was sixteen. My schoolwork was poor and unfocused, as I felt alone, even though I had a lot of friends at home in Devon.

My body continued to grow breasts, emphasizing to me just how different I was from other boys and how differently I looked at the world. I made lots of excuses as to why I could not join in games or physical education at school, as I was ashamed of my body and did not want to be seen undressing in front of other boys. Although I had been brought up as a boy, I had crossdressed since the age of eleven, and did not relate to the world through the eyes of a boy, but I never came to terms with what I was until later in life. I was held back in my schoolwork as I had to deal with my secret, but I threw myself into my schoolwork from the age of fifteen, and I left school with A-levels and went on to university.

A lot of the fears of my teenage years and early adulthood were to do with my crossdressing and relationships, which were very confusing. I still did not understand myself or accept myself, as I did not know what I was. I struggled with the fact that I liked girls and preferred their company, but only when I was crossdressed. I was really scared when I ventured out in public as a woman for the first time at the age of nineteen when the rest of my family were away on holiday. It was just a walk to the local shops, and although I did not go inside any of them, it was a frightening experience. There were no hassles, but I was nevertheless paranoid that people would see through me.

At university I had my own room and so was able to crossdress from time to time and to sneak out as well. I succeeded at university and went into a career in banking. Despite the front that I put out, I was plagued by self-doubt and struggled with many feelings inside that I could not understand. I felt very lonely inside, but I continued to crossdress in secret, and I ventured out in public on occasions when I could, having bought a wig and become better in applying makeup and choosing clothes from catalogues. As I grew in confidence and looks, I was alarmed when I got approaches and wolf-whistles from men when I went out in public. The fact that I was seemingly attractive as a female was very disturbing to me, as it brought on other feelings inside me that I could not explain. But what was I? Was I female or male? I did not know other than that I was physically and psychologically a mixture of both, but I thought I was alone, and until I had a girlfriend at nineteen, it was a secret that was never shared or revealed to anyone else.

Appearances Can Be Deceptive

I learned in my early adulthood that how a person looks or presents is often the basis of discrimination in human beings, whether a person is disabled or is black, white, or brown. In the case of women I began to realize that they were judged largely on their appearance and not on their intelligence or ability. I have come to appreciate that beauty is an asset or quality that females have, and have observed that it is those females who are more attractive that appear to have good jobs, good monetary reward, warmth from friends and family, and fulfilling sexual relationships. I believe this is also true of transsexuals, in that it is those who are pretty and attractive who are generally the ones that are successful in the female role.

Whether we like it or not, a transsexual woman or an intersexed person who identifies as a woman will be judged on her appearance, and those who are unable to pass as women are unlikely to be accepted as women in society, and face anger, hostility, rejection, and even violence. Society in 1983 did not give men permission to be more feminine or sensitive like they can be today. There was, and still is, great pressure on both men and women to conform to the norms of society. I had a very compartmentalized life that was not integrated, as I did not accept myself and was very fearful of exposure.

My own self-acceptance in coming to terms with myself in what I was or was supposed to be was a journey that lasted until I was twenty-six. It was my big secret that I did not share with many others, and although I had read about people like myself, I had never met any of them. I did, however, do a lot of soul searching in 1983, as I was crossdressing a lot in public without any problem and going shopping as Melanie. I found it natural to go into the female changing rooms, or to be measured for a bra. I could no longer ignore the fact that I had some fantasies and feelings that came on very strong whenever I was Melanie—it seemed that a lot of feelings, such as vulnerability, went with it. I just did not understand and continued to suppress a lot of my emotions and feelings and learned to contain and manage them. I split my gender roles apart to cope with life. For the first time I went to a TV/TS support group and began to meet others who had similar issues.

Many of us who are transgendered live in perpetual twilight. We inhabit a space between man and woman, boy and girl. I've come to think that the larger part of our drive to change genders is not as much because of who we wish to be as it is realizing who we aren't! Of course, the great difficulty is that we just want to belong somewhere. But there's a problem here. Part of what makes you "you" is the inner self. It gives you that feeling that tells you when something feels right to you. Unfortunately, I have never felt comfortable in being part of the male segment of society, but unlike some transsexuals, neither do I despise my male presentation or upbringing. If I had a perfect choice, I just would rather not be a part of it, but I have come to believe that the line between male and female is, in reality, very thin—that it is society that has created the bipolar gap, and despite biological differences, anyone with a neutral upbringing can be both genders.

I believe it is the upbringing and socialization process of gender in society that is the greatest determinant of gender, and not biology or hormones. The upbringing that a male-to-female transsexual will have is likely to be male, and the longer they remain that way psychologically, the more difficult it is to change over. I see too many transsexuals who still look at the female role through male eyes, and I believe that it is the area of interpersonal and intimate sexual relationships that marks the real difference between male and female, and not genitalia or hormones. Many of these differences between the sexes only became apparent to me after spending time in the female role to gain an understanding of female interpersonal relationships. I find the area of female and male interaction to be the most difficult of all, as interaction and communication from males is often made with sexual signals and innuendo.

I have come to realize that sexuality is also a powerful force on the identity of self. To me, this is probably the scariest area of all, in that there are two opposing forces. This is most apparent in my dreams, where the erotic or romantic nature could be with me being either female or male. Since I have not had surgery to my primary sex organs, I can only contemplate sexual relationships with a woman, which I am comfortable with, as I prefer both the intimacy and the company of other women. If I felt that the force of female sexuality in me were to become greater, then

I would certainly consider surgery to my primary sex organs. Sexuality is always heterosexual for me, as I cannot understand or contemplate same-sex relationships. I regard touch more stimulating than penetration, but unlike some transsexuals I am not uncomfortable with my duality, which is a gender duality and not a sexual one—I am not bisexual.

Although anyone with a neutral upbringing can be both genders, there are some formidable barriers in the form of secondary sex characteristics rather than the primary sex organs. My secondary sex characteristics are female, which I have had since puberty, with only some facial hair. I have no Adam's apple, no deep voice; I have soft skin, soft facial features, and normal female breasts. I believe that voice and speech are the two hardest things for any transgendered person to change. I have ventured out in public as female from the age of nineteen, and from my own experiences I have come to believe that the true determinants of our perceived gender are attitudes, our faces, and voices, which have nothing to do with the clothes we wear or the shape of our genitals. If one is purely male, then it is very difficult to overcome those secondary sex characteristics to be female, even part-time. I have a body and a mind that are mixed, and have since puberty been like a preoperative transsexual, but my situation is biologically imposed. I live part-time in both genders and I have come, after many years of self-analysis, to consider myself as both female and male, and I regard myself as in between, being able to identify as and be both genders, as some other intersexed persons also do.

An In-Between

Although I have sought help in dealing with my own gender issues and have been diagnosed as transsexual by a psychiatrist, I do regard myself as an in-between, and do not believe that I am a woman trapped in a man's body. My mind, body, or the shape of my genitalia do not determine who or what I am. Some people ask me whether transition is choice or destiny. I think it can be either. For me there is no destiny that I may transition entirely to the female role, for I believe that I can manage the choices I have.

In my case, there is no "big bang" transition, as I have always lived, since the age of nineteen, part-time in both genders, and have always sought to maintain a balance between my male and female emotions and values. These emotions and feelings must be expressed, as my balance of both the yin and the yang is fundamental to me. Without balance, these emotions and feelings can push and pull me from one pole to the other. No matter what gender I present, I am the same person with the same feelings, emotions, values, hobbies, and interests. I cannot be or become a different person, because my characteristics are all within me, whether they are female or male, although I can enhance or suppress them within limits.

Once I began to accept myself during the years from 1986 to 1988, I began to develop a social life in both roles, and I socialized as Mark and Melanie, but with different people. However, this period of my life was one of instability in that I confronted myself again about my gender conflict and identity, but I did not always manage to deal with it particularly well. I had a girlfriend who was very strong in terms of personality—which she had to be as a social worker. Unfortunately, she suffered from bad health, and though we subsequently got engaged, it came to an abrupt end in 1987, as she felt she could not cope with my being an in-between. The breakup caused me to reexamine myself, with all the inner struggles. My emphasis changed to management of my roles and persona and trying to use them both in the most effective way.

I also had to deal with tragedy in that I lost my father in 1987. In fact, I lost not just a father, but a friend who had helped me and supported me in my life. It was a big loss to me. The one really happy event during this time was that I met my Julie, my new girlfriend, the same year. This relationship blossomed, and we did a lot of things together, including holidays and travel. Things started to get better on the job front and also on the personal front in that we got married in 1990, and she became my wife.

As my life became a dual life, I socialized a great deal as Melanie, but I did discuss this with my partner, Julie, before we got engaged. Her attitude to most things was "live and let live," except with her partner. She was uncomfortable with me as Melanie and wished not to see that side of me, or as she called it, "my secret life."

I then got more involved with various activities and became a trustee of the support group for trans people, the Gender Trust, in 1992, and legal adviser to another group, the Beaumont Trust. At the start of 1994, my first book, which I cowrote with trans activist Stephen Whittle, was published. Titled *Transvestism, Transsexualism and the Law,* this book was a world first in the subject, and I continue to write many articles for the magazines *Gems News* and *Transliving.*

Life was very happy, and at long last the overall balance and stability that I had craved was finally slotting into place with all the hard work and soul searching of the previous decade. Tragically though, 1994 will probably go down as the darkest year of all. It started on a high with the birth of my daughter, and then my life fell off a cliff edge only a few months later with the death of my beloved wife, Julie. Life can be very cruel; just when you think that you are on a high, it can deal you a crushing, unexpected blow. Julie died from a brain tumor; she would never see our child grow up, and she was so brave in death. Julie passed all care of our child into my hands and made me promise to look after her and also to look after myself, and to find someone else, as I deserved to be happy. She told me that she loved me and that she could think of no one else who could have made her happier. Julie said she had had a good life and that I had made her very happy. I cried so much over Julie, for the loss of my soulmate, and after her death I felt so empty.

I was left with a baby daughter for whom I had sole responsibility. Although my life had crashed, I had a lot of support from my friends and family, who rallied to me. Annette, a friend of mine, was with me when Julie died. My mourning was episodic, and I knew that I must survive this crisis and that I must rebuild my life from the devastation that Julie's death brought on.

A Dual Nature

During my life journey toward self-acceptance I have had to come to terms with disclosing my duality to my family, partners, friends, bank manager, one employer, and the tax authorities, and cope with the fear of rejection or ridicule, which is something that almost all trans persons must face. Unlike many trans persons, I have disclosed my status and my dual life to my partners before being intimately involved. I cannot hide my body, since it is not a pure male body, from a potential partner. My coming out to my family and friends has been done over time and has given people time to acclimatize to me. My mother has always known about my crossdressing and has met me as Melanie, and I am fairly close to my sister. Being open and honest with my friends and family has helped me enormously in defining my sense of self and has led me to be able to integrate my transgender lifestyle into my whole life. My late wife's mother, her son, and her sister have also all been supportive and accepting.

The fact that I have natural feminine features, including a pretty face and a body structure and a lot of attitudes that are female has helped enormously in my family and friends' accepting me for what I am. However, I am certainly not a role model for others, as many transsexuals could not possibly live part-time in each role for too long. Some of them have a hard time trying to eradicate their male secondary sex characteristics, let alone acquiring female ones. I have only female secondary sex characteristics, and I attend medical examinations as a woman and have had a mammogram, as I face the same cancer risks as any other female.

I have always valued relationships since I was a child, and investing in people is very worthwhile because in life it is a good thing to build a support team from which you can gain emotional support in times of crisis. I very much value my friendships with others, and I count myself fortunate to have a best friend Annette, a genetic woman, who is warm, friendly, intelligent, and the most highly perceptive person I have ever met.

However, I think that all transsexuals or intersexed persons have choices about how to deal with their sex or gender issues, and like any other medical disability it should be actively managed. Transition is not the only solution, and for some transsexuals transition will not solve their problems. If there were a no-cost solution, then yes, I would like certainly to be a woman and have SRS surgery. On the physical side, I like most of the fashion opportunities available and the female body. On the emotional side, I like the greater emphasis on people's feelings and on personal relationships. Although I have thought about living full-time as female and having surgery, I have thought equally about the losses as well as the gains. Those losses would be emotional, as I do not feel that I could deny the male side of me. My life is a compromise and a mixture of male and female. My friends consider me womanly and attractive as Melanie, while as Mark I am unremarkable, but neither macho, laddish, nor effeminate in behavior. The confusion for others is that I am the same person, even though the visual appearance is markedly different.

My birth certificate states that I am male, but under Scottish law, unlike the position in England, I can change the forenames on my birth certificate to Melanie Sarah upon application to the Registrar General's office if I wished, but I cannot change the gender without petitioning the Court of Session in Scotland. I believe that some petitions have been successful in Scotland but that success is dependent upon the medical evidence that is presented and having SRS to the gender of choice. Whether I would succeed in a petition is uncertain, as the fact that I have married as a male and am fertile in fathering a child may count against me in a petition before the court.

This may become academic, as the British government recently lost a case in the European Court of Human Rights that will lead to the ability for any transsexual or intersexed person to amend their birth certificates. This reform is long overdue and will remove the legal discrimination against trans persons in the United Kingdom. However, changing a birth certificate will not necessarily lead to greater acceptance of individual trans people in society, as that depends on them as individuals. This is the reason why I am not hung up about my birth certificate, as changing it would not add anything to either my own self-acceptance or others accepting me.

Whether a person identifies as a male, female, or both, it is, unfortunately, society that will validate whether we will be accepted as male or female. In the case of any person presenting as a woman, society must see a woman, otherwise, despite any sex-change surgery or changing of birth certificate, that person is unlikely to be accepted as a woman. This may sound harsh, but society will not accept any male-to-female transsexual or intersexual who either looks or acts like a man in a skirt. Anyone who derives their identity from their genitals is in for a shock, as that is not what determines gender—people are not the sum of their genitalia. My friends have said to me that if I did look like a man in a skirt, I would have probably lost a lot of friends. I am thankful that I am not an embarrassment to others.

In my life I have also learned that the more successful you are perceived to be by others, the more accepting people seem to be, which even borders on respect and admiration at times. I describe myself as an optimizer, as opposed to a perfectionist, in that I seek to get the most out of something for the least use of resources, be they time or money. I have a very busy life and a very diverse life, not only in terms of gender but in everything I do. I have eight jobs, one of which is full-time, and I straddle two career streams. Although I published my first book as Melanie, I have also published many as Mark in various legal and financial texts and have even written for television. I am very fortunate that nature has given me a good brain that I use. I have learned to use the male and female within me to the best advantage. My male presentation has established itself, and I am perceived to be successful by others, despite being individualistic and not typically male. My female presentation has established itself as trying to help my sisters and brothers to succeed.

Now I have rebuilt my life with Rona, my new partner, who was told all about me before we became intimate. She is a very feisty and independent woman who does not generally like men and has had lesbian relationships in the past. My duality of life continues, and I do not conceive of a time when one day I will cease to be male and become female. I cannot comprehend this, as I would always be me. My life is, indeed, a compromise and a juggle, but I am a happy person on the whole, and hence my views and experiences are slightly different from others. We are all different.

For me, there are three great barriers to crossing the gender divide, particularly for male-to-female transsexuals: the first is accepting ourselves, the second is passing as females, and the third is in being female and being validated as such in terms of interpersonal relationships and, if possible, intimate sexual relationships. Each one of these barriers will exclude a certain number of trans persons to the point where it is very sad, and

I say this with a heavy heart, but too many male-to-female transsexuals remain transsexuals and never become women, even after surgery or hormones. As more people become educated about intersexuality and transgenderism, the situation will improve, but the road is long and slow. Intersexed and transgendered people have existed since time immemorial in all cultures around the world.

Finally, I have come to realize that it is truly an exceptional person who is bigendered—who is, in effect, a duality of both in body and in mind.

CONFESSIONS OF A SHE-MALE MERCHANT MARINE

Vera Sepulveda

I WAS A LATE BLOOMER. I envy all the people who were caught trying on their sister's underwear when they were nine years old. So many trans people know who they are at a very young age. Had I figured things out that early, I could have planned my transition much better. Instead, I took the long way around. I made it all the way through puberty, dating, high school, and the U.S. Navy without gaining the slightest clue as to my real identity. But then again, maybe it's all for the best. Would I have been able to handle it back then? Would my parents? I honestly don't know. I'm a survivor; that's one thing my life has taught me. I pay the bills, I make the rules, and when it suits me, I break them.

Looking back now, I can see that there were signposts. My fourth-grade teacher was concerned that I always played with a younger boy at recess. I remember Ricky saying, "Gary, if we're not married when we get older, let's shack up together." Ricky and I spent every recess playing together until my teacher split us up. I couldn't understand why at the time. Then there was Doug. My fifth-grade teacher knew I was a flirt, so she stuck me next to the kid nobody else liked. Doug was the fat kid, and he was black. Of course, we became the best of friends in no time at all, and were more inseparable than Ricky and I had ever been. The teacher didn't separate us, nor did she seem to worry about it, but she did send us to "screening council." For an hour every other Friday, we were encouraged to talk about our troubles and issues in a group setting. I had no clue what my issues were—I was only ten years old. I tried to oblige, and griped about my little tagalong brother (that seemed to be the popular theme), but honestly, I had no problems, not then. I had Doug.

I was in love. I didn't realize it then, but I can see it now. I had dreamed of and lusted after girls, since even before kindergarten. I used to get beatings for playing doctor with little Suzy next door, and still I kept going back. I was maybe five. But looking back, it's obvious to me now. I lusted after girls, and fell in love with boys. What a glorious beginning.

My mom unwittingly gave me an introduction to the great world of homosexual culture when she took me to my first Gay Freedom Day parade when I was thirteen. That's what it was called back then, in 1978. She had taken me on my first trip to San Francisco, and you can imagine our surprise when we emerged from the Powell Street BART Station to find ourselves smack in the middle of the festivities. It was beautiful. I remember a Peter Frampton look-alike standing on a float and tossing handfuls of gold coins into the crowd. I picked one up and read the inscription: "Bulldog Baths—111 Turk Street."

Maybe if I had been exposed to trans culture earlier, things would have been different. I remember when I first heard about the "sex change," but I didn't believe it was really possible. It wasn't until much later that I found out that sex changes were for real. I was discussing music with a friend and mentioned a favorite artist of mine, when he told me that "he" was now a "she." When I checked on my next trip to the record store, I found that he was right. The album cover was identical, but the first name had been changed. The rumors were true—it was possible. Even then, it rang a bell somewhere inside of me. Still, it would be another decade before I put it all together.

I became fascinated with masculinity. My first summer job was on a cattle ranch. I got three dollars an hour, and I chewed tobacco and fixed the barbed-wire fences. I drove a tractor, took care of the turkeys and hogs, and worked the cattle. It was a small ranch, but it was still an adventure. I came home from the fields tired, smelly, and covered with ticks. And though I bitched about the pay and the work, I loved every minute of it. The only problem was that I was so isolated. On a small ranch outside a small town, I was in a social vacuum. What fun is being a cowboy if only the cows know you? I briefly considered becoming a rodeo rider, but finally settled on a more practical solution in 1982, at age seventeen: join the Navy and see the world.

I have always been a sucker for romantic adventure. I loved the thrill of danger and wanted a job that gave me an excuse to be reckless. To this day, the image that most often comes to mind is the time we arrived in Okinawa after a typhoon. There were palm trees lying all over the beach and fish all over the decks, and as we readied the mooring lines, warm green waves crashed over the bow and soaked us. I held on and spat out salt water and was as happy as I could be. I was a sailor. And every now and then, the reality lived up to my fantasy. Maybe that's why I didn't last very long. When reality got in the way, my fantasies all fell apart.

I was in love in the Navy too. Rene was just a kid, like me, and we got along well. We worked together and goofed off together. We were the best of friends and we enjoyed each other's company. We even looked alike. When I show people a picture of my division, to see if they can point me out, the person they most often point to is Rene, standing right beside me. At the time I was far from being in touch with my feelings, and I never really considered the nature of our relationship. I never questioned it, I just enjoyed it. I had always had my "best friend" back home, so it seemed natural that I would have one on the ship too. I suspect Rene was more aware of our relationship than I was. When his enlistment was up, he tried to leave without saying goodbye. When I ran into him on the pier and wished him well, he was too upset to respond. All he could do was walk away without a word. Whether he loved me or hated me, I'll never know.

Figuring Things Out

I was kicked out of the Navy two years after I joined for "disciplinary" issues—I was a troublemaker and a rebel. I then went to community college, and it was here that I started wearing women's clothes. Nothing so you'd really notice, but I was shopping in the "misses" section. I stuck with pants and sweaters that were more androgynous than anything else, and never even considered wearing a dress. I just liked that there was so much more of a selection and that the jeans were so much softer. I still wore men's underwear, but let my appearance become gradually less masculine. When people asked why I shaved my legs, I never had a real answer for them. As I said, it took a while for me to figure it out. In a way, my transition had begun without my conscious knowledge, and I had to discover the clues on my own.

Clue number one: the first real eye-opener came when I found myself admiring a girl's purse. It had an Egyptian design printed on it that fascinated me, and I wanted so much to find out where she got it so that I could get one. And that's what got my attention. What would I do with it? I had no use for a purse, but I wanted one. That struck me as odd, and it actually caused me a little anguish. I would have been thrilled to have the purse, but the idea that I would have to leave it at home bothered me.

Clue number two: when a very attractive girl practically threw herself at me, I was repulsed. It was in a huge auditorium class, and she plopped right down in the seat next to mine. I can't remember what she said, but she was aggressively chatting me up. I gave her short and polite responses, but nothing more. The odd thing was that while I was creeped out by her advances, I felt a wash of discovery. For the first time in my life, I had overruled my dick. I found her attractive, but I couldn't handle her assertiveness, and so I was completely turned off. Here was a clue that maybe my fascination with women had nothing to do with sex.

Clue number three: Tom Cruise. I had seen the film *Top Gun* before, but this time the sight of Tom Cruise racing the jet on his motorcycle almost knocked me out. I imagined riding behind him with my arms clasped around his waist. I imagined touching his hair, tasting his breath, and feeling his stubble as he kissed me. It was the first time I consciously considered kissing a man, and while the idea was scary and new, I suspected that I liked it. I remember actually toying with the idea that I might be gay, and from that moment forward, whenever the subject arose in conversation, I would admit the possibility. "Who knows?" I would say. "Maybe some day I'll fall in love with a man. Maybe I'm gay, but I just haven't met the right man yet." I was getting closer to the truth.

Sex with women never really worked for me. I had a few experiences over the years, ranging from mediocre to disastrous. It was really hard for me to figure out the exact problem. Physically, everything worked fine, but there was something else that I couldn't quite figure out. Looking back it seems so obvious to me now, but at the time I was blind. What I mistook for sexual desire was the desire to have a woman's body. It was all about possession, which makes for bad relationships. I wanted to have a woman's body, rather than just have sex with one. This came to be one of the most important discoveries I would make in terms of defining my true self.

After college, I had several part-time jobs. Then, around 1992, when I was working on a Unocal oil tanker, I first started feeling the unmistakable pull of femininity. As a Navy veteran with shipboard experience, I was qualified to work in the merchant marine. I joined the Sailors' Union of the Pacific, and once again I was back at sea. Merchant service is nothing like the Navy. You work twelve-hour days, but there's no military crap to contend with. Since I was the new kid, all I could get was a job washing dishes. I didn't care; it was more money than I had ever seen before. I served meals, cleaned state rooms, swabbed the decks, and scrubbed the pots.

The most menial jobs allow the greatest freedom of thought. I spent hours each day with my hands in the suds while my thoughts roamed the universe. After a while it became almost meditative, and the more I worked, the more thoughts arose. I found myself thinking about who I was and what I wanted out of life. I let my mind become a blank slate—an arena where any idea could be entertained, and the ideas that started to form were real eye-openers. There in the galley of the SS *Sierra Madre,* I began to assemble the little clues that I had missed all my life. It would still take time to figure it all out, but I began to see in what direction I was going.

I became more and more fascinated with androgyny. I had been listening to the Eurythmics and David Bowie, and I found their gender blending irresistible. Annie Lennox's butch/sweet combination seemed close to the image I was trying for, while Bowie's unashamedly queer lyrics gave me much to think about. I was still wearing girls' jeans, and I wore them tight. I wore a woman's motorcycle jacket and cut my hair like Annie Lennox—shaved on the sides but long on top, with bangs in my eyes. For the first time it was beginning to show, and people began to notice.

The first time someone called me on it I was thrilled. He was just a cocky kid, whose dad had pulled some strings to get him into the union, and we worked side by side in the galley. He mouthed off to everyone, but found me an especially tempting target, and so he took to calling me a faggot. The funny thing was, I liked it. Part of the thrill was his shock and disgust with the fact that I never denied it. Had I ever complained, he would have been fired, but I didn't want that. He was my herald, my annunciator, and I would be lying if I said I didn't love the attention. In denouncing me as a faggot to the rest of the crew, who really couldn't have cared less, he handed me my queer membership card. I was thrilled. In my mind, David Bowie put a glittered arm around me and welcomed me to the club.

Imagine my situation. All my life I had been infatuated with masculine jobs. I loved the danger, the adventure, and the toughness. Why? I used to think it was overcompensation, to prove that I was really a man, or maybe that I was trying to hide from my true feelings. But now I know better. I call it the Schwarzenegger principle; next to Arnold, just about everyone else is a sissy. Among cowboys and sailors I appeared unmistakably feminine. Not just to myself—now I had evidence that others were picking up on it as well. Homosexuality is as common in the merchant marine as it is in the Navy, but since it's not prohibited by military regulation, it's more visible. And while the term *homosexual* was not quite accurate, it served me for the time being.

Having made a few trips with Unocal, I found myself with more money than I could believe. The long hours and hazardous conditions, combined with union wages, were enough to get me into an apartment on San Francisco's Nob Hill. I bought a motorcycle and toured the state in my leather jacket. In the spirit of sexual rebellion, I wore a barely legal half-shell helmet and red lipstick below my goggles. I wore women's equestrian boots and let my ponytail fly in the wind. I crossed California like that. From San Francisco to Los Angeles, through the Sierras and the Mojave Desert, I proclaimed my arrival from the back of my Honda racer. It was an exciting time that I will never forget.

Living in San Francisco really opened my eyes. Before the apartment, I had lived in a fleabag sailors' hotel in the Tenderloin district. I knew where the drugs were sold and where the whores could be found, mainly because I could see it all from my window. It was a big change from my suburban and small-town upbringing, and a real eye-opener. I discovered Polk Street, the original gay neighborhood before Eureka Valley became known as the Castro. It had an older, seedier feel to it, rather than the more polished commerciality of the Castro. More important, it was (and still is) the center of the transgender neighborhood. For the first time in my life, I saw transvestites, transsexuals, drag queens, and she-male prostitutes.

Time for Change

Things really began to change when I went to work for Chevron, where I stayed until 1997. Never before had I been treated so well by an employer. Big corporations are terrified of lawsuits, and that worked in my favor. They were emphatic in guarding my right to express myself without harassment from any other crew members. The job was basically the same as at Unocal, though now I had a more regular rotation. I always worked on the same two ships, and I got to know the officers and engineers quite well. The captains all liked me because of my hard work and cheerful attitude, and this won me the approval of the commodore. Through hard work, I managed to carve out a position of respect and freedom.

The captains never minded that I wore long hair and earrings. Once, when a customs agent came aboard in the middle of the night and I presented my passport with my hair in curlers, there were a few muffled giggles from the crew, but little else. When company officials came aboard, they were always friendly, and the human resources people always made sure to ask me how I was getting along with the crew. As I said, they were terrified of a lawsuit, but if terror creates acceptance, who am I to question it? For the most part, the crew left me alone. When I walked into the room, conversations always hushed, but I got used to that. I firmly believed in their right to talk about me behind my back, and appreciated their restraint when I was around.

One day it all broke the surface. A good friend of mine said, "You know, you've got them all buffaloed; they don't know what to think about you." I loved it. I had known they were talking about me, but now I had an inside informant. He filled me in on the discussions and opinions, so I filled him in on my side of the story. I told him I was a transvestite. "Well, duh!" was his only reply, and we laughed about it.

I came out on my thirtieth birthday. Not that I had been closeted in any sense of the term, but I had just started consciously dealing with my gender issues. As soon as the opportunity presented itself, I proclaimed myself to the world. Mom had noticed my lack of a social life. Believe me, so had I. She asked why I never talked about my friends. It was a tricky question to answer, but it really boiled down to the fact that I didn't have any. I had acquaintances and coworkers, but no real friends. And why was that? Simple—I was a transvestite and I hadn't yet learned how to relate to people in my new situation.

I liked the word *transvestite*. It had great shock value and it suited me at the time. When friends later suggested the more modern term *cross-dresser* I rejected it. It sounded to me like an angry piece of furniture. But while I embraced the term transvestite, I knew it wasn't the whole story. I wasn't quite ready to make a grab for *transsexual,* but I felt the pull in that direction. I still enjoyed my androgynous aspects, and wasn't quite ready to abandon masculinity all together. I suspected that my true identity lay somewhere in the gray area between the sexes.

Mom wasn't freaked out; in fact she was quite supportive. We had never really been close before, but then I had never really been close to anyone. How could I have been? I wasn't even close to myself. But when I explained my feelings to her, she listened very patiently and attentively. She let me know that she loved me, no matter what. I have been very lucky in that respect. I know so many trans people whose families shun or reject them. Some are tolerated by their family, but not welcomed at family gatherings. Some are a family secret, kept hidden from the children. Today my mother and brother are my biggest supporters. If we were distant in the past, we have more than made up for it in recent years. As I grew to know myself, I grew closer to them both.

She-Male

Somewhere between male and female was where I knew I belonged. Believe me, there's a whole spectrum of genders between the two extremes, and living in the Tenderloin exposed me to many of them. More and more I came to realize who I was: a she-male. By this time I had learned to distinguish sexual desire from sexual identity, and I recognized both in my fascination with she-males. They seemed to embody the specific quality that had guided me from the beginning: rebellion. That's how I see the transgender experience. We're challenging the most fundamental assumption of the animal kingdom, and I find that unbelievably sexy.

Most people, no matter how confused they may be about anything else, can always, as a last resort, look in their pants and know that they are either a man or a woman. They have a tangible concept that they can cling to when all else fails. But trans people don't have that luxury. Instead, we have to find our own definitions. There lies the problem. By questioning the validity of an absolute duality of gender, we shake the foundations upon which society is based. The concept of male and female goes deeper than most people realize. It's the most common denominator of the human race. By renouncing that absolute definition, we cast doubt on its validity. And that can really scare people.

It's so ironic that people fear us. Trans people are generally the most harmless people around, regardless of what you see in the movies. But fear of trans people has nothing to do with that. I occasionally encounter people who are fascinated by me, yet horrified to look at me. On the bus or train I will catch people sneaking glances at me, and when I smile at them, they flush red and look away. I have seen people so agitated by my presence that they can't keep from looking at me, yet they can't meet my eyes. I'm not talking about the ones who are sexually attracted to me, as they're a different group altogether. These people are afraid, but I really don't think it's me that they're afraid of. I smile at everyone; I'm harmless. I think they're really afraid of themselves. They feel that certainty of male or female being questioned, and it scares them.

Part of being a she-male is being a social outcast. You can say it any way you want, but that's what it amounts to in the end. I know that I am severely limited in the type of employment I can find (I'm currently working in a hardware store), as well as in the types of relationships I can form. So many of us become prostitutes for these very reasons. There we can find both social acceptance and steady work. It is as hard for me to form lasting relationships as it would be easy for me to find sexual partners. The sexual fascination with she-males astounds me. The fact that this specific fetish has such widespread appeal is readily apparent when you look at the sheer bulk of she-male porn on the Internet. I have never yet met another person who identifies as a she-male. To most, it's a dirty word beyond redemption, used only to market us in the world of pornography, and that's part of the reason why I have adopted it. Mostly I like it because it accurately describes me. I just don't feel like a "nonoperative transsexual," and I can't think of myself in that light.

I live my life by only two rules. One: never lie to yourself. I can lie to anyone else I want to, for whatever reason I see fit, but I refuse to lie to myself. This takes us right to number two: deal with your shit. I never go wallowing in my psyche, trolling the depths, searching my soul, or whatever you want to call it. I just don't care for that kind of introspection. But when feelings or issues come up, I deal with them—immediately. I never try to hide them or pretend that I don't feel them. When an issue is ripe to be dealt with, it will make itself known. Then it's up to me to work it out. This policy has never failed me. I don't pretend that it's easy, but it works. I have come a long way by following these rules, and I believe I know myself on a level that few people enjoy.

Effects of Hormones

I have never voluntarily seen a psychologist or a psychiatrist. It's just not for me. Before I was kicked out of the Navy, I was forced to see a shrink. He was a lieutenant commander and an asshole, and I told him to go fuck himself. I was forced to sit through group therapy and I hated it. To this day, any kind of group discussion gives me the willies. I had to see a social worker to get started on my hormones, but all he wanted was for me to demonstrate that I was capable of making a decision and that I was aware of the consequences of that decision. It was more than I had dared to hope for.

I had feared the Harry Benjamin International Gender Dysphoria standards of care for transgender people for some time. These standards are open to various interpretations, ultimately depending on the judgment of the therapist. I had no illusions of being able to snow a shrink into granting me permission to start hormone therapy. I also knew that no progress could ever come from such a relationship. How could I ever be honest with someone who holds the keys to my Holy Grail? My only concern would be getting that permission, and I wasn't about to risk having it denied to me. Just imagine my relief when I discovered that not all doctors follow the Benjamin standards.

My world split wide open when I started taking hormones four years ago. At first it was a quiet relief, as though I were lightly sedated with a hint of happy thrown in, but after a couple of weeks it hit me big time. I was working in a little record shop on Polk Street, in the heart of San Francisco's trannie community. I'll never forget the time a man walked in and I realized that I was seriously hot for him. There it was again—I was feeling sexual attraction to a man, and it knocked me for a loop. Not that I was freaked out—far from it. I was awash with new and exciting feelings and I enjoyed every minute of it. Those early months were great times. I was riding the crest of the estrogen wave and experiencing these feelings for the first time.

Then the physical changes started. My nipples puffed up first, and then my breasts started to swell. It seemed to happen overnight, though in reality it took months. The changes were so gradual that they were hard to notice, but one morning I looked down to see unmistakable breasts. Hormones affect everyone differently. Some people get great results, while others don't. Some people get boobs, some don't. Some get fat, some don't. I'm one of the lucky ones who got pretty much exactly what I wanted. And while I would still love to have more of the same, I'm quite happy with what I have now.

Of course, there is a trade-off. As my breasts grew bigger, my penis got smaller. And along with my newfound sexuality came a decrease in sex drive. That ever-present need to bust a nut is long gone, and I don't miss it in the least. I traded it for the ability to see beyond mere sexual desire to the more beautiful aspects of sexual attraction: sharing, closeness, and intimacy. I can still have an orgasm but it isn't really important anymore. I am blissfully free of that need.

Oddly enough, I don't consider myself a woman. I think I'm as far from being a woman as I am from being a man. I identify as female, and want to be accepted as such, but I don't equate that with being a woman. To me, that's a different thing entirely. I've never fully understood women, and even with the benefit of hormones that give me similar emotional conditions to genetic women, I can't equate myself with them or say that I understand what it means to be a woman. Sure, I use the same bathroom, but there the similarities end.

I don't try to hide my previous identity. I'm very proud of the man I used to be, and I know that he will always be a part of me. Oddly enough, I think of him as a different person. When I look at pictures from my previous life (that's how I like to say it), I feel a fascination and a love for him. He was a great guy, even if he was misunderstood, and he stepped aside to let me enter the picture. For that I am eternally grateful.

I wish I could understand why society is so concerned with what's in my pants, as though that were the only distinguishing mark between men and women. If I were to have sex reassignment surgery, I could have all my records changed to reflect my female gender. As it stands, my driver's license is the only document that lists me as female. Will there someday be other options? Maybe an M/F designation, or MTF? I think that day will come, but not in my lifetime. As far as we have come, we still have a very long way to go.

In the seven years since I began my transition I have learned a lot about myself, but I'm still a long way from knowing everything. But I don't worry about it, I just live it. The bottom line is that I'm happy. I walk down the street with my head up and a smile on my face. In spite of all the difficulties involved with living as a she-male, I can finally say that I know who I am, and that is worth more to me than anything else. I'm finally doing something right. Of this I have no doubt.

DREAM ON, AND DON'T WAKE UP TO THE NIGHTMARE OF REALITY

Natalie Murphy

LIFE . . . I'VE OFTEN WONDERED what my life is all about, and what I am doing here. It appears we all struggle to get through it, take the knocks, accept the blame for all the problems that our parents cause, and then on top of all that, we die.

It all started for me in 1952, a year that saw the coronation of Queen Elizabeth II in the country I was born and later brought up in: England, that green and pleasant land somewhere near Europe. The month of February can often be one of the coldest in England; it is midwinter with an extra bite that gives way to spring in March—it's almost as if winter wants to have that last big gasp of power. February was the month I was born, it was the month my father hated the most; it was the month of doom.

My dad didn't want me. I was an accident that would haunt him forever, and I would hang round his neck like a millstone, like a debt never paid off—even though you cut back on your spending to pay the extra, the interest mounts up until you just pay for the service charge. I was the devil child sent from hell to annoy him, not like my older brother who would become my dad mark two, in many ways. My sister, the oldest of the three children from this postwar baby-boomer family, turned out much like my dad too. She was handed the same attitudes and behavior patterns, and my siblings both had the dimple in the chin that I missed out on.

My dad didn't like children. He liked beer, although he always made sure we were all well fed and clothed, something that he didn't have in his early life. He would tell us stories of how he would go out looking for food and sometimes be without the basics of life—barefoot and almost urchin-like through the dark days of the 1930s. He worked hard to become successful in his chosen career—a bricklayer—once the war was over to provide for his family that had come along, even though he didn't really want us. He was always a practical man, proud of what he had and what he achieved, even if he did not have the ability to read and write. He was dyslexic, but it never stopped him being able to read a construction plan and then build a complete office block or new housing estate.

My mum came from a family where there was a lot of love and which was wealthier than my dad's, and his jealousy would lead to bitter rows driven by alcohol. She suffered so much in an abusive relationship, unable to control the rage of her husband, who would dish out verbal and physical beatings to all of us. Over the years, mum's family would try to convince her that leaving this miserable relationship would be the best thing to do if she wanted any true happiness for her and her children, but she would not leave my dad, even though she threatened to several times.

My life was a mess right from the start, really; Dad wanted to name his sons after him; my brother had taken my dad's first name, Reg, and I was to have his second name, John. My mum didn't want this, instead wanting to call me Shaun. That was the first disagreement, and it caused a lot of resentment from my dad as they argued about it fiercely, each with their own selfish reasons and motivations. My mum won the argument in the end, as a few days after I was born she was rushed into hospital with septicemia. The afterbirth had been left behind and had festered, and as she lay in dreadful pain, expecting her life to slowly ebb away, her dying wish was granted: I would be named Shaun. After weeks of antibiotic therapy and dedicated care, my mum recovered and returned home to look after her new baby, whom she thought of as her special son, and I was constantly reminded of the events throughout my life.

Until I was five, my grandmother, who lived literally across the street, cared for me while my mum was out earning the daily bread and my dad was earning his daily beer. I never saw much of my dad, as he was out of the house by the time I awoke and when he got home I would be in bed. Weekends would be the only time I would have any contact, as he was never a caring sharing type of man, except of course with the beer he cared for and the punches he would share with us. I had plenty of male role models, however, as mum's brothers were very influential throughout my early life in many ways.

My experiences of early school life were dreadful, as I felt so confused about how to react to other children. Other boys were rough and tough, and I would play with them only because I was expected to conform; boys played with boys, girls played with girls, and if anyone strayed into the other camp, they were thought of as a bit odd. I didn't like boys, and after a while they didn't like me very much, as most of the time I would choose my own company and found that girls were much easier to play with. I was on their level; they didn't try to beat me or shout abuse, they enjoyed the way I joined in and played the same way they did. Mum, of course, thought that the fact that her son was so popular with girls was a good sign for the future. She considered that it was because girls were attracted to me, and often said that I would have no trouble finding a romantic partner when I got older. She would come home and find my girlfriends and I playing happily, and so she was satisfied that life was great and everything was working out just fine for me.

The Great Sex Divide

But as time went on, my girlfriends drifted off as puberty approached, and they were attracted to boys for other reasons; it was almost as if I was one of them and should join the migration. I began to understand that something about my personality was not the same as other boys. I felt isolated as my peers pushed me away from both sides of the sex divide. It was at this time that something was beginning to make sense in my mind about boys and girls, why they were different from each other, and why I was different from all of them. Mum would encourage me in the kitchen to help her with the cooking as I showed so much interest and was always willing to be her gopher. She referred to me as her "right-hand boy," indicating how much I helped her and how well we worked together; of course, all I had done was to replace my erstwhile girlfriends with mum— I was on her level. She always wondered why my sister was not as domesticated as I was; it was probably because she never got a chance to, as I was always the one with my hands in the sink.

Puberty is a terrible time to experience for any child, as their body starts to change and strange feelings start to invade their childish minds. My early pubescent experiences and feelings were stranger still as I became even more confused as the changes took place within me. I started to desire the clothes that my mum and sister had, although I didn't talk about these feelings with anyone. I would sneak off and crossdress, usually at bath time when I could lock the door and indulge in my fantasies of being a girl. I could look at myself in the mirror and see the girl I really felt inside, and not the boy that I appeared to be. I wanted so much to tell my mum how I felt, tell her that something was very wrong, and how unhappy I was with being thought of as a boy.

School was no better, as I was being picked on and bullied; boys didn't like me, and girls found me strange and aloof. Added to this was the dreadful home life I was suffering because of my dad's alcohol abuse that was getting worse and causing us all problems. He would come home drunk if it was a wet day, as building work stopped if it rained; the workers would end up in the pub with nothing better to do than drink themselves stupid. He would be suspicious of everything and everyone, believing that we were all out to get him. He was unable to reason with, and it usually ended up with someone getting the feel of his fists as they slammed into your head. His specialty was a hard slap on the back or side of the head if he thought you were lying about something, or nothing— or anything he deemed to be "not quite right." At night I would lie in my bed and listen to the yelling and shouting of two people who appeared not to worry about the children they so carelessly brought into the world. Love was something I knew nothing about, and I can't remember my dad ever saying that he loved me, or anything else.

My brother was no help, as he was trying to deal with his own problems; he was into stealing and other criminal activities. By the time I was fourteen, Reg was in a government facility for children that were out of control, known as an "approved school," equivalent to a modern young offenders institute of today. My sister, who was four years older, had moved out to live with my grandmother across the street, so I was left alone in the house from hell with a mother who was only interested in surviving the next battering and a father who didn't care about what pain and suffering he caused to his family. My mum expected me to help her when the beatings occurred, even if it was in the small hours; I would lie on my bed fully dressed, ready to rush down and somehow stop my dad using his fists against her. More than once I got the shit end of the stick for interfering, attempting to help and getting abused for my efforts.

My problems were getting worse as puberty moved into a full-blown assault on my body; the flood of testosterone through my system created even more confusion for me as everything changed from the boyish looks to the resemblance of my mum and dad together. I found my muscles developed quicker, especially those in the legs, as I did a lot of roller-skating. I loved those skates, and I would go for miles just skating around, up the hill, down the dale. I suppose it was a way of getting out of the house and forgetting all the other problems that were threatening to engulf me. Other kids had skates, but no one could get anywhere near the speed or the skill I had, even if they tried to catch me on their bicycles.

At fifteen I was praying to God every night, hoping that I would wake up in the morning the way I felt nature had intended me to be: a girl. It never worked, but it never stopped me from believing that God could change everything that was bad in my life, including the death of my dad; oh yes, I prayed for that too, so desperate to be rid of him and his brutality. I crossdressed as much as I could to satisfy the need in me to be real, but it was a dangerous risk, as my dad would have completely flipped, had he found out what I was doing and why I was doing it.

I left school thankfully at last in 1967, pleased that I would be able live my life away from the school bullies. I wouldn't have to face the daily round of ridicule and isolation I had felt, but what was in the future was far worse than that. The family, which now consisted of me, Mum, Dad, and my brother, moved to a village in the New Forest, which meant I would have to find work locally, and not in the city I grew up in. If I wanted the bright lights, I would have about twelve miles to travel, so at first it put me off. I soon found the pull of the city was too much to resist and started to go ice skating. I needed to keep contact with city life, and soon I began to realize just how good I was at skating. The years I roller-skated had given me a good head start and the balance I needed. I joined the Southampton Ice Speed Skating Club and enjoyed every thrill and spill I experienced; this was one of the better times of my life.

At the age of eighteen, although I had a great social life, my home life was miserable, and I would do anything so I could get out of being there. I had experienced a couple of romantic relationships with "girlfriends," but each time I was dropped like a stone because I didn't have any interest in sexual matters whatsoever; I can't even remember it crossing my mind, and they all found this so weird—not that any of them made a move on me at all. My sister made a suggestion to me that would change my life forever in some ways. She was concerned that I was so unhappy and wondered if I should move away from home. I explained that I was not earning enough to support anything like that, and then she came up with the idea of joining the armed forces! Well, at first I didn't know what to think, as being a soldier was not one of the careers I had ever thought about. My mum thought it was a good idea, as from her point of view, having a son in the army would, as she put it, "make her so proud." I decided, after talking to my sister again, that it was not the ideal situation, but it would solve a few problems; little did I know that it would cause far more problems and lead to my attempted suicide.

Join the Army and Become a Man

I signed up in the summer of 1970 with the Royal Engineers. This choice was because my dad had been a Royal Engineer, and so had my uncle and his dad before him, so it was a bit of a family tradition. The first few weeks were heavy slog, as it was the worst thing I could have done, and I knew then that I had made a grave mistake. I wondered how my parents would feel if I gave up—all of the people who backed my decision in the first place, including a major general my parents worked for. I decided that I had to carry on for them, and so I stayed, although I hated it so much. I was bullied by just about everyone from the top rank down, yet somehow I managed to get through eighteen grueling weeks of basic training, including being licensed to drive a truck. It was the only thing I took away from the army experience that proved to be of any use.

I was sent to West Germany in January 1971 to join a field support unit, and my troubles went with me, more or less. I still felt so wrong in the guise of a man, and it was soon noted that I didn't exactly fit that description. I still wanted to dress in female clothes, although it was impossible to even think about how it could be achieved. After some time, though, I did find a way, and that was to become a baby-sitter in the evenings for the soldiers who lived away from the main barracks. I would "borrow" their wives' clothes to dress in, plus I made an exceptional childminder, as it was something that came to me naturally. No one ever knew of my desire to be female, and I never got caught with the clothes on. What changed my outlook about doing this was the story of another soldier who had been caught, and this frightened me so much, I decided that I must do something about my problem.

After some consultation with the medical officer, I was offered help to stop these feelings of being a woman occurring. I was convinced that there was some kind of treatment that could "normalize" me; after all, I was a deviant, abnormal, loony toon. The psychiatrist I saw told me that it was something he could help with, and so I was sent to a psychiatric hospital where they treated all kinds of disorders, including homosexuality. Oh yes, they could cure anything—that was the British Army; as the adverts used to say: "Join the army and become a man." It was the easy way out for me, as to tell my parents that I had been discharged because I insisted on being a woman would be just too much for them, and although that is what I really wanted to do, I felt I could not put them through the trauma that it would surely bring.

The army's way of treating sexual deviants was probably in contravention of human rights, but we didn't have such legislation to fall back on at that time, should we find the treatment unacceptable. They used brainwashing techniques to cleanse the mind of all abnormal behavior, but I didn't know at the time that was how it was done. In a few weeks I started to feel different: the treatment was working, but I didn't realize what the doctors had done and what the consequences of their actions would lead to. I was sent back to rejoin my army unit and given a clean bill of health, but within weeks I was back in the hospital after attempting to kill myself when the treatment failed to work as they had hoped.

I left the army in August 1973; in the intervening time I had found a woman who said she loved me, and at last I had a decent reason to leave. The romance was swift, and within a few months of leaving the army, we were married, and that proved to be life-changing mistake number two.

By 1978 the marriage was doomed to failure, although as usual I tried so hard to get it right, to stop any hurt and be what I was told I should be. It was a stormy relationship that produced two children, and I was dreadfully unhappy with the whole situation; I had told my partner about the problem of my dreams of being a woman, but I had also told her that I had received treatment and it was gone for good. In 1978, after I had seen a gender psychiatrist who had confirmed my transsexualism, I left the marriage and went to the city of Leeds in West Yorkshire to live my life as the woman I felt myself to be. After my divorce, I felt so ashamed of the marriage farce, the fact I had helped bring two children into the world, who now no longer had a father, as the divorce conditions included an almost outright ban on any contact. I was unemployed, as in the dark days of the 1970s, transsexualism was not exactly something that even family doctors had any knowledge of, so potential employers weren't likely to understand at all. I missed my children badly, so badly that I wanted to be with them, just like any other parent, and the only way was to stop living the life I wanted to live, give it up and return to Southampton as a man; at least it would please my children, my parents, and all of the people who thought I had made the wrong choice in the first place. Some choice, huh?

By the end of 1978, I was back with my ex-wife and my children. The decision to return and try again to be a man was not an easy one. In one way it was what I wanted to do for them, in another it was an escape from the discrimination and prejudice that I had suffered, simply for being different. The relationship, now a live-in common-law one, struggled from one disaster to another with the transgendered feelings never going away. There were several suicide attempts to resolve what I saw as a hopeless situation. I wanted so much to be real, but I had to suppress that overwhelming need to be out and free, for the sake of others. Another child came along in 1982, but it didn't change the way I felt until eventually I left for good in 1986. I was broken and defeated, and full of bitterness for the way my life was turning out. How much more could I take before something good happened? What the hell was next around the corner, and how would I ever find peace of mind?

In the following year, life became a little easier. I had full access to my children, who were now growing up, and I did not have to hide quite so much behind the wall of pain and depression that had been my life up to then. I decided that I would have to live as best I could with the feelings I had, and I had found ways of juggling them around and keeping myself sane. In reality, I was in denial, and it would soon catch up with me and threaten to destroy everything I had always dreamed of. Transsexualism is the kind of condition that feels like it has a life of its own, as the feelings are uncontrollable, even when you think you can control them. I know at the time I was not looking for any romantic encounters, as that was the past, but once again I found out that life has a way of dealing its own set of cards from the bottom of the pack.

Over the years the one thing that remained constant was my love of ice skating. It had never abated, and I had somewhere to go to enjoy myself, perhaps make some friends, have a great time keeping fit, and share the enjoyment of watching my favorite sport, ice hockey. The group of people I had gotten to know were all hockey nuts, and our friendship was solid and based on mutual respect. In a funny kind of way I had become their leader, the person they all looked up to. None of them knew what secrets I hid and the pain of my reality; they just thought I was a good guy. We would all travel together to away matches of our local hockey team, the Southampton Vikings, mostly in the back of a large white van owned by one of the group. Sometimes we would choose a little bit of luxury and go on the bus provided for the traveling team and supporters. It is on one of these trips that I met a woman who would suck me into a torrid love affair and marriage that has lasted to this day.

True Love

Fate is something I have always believed in, and it was fate that played its wriggling game when Karen appeared. She was waiting to board the bus when she caught my eye. I asked her name because she was a stranger that no one had ever seen at a road match. Something inside me reached out to her, something knowing and wanting; she was just . . . there. It was her first trip away, and by the end of that trip, she would be a part of my life I could never let go of, and never have.

Our love for the game and for each other drove us on, and within a year of meeting we had become engaged and soon to be married. In 1988 I said those words once again that I had uttered in 1974: "I do." This time, it was not the impending disaster I felt, but a coupling made that I felt would last forever. I was happier than I had ever been, and even though I knew that my gender dysphoria was waiting to emerge from its hiding place, I couldn't stop the growing love for Karen. Before we agreed to wed, I told her of the dysphoria that I had fought all of my life. I told her it was her choice if she wanted to walk away, but she stayed; we tried hard not to let the prospect of transsexualism ruin our lives, and that is how it was for the first few years.

After a while it did make its comeback, but Karen helped me through the bad times it gave me as I struggled with the identity, the real me that wanted to and would have its way. It was a private hell that only she and I knew about, and all our friends still had no idea that our secret was so extreme. We planned our first child, and Andrew was born in 1990 to a proud and happy set of parents. In the years that followed, we spoke often about what may happen about my feelings of being in the wrong body, but it didn't stop us, it just reminded us that life can play some cruel tricks. Our second child, Aaron, was conceived in the knowledge that my growing feelings of femininity were about to engulf us both, and by 1994, the year of Aaron's birth, I would be living full-time as a woman.

Telling children about yourself is something I still find difficult, even though I have now done it four times. My older children from my first marriage, under the guidance of their mother, rejected me, and I never see them. My two children from this marriage, told at early ages, have accepted the change completely and comprehensively. They are fiercely defensive about their "other parent" and tell others if they feel it is necessary. Andrew was told when he was four. He never batted an eyelid, and after I gave him the choice of calling me Daddy or Natalie, he immediately said the latter. I don't know if every child would be the same, but we have found such understanding and love from both our kids.

In 1999 I had my dream come true when I was wheeled off on the gurney to the waiting surgeon at Charing Cross Hospital in London, who performed the gender reassignment surgery to change my body on the outside into the woman I knew I was inside. That year was also the year we told Aaron of my past and who I was. It came after we realized Aaron was making up stories of who his dad was. He was four when we sat him down and told him that I was his dad, and that I had needed to change into a woman. I told him that I had always been a woman inside, and that is why I had to do what I did. At first he just sat and thought about it, and after a few minutes he said, "You used to be my daddy." I confirmed this and he then said, "I love you Natalie. It doesn't matter, I still love you." I burst into tears, Karen followed, then Andrew and Aaron, and we all just hugged each other in the knowledge that we were a family with an extraordinary life.

In our life together, we have faced many tough times, and the children have shared them and overcome the prejudice and bigotry that are always there. Other parents at the local school have discriminated against Karen, and friends and family have turned their backs on all of us. The children have fared a little better because they have not been afraid of telling those who poke fun at them the facts of what has happened. It appears to us that telling children at an early age causes no harm to them, no abreaction, and less rejection of people who are different.

Andrew, who is now twelve, has a deep and knowledgeable understanding of transgender issues. It has also led to his having a greater understanding about life in general than his peers. He is not afraid to voice his opinions about these issues, even though he suffers from his own private hell that we believe is Asperger syndrome, a developmental disorder that falls within the spectrum of autism. He is bright, with an eager interest in computers and science. As with all people with this condition, he finds it hard to communicate effectively, which brings a whole set of social problems. However, he is in the local youth brass band and is doing well in school academically.

Aaron is nearly eight and is a brilliant artist and a steadying influence on his older brother. His take on transgender issues is one of total acceptance. He is developing into an intelligent and balanced person who is caring and loves to play the joker. He is well respected and liked by his peers, who look up to him. His artwork is fascinating for a child so young and he leans toward cartoon drawing.

Karen works at the city council as a librarian and is also a spiritual healer. She is a wonderful person to whom I owe so much for standing by me for so long. She is the person I would die for and whom I love so deeply.

And me? Well, nearly four years ago I started working for the local authority at a large reception area. I am a happy, well-balanced individual who loves people. I have a few special friends who have shown themselves worthy of my unconditional support. I reject discrimination of any kind and fight hard against all bigotry and prejudice.

JACK'S STORY

Jack Powell

MY NAME IS JACK, and most people reading this story will think of me as sex and gender diverse. But I don't believe I am. To me, this is normal, this is the way I think, this is who I am. I have always questioned gender; I can't imagine what it would be like to not question gender, to have a fixed, stable gender identity—to know, beyond any doubt, that you are female or male. To know what a man is, to know what a woman is. Anyway, I am jumping ahead.

I should start at the beginning. I was born female. The doctor said, "It's a girl," and my parents said, "We will name her Jean-Marie." Family and friends came to see the new baby girl, I was taken home, and my life began. I had a relatively normal childhood, growing up in the 1970s with Mum, Dad, two sisters, and three brothers in Sydney, Australia.

When did I know I was different? Probably not until I was twelve or thirteen years old. I think that most teenagers feel that they are different— very few actually fit in and are secure in their identity. It is a time of discovering yourself as a young person, pushing boundaries and challenging ideas in order to develop your own sense of self. It wasn't the feeling of difference that was the problem, it was the not knowing what the difference was. I had never heard of the word *transgender,* and at that time I didn't really understand the concepts of gender, sex, and sexuality.

When I started high school, I hung out with a bunch of guys and girls. We played football during our lunch break, we smoked, and we all sat around together. Within the first year of high school, the guys and girls started to pair off. They would hold hands and kiss; I was never interested, as I didn't find any of these people sexually attractive. I was a tomboy.

I was labeled a troublemaker at school. I was opinionated, loud, and mischievous. I questioned things and this was seen as disruptive. When I was fourteen, some new teachers came to the school, and they were younger than some of the previous ones. They came with an approach of respect rather than dominance, and they asked us to do things rather than demanding tasks of us. They could see the questioning in me and didn't try to suppress it. They respected me as a person, and I respected them. This was a crucial time in my life: hormones were starting to kick in, changes had started happening to my body, I started to grow breasts, my shape started to change, I was no longer allowed to run around without a shirt on, and then to top it all off, I started to menstruate. I spent the next six years feeling suicidal, just getting through life, just staying alive.

Throughout my childhood, I developed few close friendships. One friendship was with a girl called Nicola, who went to the public school, while I went to the Catholic high school. We were very different, yet remarkably similar. Nick was weird—she dyed her hair, had strange haircuts, and wore different clothes. She was an outcast and everyone knew it. I was also an outcast but no one knew it. I was popular at school. I stayed at people's places, I was invited to parties, we all went to the movies together, all the things that kids in high school do. I got along with everyone. I had friends in the popular crowd, the smoking group, in the computer nerd crowd, I was friends with the good girls and I was friends with the bad boys. I knew everyone and everyone liked me, and this allowed me to hide. I had many friends, although none of them close friendships—I didn't want to let people inside because I didn't like me, so how could they be my friends if they knew?

Meeting Lesbians

When we were about fifteen, Nick told me that she was a lesbian. She didn't like men sexually, so I thought that must be me too, I must be the same. So over time, we talked and I came out to her. At the end of year ten, when I was sixteen, I started work at the Reserve Bank of Australia, which was my first full-time job. There were several lesbians in the department where I worked, and I managed to sit and talk to one of the older ones, Jane, one day. I told her that I thought that I might be a lesbian and that I had a friend, Nick, and that she was "out." I also wanted to tell my family. Jane suggested that I work things out a bit more before I tell my family, and suggested that I go out and meet some other lesbians. She knew I was not comfortable with the label.

So it took a while, but one night I went to a bar and met some other lesbians. Around the same time, Nick had fallen in love with one of my coworkers and they started spending a lot of time together. Through them I met a whole bunch of dykes, and I started seeing Doris. I was only sixteen. I was young and naive; I liked Doris and I enjoyed the company, but again there was nothing sexual in it for me. She tried to get me sexually involved but I wasn't really interested. She was around for a while, but eventually the relationship broke down.

So for the next few years I had flings with straight girls, I worked and studied, and had a miserable existence. Very early in life I learned to smile, regardless of how I was really feeling; even now when I am having a hard time or a bad day, it is difficult for me to express that.

I felt like I was living two lives: one where I was dating straight girls in an attempt to find my identity, and another life where I was dating straight guys, wearing skirts, and being a girl, to keep society happy. I tried very hard to be the person everyone wanted me to be, to play the part that society expected, but I couldn't. I felt like I was going mad!

So at eighteen I decided to leave, to go searching for my true self, as I knew that I couldn't find myself in Sydney. I had to break away from my family and everyone that I knew and be by myself. I was petrified. On my last night in Sydney, I cried myself to sleep. I was starting to allow myself to feel, I was starting to allow myself to "be," and that was scary. I knew that life was about to change, but I didn't know how or why. I clearly remember the morning that my mother drove me to the bus station. As we reversed out of the driveway, I knew that this was no longer my home; I was leaving the safety net of my home to start an incredible journey.

I left Sydney and started to backpack my way up the coast. I stayed in backpacker hostels and met people from all over the world. For the first time in my life I felt like no one had any expectations of me. This was probably the first step toward discovering my gender diversity. It was a strange time for me—I was excited about the journey I was on, but at the same time, deep inside me was a profound sadness. I was grieving for what I could not be, I was grieving because I was different but I didn't know why. I was lonely, but for the first time, I felt a sense of freedom.

After several months of traveling, I landed a job on Hamilton Island. This is where I met Althea, while she was on holidays visiting a friend. For the first time in my life I was attracted to someone. She was a female and I was female, so I must be a lesbian—I thought I had found my place in the world at last. She went back to Brisbane, and a few months later my friend Tracey and I followed.

We arrived in Brisbane in December 1992; I was twenty. Althea and I started seeing each other and I fell in love. During this time I met and formed friendships with a group of women known as the West End dykes. Some of them were butch and behaved in a masculine way. But although they looked masculine, they didn't want to be men—actually they were happy being women. I found this very confusing, as I wasn't like them. One of the women I met was a male-to-female transsexual, and the moment I met her I knew it was gender that I had issues with, not sexuality. I knew that I wasn't a woman, so I thought I must be a man. I felt that I really was a man inside. The more that I thought about gender, the sadder I was. I thought that my whole life would have to change, my family would disown me, my friends would not talk to me, and I would be an outcast forever. I had never met any FTMs, I didn't know much about transition—I knew nothing. I had spoken to Deni, my MTF friend, but I didn't really know much about transsexuality. I felt that my only choices were to transition and lose everyone and everything, or stay living a miserable life where I didn't feel right. I decided at that time to stay female and revisit the gender question in a few years. Deni had said to me, "You will be sitting on a cliff with a gun to your head and then you will know what to do." At the time, I thought this was a bit melodramatic; however, I never forgot that statement and eventually I understood it. I devised strategies to get me through the next few years. I decided to broaden my friendship circle, to move slightly out of the West End dyke community, and start a carpentry apprenticeship. I thought if I allowed myself to be as masculine as society accepts, then maybe I would be happy.

I really enjoyed carpentry. I enjoyed being on a building site with the blokes, and the blokes accepted me. One day I turned up to work on a new site. I went to the supervisor and introduced myself. I realized that the supervisor thought that I was male. When he was told my true gender a week later, he went into a bit of a spin; he kept coming to me saying, "I can't believe I don't know the difference between a bloke and a chick; maybe I should see a psychiatrist." This was the first time that I thought maybe transition is possible and not as hard as I first considered.

Around the same time, my friend Althea went overseas for a couple of months, which meant that for the first time I was thinking about myself and wasn't worried about her reaction. And a guy called KC came into the community. He had known some of the West End women years before, when he was female. He came back to Brisbane to transition. So I met my first FTM. This was an interesting time. I watched his friends talk about him behind his back. They talked openly about transgender issues, KC, and what they thought about "sex changes." Of course they didn't know that I was transgender and that I was contemplating transition. They thought I was just like them—a woman.

Deciding to Transition

The next few months became harder and harder. I couldn't stop thinking about transition; I couldn't stop thinking about gender. I couldn't concentrate on anything, my life was falling apart; I knew that I couldn't keep up this charade forever. I got to a point where I decided that even if all of my family and friends disowned me, even if I never had another intimate relationship and spent the rest of my life alone, that would be better than living my life as something that I was not. I was sitting on a cliff with a gun to my head.

In March 1994 on International Women's Day, I made the decision to transition, while visiting friends in the country. For the first time in a long time I was smiling. At twenty-two I started my journey of gender exploration. I went to see my GP and told her everything. I got a referral to a psychiatrist, as she was not prepared to start any treatment until I had seen the psychiatrist, and I had to wait three months for an appointment. I got myself a dog, Talaska. Just in case everyone walked away, at least I would have Talaska to keep me company.

So, I started telling friends about my transition. Most of them were OK. Some of them said things like, "Well I don't think that it is the best idea and if there was any chance we could talk you out of it, we would." But they knew I was determined to go ahead with it and they would stand by me. There were some people that I didn't bother to tell, particularly after witnessing the way they talked about KC behind his back. Althea was one of the last friends to be told, and I was worried about her reaction. When I told her, she said, "I thought so. Well, let's have a beer and toast to your future." We talked for a long time, and over the next few months our friendship was tested, but we survived.

I was still working as a carpenter, but it was getting harder. I wanted to start my new life, so I took twelve months' leave from my carpentry apprenticeship and went back to work full-time in an Indian restaurant that I had worked casually in over the years. Eventually three months passed and I got to see the psychiatrist, who prescribed me testosterone tablets, referred me to an endocrinologist, and a few months later I was on testosterone injections. This is when the physical changes started. I looked in the mirror every day searching for facial hair, but the changes were slow.

I was petrified of telling my parents about my transition, as about this time my grandmother was quite sick. I didn't think that this was the time to tell them, and I certainly didn't want to tell them on the phone. My voice was starting to change, so every time we spoke on the phone my mother would say, "Do you still have that cold?" The situation was becoming very difficult. My housemates were calling me Jack and using the pronoun "he," but when my family called they would have to call me Jean and "she." Friends would often speak to me without using pronouns because they didn't want to get it wrong.

Life was very exciting at this stage; I was being treated as male by most of society. I had changed my driver's license, and life was progressing nicely. It was also a very stressful time, as I had to get used to society treating me differently. How do men interact with each other? What are the rules when entering male toilets? How do men interact with women? Society has many unspoken rules—I had to go through a whole childhood and adolescence of learning in one year.

As I was working evenings in the Indian restaurant, it meant that I had a lot of time on my hands during the day, so I started to get involved in the Brisbane GLBT Pride festival. This is a festival that happens every year. There are discussion forums, art exhibitions, films, and a march through the city, followed by Fair Day and a big dance party. I joined the Pride committee and was involved with organizing Fair Day, which was a lot of fun and got me out and about in my new gender.

One of my friends decided to organize a fashion parade as part of the dance party, and I was asked to be a model. The group involved with the fashion parade got together, and this is where I met Michael. He was the hairdresser and makeup artist for the night. I remember at one of the organizing meetings sitting next to Michael, and we talked and laughed. I felt something that I had never felt before. I was high—I was on cloud nine after talking to him; we connected. This was really strange for me. I had only dated girls, I had never thought about men sexually. For the first time I was contemplating a sexual relationship with a man, with a gay man. I really didn't think that he would be interested in me. If he was a gay man, then how could he be interested in a man without a penis, or more to the point, a man with a vagina? With clothes on I could pass as a male, but naked, how could he possibly find me sexually attractive?

So we went on a few dates and we talked about different things. I was incredibly confused. When deciding to transition, I had come to a point where I decided that I would probably never have another sexual relationship. I thought that no one would ever find me sexually attractive and then I had this man pursuing me. Gender and sexuality are very different things, but they are linked together. So at a time when I was still trying to sort out my own gender identity, I was also forced by circumstance to try to sort out my sexual identity. Heterosexual, gay, lesbian are all identities based on gender—by definition you have to be two women to take on the identity of lesbian, two men to take on the identity gay, male and female to be heterosexual, and I wasn't sure how I fitted into these definitions. I had always thought that I would have intimate relationships with women, because that is what I had done in the past. I was way outside of my comfort zone, and I didn't know how to proceed or even if I wanted to proceed with this relationship.

In August 1995, after a night out, Michael asked me if I would consider having a relationship with a male. Unfortunately at that point, I laughed because I was thinking: "How can I ask him if he would consider having a relationship with a trans man?" He got out of the car and ran into his house, as he thought that I was laughing at the prospect of having a relationship with him. Oops. So I got out of the car and followed him inside, and we talked. I said that I didn't know if I could have a relationship with a man, but that I was willing to give it a go. This was the start of a long relationship; we are still together seven years later.

My biggest concerns were being naked in front of him and having sex with a male. So, we proceeded slowly. I had only been on hormones a short time; it was only five months after the decision to transition and I had only had one or two hormone injections, so my body was still very female. I was uncomfortable with my body and I was worried about how he might react, so we took things one step at a time. Michael stayed over for a few nights and we slept in the same bed; slowly over the next few nights, I took off articles of clothing. As I felt more comfortable with him I was able to expose a little bit more of my physical body until he had seen it all. The whole way through this process, I expected him to get up and leave—I expected him to say, "You are not a man, you are a woman; no, you are not a woman, you are a freak and I cannot be with a freak." I guess this says more about my state of mind at the time. You see, when I was seen as female, at least I had a body to match and everyone thought that I was normal, but by deciding to transition I was telling the world that I didn't match. I felt like a freak. How can I be a man with breasts and a vagina? It took a long time for me to understand how Michael could still see me as male, even when I was naked.

When a trans man starts hormones, a number of things occur. Fat redistributes around the body to give a more masculine shape, muscles develop, hair grows in a male pattern (which includes male-pattern baldness for some), facial hair starts to grow, the clitoris grows into a micro penis, and the person's voice deepens. If you see a picture of a naked trans man, particularly after his breasts have been removed, you probably won't even notice that he doesn't have a penis. It was only after I had seen such a picture that I could understand how I could be seen as male, even when I was naked. At this point in my life, it was important to me to be seen as a man.

Telling My Parents and Friends

In October my parents came to visit. I didn't want to have to tell my mother at this time, but the changes were happening, and when they saw me, they knew something was different. I think parents, especially mothers, know when their children are having a hard time, so my mother had been worried about me for many months. So I took them out for a coffee and told them what I was doing. I talked all about the transition, the psychiatrist, and the endocrinologist. They were upset, but they kept it together and we parted on good terms. When I walked them to the car, they got in and drove off. I never knew if they would speak to me again.

A few weeks later I got an amazing letter from my mother. I still have it. She wrote and told me that she loved me and she would always love me. She said that she recognizes how hard it must have been to make such a big decision and that I can always count on her for support. She has always been there for me and I love her dearly.

Over the next year or so, I spent a lot of time seeing doctors and psychiatrists, and changing documents. I spent a lot of time trying to understand transition and myself. Michael and I spent a lot of time together—we did all the things that new lovers do, we discussed gender, and generally got to know each other.

About one-and-a-half years after I started my transition, Michael and I moved to the Sunshine Coast in Queensland. This was the first time that we had lived together. The move was one of the best things we have ever done. We had been living in inner-city Brisbane in the queer ghettos. Moving away allowed me to enjoy the environment (we lived a short walk to the beach), and I started to look toward the future. When I was living as female, it took all of my energy just to survive, just to get through the day. I never had any concept of the future, or even thought what I might be doing years from then.

It was also a chance for me to start making friends with people who didn't know my past. To these people I was a man and that was all. At this time I still had breasts. Early in transition I decided not to have any surgery for the first two years, as I felt that this would give me time to adjust to all the other changes and to preserve my mental health. The two-year time restriction that I had placed on myself still had six months to go, and my mental health was declining. I needed to have surgery; I needed to have my breasts removed. I went to see a doctor who had operated on only one FTM before; I liked him and could afford his fee. I only had to wait six weeks from the first consultation for a surgery date—I was so excited.

The day before the surgery, my mother picked us up and took Michael and me to Brisbane, where we stayed with my sister overnight. Early the next morning we went to the hospital. The doctor warned me that after surgery my chest would be heavily bandaged. He told me this so that I didn't panic and think that they had performed the wrong operation and put in breast implants! Mum and Michael sat with me while we waited for them to wheel me off to surgery. The next thing I remember is waking up in the recovery ward; I was still groggy, and I kept pulling the blanket down. The nurse would walk past and pull the blanket back up; I would then pull it back down. This happened several times until I managed to say, "I have been waiting my whole adult life to be in public without having my chest covered, now go away and leave me alone." At this point they decided that I was OK and sent me back to the ward. I slept for the rest of the day, and the next day I was able to go home. Mum and Michael came to get me, and home we went. Mum stayed for about a week to look after me, but after a few days, I was fine. My chest was bandaged for a week, but eventually the bandages came off and I was able to see the results. My chest was incredibly bruised and sore (I had a reaction to the elastoplast and my skin was raw) but that didn't matter—my chest was flat. So home I went and life continued as normal, but with less stress.

While living on the Sunshine Coast, I completed a diploma of applied science in community and human services. This was a two-year course. The class started with more than fifty students, and only eight of us graduated after two years. We became a very close group, going out together, studying together, and going camping during one of the semester breaks. No one ever questioned my gender, and when I eventually told them, their initial reactions were of disbelief. I never had any problem with using public toilets or anything else. One time when we were camping, one of the women said to me, "Why do you walk all the way to the toilet block? Why don't you piss on a tree like the other guys?" I replied simply, "If you were a tree, would you want me to piss on you?"

After completing my studies I started working in the community sector. Five years after starting this journey, Michael and I moved to Sydney, and I immersed myself in the transgender community. This has been good for me, as it has allowed me the forum to discuss the ideas and issues that I face as a trans man. It has also given me the opportunity to explore my identity in a safe place with people who understand. I now have a balance of people in my life—those who know I am transgender and those who don't. Some of the people around me are transgender and others don't even know what the word means.

It has now been seven-and-a-half years since I first started my transition, and my thoughts and ideas on gender have changed dramatically over this time. I would like to leave you with some of my thoughts.

Thoughts

Many people have trouble understanding how I could have relationships with women and then start having a relationship with a man. I don't have relationships with men or women, I have a relationship with a person that I love, a person that I am attracted to for many reasons—I do not love Michael because he has a penis, and his genitals have nothing to do with my attraction. I think that most people are attracted to people. However, we are raised with such strict rules about how men should behave, how women should behave, how all people should behave, and who we are allowed to be attracted to. When we first meet somebody that we are attracted to, we do not know what genitals they have—all we can do is assume. We are attracted to other qualities.

When I started seeing Michael, I briefly identified as a gay boy; however, I quickly lost that identity because it simply didn't fit. I don't have anything in common with the gay scene, and as a whole I don't objectify men. I have never liked the term *bisexual,* as it implies two genders—I know that there are so many more than simply male and female. Gender is much more fluid.

So I have taken on the sexual identity "queer." I do not believe that there is much difference in the sexual practices of lesbians, gay men, or heterosexual men and women. People are individuals and participate in different sexual practices; society would benefit enormously if people were open about sex.

During my life, I have had the opportunity to be part of women-only spaces, to talk with women about women's things, to be involved with women intimately as another woman. I have also had the opportunity to be part of men-only spaces, to talk with men about men's things, to be involved intimately with men as another man. I have also had the opportunity to be part of a gender-diverse community, to talk with people about things we commonly share, to be involved intimately with gender-diverse people as another gender-diverse person. I have found that men and women are not fundamentally different. There are some differences, but

I believe most of the differences are barriers put in place by society and reinforced by us. If we believe that men and women are different, we don't have to take responsibility for not trying to understand each other—we don't need to share our thoughts and feelings, our beliefs, our hopes and fears.

These days I see myself as Jack. Some days I am more feminine than others; some days I am more masculine than others. I have a wide variety of interests and skills. What I am doing and who I am with will depend on how I am and what personality traits dominate. When I first started this process, I thought I was male and I believed this for a while. Then I read something and I realized that I thought that I was male because I knew that I was not female. Once I realized this, my life opened up: I didn't need to take on the identity of male; I could be me, Jack. Jack is definitely masculine and presents to the world in a masculine way, although I do not consider myself to be a man. I am reluctant to use any labels, especially a label like *man;* everyone (except me) knows exactly what it means, yet no one can define it. I don't think that the label *man* adequately describes my reality.

You see, there are many things that I have and haven't experienced. I know what it is like to be treated as a man and as a woman in this society. I do not know what it is like to grow up as a little boy. I don't know what it is like to go through puberty as a teenage boy. I don't know what it is like to have a penis or to orgasm with a penis. However, I do know what it is like to grow up as a gender-confused little girl. I know what it is like to go through puberty as a biological girl. I know what it is like to have a vagina and to orgasm with a vagina. So, somehow the title *man* doesn't adequately reflect my experiences. I have lived my life as a female in this society, and I have lived my life as a male in this society. I believe this is something to be cherished, and I feel privileged to have had these experiences.

For me, being transgender means more than identifying as male and/or female. It has allowed me to see gender as fluid, and in doing so has given me the opportunity to really look at myself. This has not always been easy. I have found parts of myself that I don't really like, and I have had to work really hard to change those parts or to accept them if they can't be changed. I feel that I have grown enormously from the gender diversity in my life, and I would not change any of it.

TRACY'S STORY

Tracy Deichmann

I AM A WOMAN, similar in most ways to millions of others, but I am also different because I belong to a group of women who were born with a physical defect, a defect that some in society find hard to deal with—I am a transsexual. A transsexual has the body of one gender but the brain of the other. In my particular case, I was born with a male body but a female brain.

There is much confusion about transsexuality. For me, it has nothing to do with sexual preference, nothing to do with crossdressing, it is not infectious, and above all, it has nothing to do with sexual activity. Transsexuality is nothing more and nothing less than the mismatch of mind and physical gender. I am happy now because I can live and function as a woman, but I am not allowed the basic human right of marriage, and the bureaucrats refuse to change my birth certificate—I always thought my country enshrined equality, but some people are deemed less equal! This is my story . . .

Confusion (1952–1972)

I was born into a conservative, sports-mad, and male-dominated Australia in 1952 from Dutch parents. I was educated in Australia and Holland and have also lived and worked in Nigeria and South Africa.

My first memories of sensing that something was amiss began around the age of six. I can remember how uncomfortable I was doing many of the things, such as sports, that other boys seemed to enjoy. It just didn't seem to come naturally, and I often felt like an outsider. I liked to climb trees and play in the sand as much as anyone, but when it came to the important things in a young male's life, like catching a ball or kicking a football, I both lacked interest and was hopeless.

At the time, girls seemed to be mysterious figures that did interesting things I wasn't permitted to join in with. Having no idea what the problem was, I desperately tried to blend in. I was typically the kid who never got picked for the team and was often overlooked at school if it involved any boyish-type activities. Even though I was somewhat of an outsider at school, I never lacked for friends and somehow was never troubled by bullies—something that (luckily) was to carry over to adult life. Later, when I did have opportunities to join in activities with girls, I remember it used to feel so much more normal, and I didn't have to act.

By the time I reached puberty, I had worked out that I should have been a girl. What I remember of puberty is a nightmare—my body was deforming and growing more horrible every day. There was nothing that I could do about it, and I had no idea who to see or what to do; I had a constant feeling of "wrongness" and a fear that somebody would notice.

I tried my best to act as was expected of me, meanwhile trying to sort out my own feelings and emotions. I looked at girls differently than how my friends did, not with lust but with envy. Talking with and being around girls was easy as a friend, but if I had to act the male, like on a date or at a dance, I became very uncomfortable and self-conscious, not knowing how to act. With boys it was different; in a one-on-one situation I got along fine, but when a group got together and it got to "boy talk," I just seemed to fade out, trying to show interest but invariably being bored and having the feeling I didn't belong. I knew I was definitely not a homosexual, but if I secretly dared think of myself as a female, it seemed to throw a switch in my mind, and the thought of a relationship with a male was very much of interest. Whichever way I turned, I couldn't mesh my mind with my body.

During my teens I just seemed to drift from year to year. My father had jobs in various countries, and the family followed, finally returning to Australia. I probably seemed fairly normal, if somewhat shy and bookish from the outside, but on the inside I was starting to feel more and more like life was passing me by—never being able to act in what for me was a natural way. The longing to be female was never far from my thoughts.

I felt like a hollow shell. I can remember becoming very excited when I read that there were other people in the world that were like me— I wasn't a total freak! Unfortunately, because of the fear and misinformation that were so much part of society then, I was too scared to see anyone and tell all; maybe somebody could have helped me, even then.

Anyhow, I kept quiet and pretended I was the confident male, doing things that secretly I detested and succeeding only in becoming steadily more lonely and withdrawn. Looking back now at so many wasted years, a feeling of loss still haunts me.

Hopelessness (1972–1999)

In my twenties I traveled extensively and worked at many different jobs, trying to escape from myself. Every time that I seemed to get my act together, the gender dysphoria would kick in with a vengeance and it all came to naught. Basically, I was throwing away golden opportunities for a well-paid career, not because I wanted to but because I could not handle the pain of trying to act the male.

Even though I did not lack for friends, I felt lonely—the horrid loneliness of not belonging, of forever feeling apart—I never was "one of the guys." This loneliness led to my one serious attempt at suicide. I threw a rope over a beam, tied the other end around my neck and then gave it a big tug to see if it could take my weight—it didn't! The beam came loose and nearly clobbered me for my trouble. I dragged myself off to bed and spent another night sobbing into my pillow. Why the bloody hell had I to suffer this gender dysphoria? All I wished was to be me: a girl.

Finally, rather surprisingly, I married in 1981. I thought that all my silly ideas would go, and I would finally be able to settle down to a normal life. After acting the dutiful husband for some time, I realized that my feelings hadn't changed but were growing stronger each year. By bottling up my inner feelings all these years, the strain was starting to affect my health, with constant migraines and a mounting sense of bitterness and cynicism.

In January of 1999, I could take it no longer; I broke down and told my wife, amid much hand wringing and many tears, that I could no longer continue to live a lie. Somehow, even though I was cursed by being born male, I had to become the woman I should always have been.

Being True to Myself (1999–2001)

When I told my wife, I had expected to lose her and everybody and everything I held dear. Even with that certainty hanging over my head, I knew there was no going back—if this was going to be the end of it, then so be it. I was desperate; if I must die, then at least let the world know that I have never considered myself a male, and that even if the rest of humanity turned on me, I needed to at least try to be true to myself. Anyhow, after digesting this momentous news and with much discussion, my wife became very supportive, for which I was, and am, extremely grateful. (She had always known I crossdressed, but thought it was just a fetish, not realizing it was a crutch to minimize my self-loathing.)

The possibility that I might actually finally become myself was an enormous boost to me in every possible way. The migraines that had been steadily getting worse stopped within days, the cynicism and bitterness that were becoming a horrible part of my life disappeared, and I just felt happy and alive for the first time I could remember.

After much research on the Internet, I managed to contact the right people and was soon on my way to becoming a real person. The first time that I spoke with another transsexual is something I will never forget. She was the first person who truly understood me; we shared the same pain, the same hopes, the same feelings—it was a truly wonderful experience for me. I started taking female hormones in April 1999 and was soon doing the rounds of doctors and psychiatrists that all transsexuals must endure to become our true selves.

Within weeks I started to regularly go out dressed as a woman, albeit a rather nervous one. For the first time, I felt normal and could act naturally. I was lucky in that I was never very masculine in appearance, so I could walk around without people looking at me strangely. (I was called "madam" on more than one occasion when trying to pretend I was a male, but I have never been called "sir" since I transitioned—yippee!)

The next step was telling friends and family. That was a very scary thing to do, but it had to be done. After much talk and many in-depth discussions, I was fortunate enough not to have lost anybody and have made many new friends along the way. I knew that my transition had made it so much easier to talk to people; I could now be open and free and didn't have to filter everything I said to see if it is what a male would say; I now enjoyed people's company.

The reaction of my family was especially gratifying: my mother was an enormous help to me after she had digested the news and realized that I was still her child. We could now talk—really talk and get to know each other so much better. My little niece in Holland summed it up when she heard that I was now her aunty: "Of course she wants to be a girl, who'd want to be a boy—yuck!"

In August 1999 I changed my name and started to live full-time as a female. This was one of the most momentous and satisfying things that I have ever done. Expecting to be subjected to many forms of ridicule while changing my details, I was pleasantly surprised at the friendly and courteous service I received from most levels of bureaucracy—maybe society is slowly becoming more compassionate and understanding? There is still much discrimination against people like me, but at least I could get on with my life as a female.

About a year into transition, I lost my best friend of twenty-eight years. At first he seemed to have no problems with my transformation. We still had our regular rave sessions about computers, and whatever else was of interest. Then, literally from one day to the next, without explanation, the friendship was over. I don't know what happened (maybe I was becoming too feminine for him), but it hurt that I was not deemed worthy of even a goodbye. Regretfully, I have now learned that, apart from family, you will most likely lose some friends eventually—luckily they are often replaced with friends with fewer hang-ups.

My wife and I divorced in November 2000. We remained living under the same roof, but began to lead steadily more separate lives. I had already begun to date men, as had she, and found it rather exciting to act in a natural way with another person romantically—a totally new experience for me.

Chaotic Months (January–March 2001)

In December 2000, I received a very welcome letter in the mail—my surgery date. I was to have gender reassignment surgery on February 23, 2001. Needless to say, I was excited beyond belief—it felt like a lead weight had been lifted from my shoulders. I frantically filled out all the paperwork, got the appropriate people to sign in the required places, paid the money, and sat down to wait. Then my life took a turn that was both totally unexpected and was at least as profound as the upcoming surgery: I met Andrea.

Saturday, January 13, was a warm day. The Seahorse Society, a TG support group, was having a barbecue that afternoon, not far from where I lived. Having nothing better to do, I thought I may as well go along and pass a few hours in idle conversation. After a couple of hours, I was totally bored. Nearly everyone there was a crossdresser, and even though they are nice people, we have little in common. Sitting in a semidaze, I was on the verge of leaving when I heard somebody mention the word "hormones." Instantly awake, I focused on the rather attractive young lady who had said the aforementioned word, and joined the conversation.

Before much time had elapsed, Andrea and I were in deep discussion— the rest of the guests just seemed to fade away as we concentrated fully on each other. The conversation was along similar lines to many that I had had with other transsexual girls, but there was more . . . much more.

We seemed to be very much on the same wavelength, finding a very close similarity in how we thought. At the same time, I felt an almost over-powering attraction to her, partially in a physical sense, but mainly for her as a person, the inner her, her mind.

Early in the evening, I had to leave. I left my card with her, hoping she might want to talk some time in the future. My feelings were very con-fused, and I felt both scared and annoyed with myself. What was I? Some type of idiot for even daring to be attracted to somebody who was not only smart and attractive but also much younger and female too—I thought I liked only guys. Trying to shrug it off as just some type of silly fantasy, I spent the Sunday working on my computer—unsuccessfully try-ing not to think about her. That evening, I nearly had a heart attack when up popped a message on ICQ (an instant messaging service) from Andrea—she had contacted me! Excitement clutched at my heart and impossible thoughts rushed through my mind at breakneck speed as I quickly replied to her message. I had never, ever felt such deep emotion in my life, and it frightened me with its intensity.

Over the next couple of weeks we corresponded every night over ICQ. It became apparent that a friendship was developing, and that was as much as I could realistically expect. Two weeks after our original meeting, we held a barbecue along with another TS friend. We spoke without a break for more than twelve hours and became firm friends. Over the next few weeks we began to get together more and more, and we realized that what was developing was more than just friendship; we had started to fall in love.

Shortly before I was to go in for surgery, we realized that we could no longer live apart—we needed each other, and both felt lost when we were not together. Andrea moved in with me and my ex-wife, and I spent the last few preoperative days frantically helping her move all her stuff over. Things on the home front were beginning to get rather hectic, but first I had to get through the surgery.

I was to be admitted to hospital on Thursday, the day before my surgery. My ex-wife wished that she alone could take me in, and with mixed feelings, I allowed her to do this. Andrea would visit her family in the country and come back to me on Saturday, the day after the opera-tion. After being admitted to hospital, I was given a nice room, where after some talking, my ex left and I was left to face the big day feeling very much alone. The nurse came and gave me a glass of "Fleet" to drink—tastes awful and is designed to clean you out prior to surgery. The evening passed with alternating trips to the loo and watching television. The upcoming surgery, funnily enough, did not worry me as much as expected, which was a relief.

The next morning, as I was getting ready for surgery, I was hit by an overpowering sense of loneliness—Andrea was miles away and I needed her more than ever; I felt very small then, sitting on the edge of the bed wearing that silly surgical robe they make you wear, and looking out the window, waiting for them to come and get me.

By the time I was wheeled toward the operating theater, I was happier again as the realization hit me that I was about to finally become a whole person. I felt hardly any fear, just a "rightness" as to what was about to occur. As I was being wheeled along the corridor to the operating theater, I had to smile as I caught myself humming, "I'm a lesbian and I'm OK," to the tune of Monty Python's lumberjack song—Andrea was on my mind! The operation went very well and seemed to be over in a flash (actually about five hours had passed), with me awakening in the early evening muttering, "Thank you, thank you," over and over again. At last, that horrid "thing" was no more!

The following day, shortly before visiting hours began, I was thinking of Andrea, hoping that I would see her soon. I glanced up, and like a wish fulfilled, there she stood, framed in the doorway, a big grin on her face and looking gorgeous beyond belief. I squealed and she rushed into my arms—we were together and nobody would ever part us again. We were happy, very happy.

Many friends came visiting over the next ten days while I lay recovering in hospital. The highlight, though, was Andrea. She came every day before visiting hours began and stayed at my side until well after all other visitors had left. We grew very close over that time and seemed to fall deeper in love every day. Andrea came and picked me up on a warm Monday ten days after surgery, and took me home. We must have looked like a couple of Cheshire cats, grinning and laughing, as we pulled into a McDonalds drive-in to stock up on burgers and fries.

Settling Down (2001 and Beyond)

Around the same time that Andrea had moved in, my ex's boyfriend also moved in—luckily the house could accommodate all four of us and give us some privacy, but this situation could not last for long. Even though we tended to stay out of each other's way as much as possible, over the next few months, things became steadily more hectic, and there was an underlying tension that we all felt.

As I regained my health, Andrea and I started to review our options and came to the conclusion that we needed our own place. Eventually we decided on moving out to the country, as we detested the city with its traffic and pollution, and above all, the heartless corporate culture that seems so prevalent these days. We would miss being close to our friends and the big shopping centers, but the city was no longer an option.

We sold the house about six months after my surgery, and with my share we had just enough to buy a nice little cottage in the country. We settled on a small town in Victoria, about a two-hour drive from Melbourne, but within close proximity of large local towns. It was a risk, because you never know how people will react, especially in a semirural type of environment, but luckily, sizable parts of the town's population are also escapees from the city, and people seemed to accept us. Most of the people that know us here know that we are lesbian, because even though we don't make it blatant, we also don't try to hide it. As to our being transsexual, a smaller but growing number do know but seem to accept us, probably because they can see we are doing our best to blend in, and we pose no threat. Anyhow, we are starting to feel very much at home here.

Andrea is working locally with computers and has settled in very well with her job. I'm studying for a science and information technology degree, using the Internet to save on travel. We are beginning to get a social life and enjoy going out regularly, but we also enjoy spending time at home, being nerds with our computers or just relaxing in front of the fireplace and talking.

We still go to the city every couple of weeks for appointments and shopping, and to visit friends and family, but it is always so nice to get back to the freedom of the country. We're just a couple of country girls who mean no harm.

Sexuality Soul Searching

One of the hardest things that I have had to deal with is my own sexuality. Did I like males or females? I had so much love that I wanted to give, but I was always in a state of confusion about how to relate to either sex. Both were of interest, which in itself was confusing, but I had to hide my true self from both.

Pretransition I think I could have only been a friend to a man, because if I had hinted at more they would naturally have thought me a homosexual—the thought of them thinking of me as male is too horrid for me to even think about. To a woman I could only present as a male with all the attendant mental torment—I had to do major mental gymnastics to even go with a woman, totally blocking from my mind what I was and pretending that it was some type of lesbian relationship.

Now that I am postoperative, I can be totally myself and let my feelings emerge—I initially thought I was a heterosexual woman and began dating guys. Then, after meeting Andrea, I knew that women were of equal interest, and I came to the realization that my love is for the person, not for what sex or gender they are. My confusion as to my sexuality has gone; I guess I'm bisexual, but I'm in a lesbian relationship, and it doesn't worry me one iota. It feels wonderful to dump the old stereotypical dogmas imposed by society and not be afraid to love—that's liberation!

What It Has Meant to Me

Transition has meant a rebirth, a chance to finally be myself. Having spent my life struggling with gender dysphoria, I have found an inner peace by allowing the woman I am to emerge. Despair has changed to hope, self-loathing is now compassion for others, and cynicism has been replaced with a joy I thought would forever be denied me. My biggest regret is for the wasted years trying to be what I am not. My biggest fear is for others like me, who may be resigned to living an empty life, as I once did—please be true to yourself before it is too late. Now, for the first time, I no longer hate myself and can say that I am truly happy.

Was It Worth It?

There are still problems in my life, but they are the normal ones that many women have—I wish my figure was better, my hair is always a mess, and so on. These are the worries I am happy to have, because they are the normal worries of life. What upsets me are the worries that are caused by society, the lack of equality to other women just because of a birth defect, and the fear of people like me. I still cry for the lost years of my life, the years of trying to be a male, the loneliness, the hopelessness, and the fear.

Transitioning has allowed me to live a life that is much closer to what, for me, is normal. I no longer have the constant feeling of acting, of playing a role in a life that feels totally alien to me. Also, almost as compensation, I have found a love with Andrea that has made me feel more alive than I ever thought I would, so to have found her and myself at the same time . . . oh yes, it was worth it!

THE SECOND TRANSITION

Christine Burns

FOR MANY YEARS there has been an increasingly diverse choice of literature dealing with the period surrounding the obvious physical transition
made by trans people. Lots of people have written about their path to the
doors of the operating theater, and all the tears, drama, and obstacles that
have come to be regarded as the natural rites of passage on the gender-
crossing road. Far less ever seems to have been written about what lies
beyond the knife, though—that time when the stitches have come out and
the physical wounds have healed, and when the newly liberated person is
set loose on the world with a blank canvas on which to paint a life. I think
it's time that omission was rectified.

I don't want to spend a lot of space speculating on why this part of
trans people's development seems to have been relatively overlooked. Historically, many people have simply sought to assimilate and disappear
after surgery. Or maybe stopping the narratives at this point reflects society's simplistic belief that gender transition is only about hacking at bits
of flesh and nothing else—an end, rather than a beginning.

If this were true, you could assess the success or otherwise of a trans
person's journey the moment they wake up from the anesthetic, which
seems ridiculous. Other people's biographies don't stop at the point when
they pop out of the womb or celebrate their coming of age, it's usually
where they begin! The assumption that things are in any way different for
trans people can lead to a false set of expectations about how you should
feel and behave afterwards. In the worst case, it can lead well-meaning
individuals to shut off the support process at the very point when it is
most needed, in the real growth phase of personal development.

"You won't need me now. The operation's over, the file's closed. Go out and live happily ever after and don't you dare say that you want or expect anything more after this much fuss. If you're not instantly ecstatic, that can only mean the whole thing was a disastrous and irrevocable mistake."

This story is therefore about the second and more profound transition in a life. The longer, most exciting but least talked-about one: what happened next. Hopefully this will encourage more people to think about the spiritual journey that the physical passage merely qualifies us to begin. That doesn't mean I want people to think of this quick recap of my own "second transition" as some sort of model, something else to fail or succeed in replicating. Trans people's lives are littered with far too many conformance models for me to dream of wanting to add another! Besides, as I'll go on to explain, the second transition is far more of an evolutionary one. There is no set place for it to begin, no right or wrong speed or direction for it to proceed, and no reason to suggest that it should have to end. All I'd like people to think about is the notion that it exists and how to make the best of it. The rest is up to each individual.

Before I begin my story, I'd like to introduce you to a folktale that I heard many years ago and whose moral you might find as useful as I did.

One day a storyteller thoughtlessly offends a gypsy selling heather at his door. She puts a curse on him, and he finds, to his horror, that thereafter everything written—all the books, magazines, and newspapers that he picks out to read—appear to him as versions of the same narrative.

The storyteller loves reading, and this is a curse that bites. He's not become blind in a conventional sense, but worse perhaps: he's blinded by the image placed between the print on the real page and his consciousness. In panic he looks for a cure, only to find that nobody can help him. The problem lies inside. Other people look at a book and see the real words. They can't envisage his reality. He contemplates ending his life, for surely there is nothing to live for in this condition. In one last desperate act, however, he seeks out the gypsy to apologize for his actions and to beg with her to lift the curse.

The gypsy readily accepts the man's apologies, but confesses that there is nothing she can now do to lift the spell. Instead, she advises him to find his peace with it. He needs to learn from and embrace his condition, she says. He must find the value in what has happened and rejoice in it.

At first the man is mystified by the advice he has received. How can you embrace and find peace with an obstacle like this? Then he resolves to try a new approach. He picks up a book and starts to transcribe the story that only his eyes can see. No longer fighting to see past the message that's there, he finds, to his surprise, that he is transcribing a masterpiece of great subtlety and depth. The substance of his curse turns out to be a thing of real beauty. At the same time, he realizes that the ideas were there all along, locked in his unconscious. They're his. What seemed a curse was actually a gift of insight into what lay waiting to be tapped in his own abilities.

The man's transcription turns out to be a best-seller, of course. And with the release of the ideas that stood between him and the world, he finds that the spell offers something, rather than taking it away. Now when he opens a book, he sees new perspectives waiting to be passed on, and realizes how this will continue until all the good ideas released by the gypsy's "curse" have been written down for others and published.

The story ends there, of course, and there's a moral in it for everyone: take what you've got and use it. Take the "curse" of seeing things differently as a "gift," and that is what it will become. Now I'd like to tell you a little bit about my own life . . .

Acceptance

Looking back, the first part of my own life story seems like a bit of a stop-start affair—for years a game of hide-and-seek with reality.

It's quite safe to admit nowadays (cliché or not) that I knew how different I was from very early on as a child. There were "incidents" from before I even started school. The other kids instinctively spotted a difference of some kind too. The boys bullied and shunned me, the girls welcomed me as one of their own. Even before my teens I ached to be one of them, with an inexplicable force that became more terrifying the older I grew. There could be no question of doing anything about how I felt inside until I had at least left home, though. And, at university, it wasn't long before I was covertly reading about others like me. (This was the 1970s, when the story of British trans woman April Ashley appeared in the newspapers because the court refused to recognize her as female, and the travel writer Jan Morris published her autobiography *Conundrum*.) Before my finals, I'd even overcome my self-abhorrence sufficiently to seek professional advice. When I was twenty-one, the advice I got from an amazingly well informed psychologist of the time was that the decision was mine. I filled all the diagnostic criteria as a "transsexual." Being young, slight, longhaired, and pretty, I could start my transition tomorrow if I wished.

All I had to do was ask. I still remember her words: "We can do so much to help you."

You'd think in hindsight, and in view of the problems encountered by so many others over the years, that I'd be overjoyed at this news. In fact, it was quite the opposite. I was terrified, and hid. It wasn't the prospect of the change that terrified me, but the consequences. I feared the loss of everything else that was important about my life at the time. I was convinced I'd lose my family and friends, all the people I cared for. The very things that underpinned my personality were at stake—needing to be valued, respected, and cared about by others. Strong as the desire to liberate my self-expression might be, this fear was stronger. What would there be in this other life if others withdrew their love and the opportunities to love in return? So it was that I embarked on a cat-and-mouse game of denial for years, becoming ever more frightened of the immense force of what needed to be expressed in me, and more and more guilty at my inability to ignore it. Like the character in the short story, the curse was wherever I looked. And, more than once, it took me all the way to the brink of decision before another psychologist came to the same conclusion.

You know the outcome, of course. Third time lucky I stepped, and found my fears to be largely unfounded. True, there were long-term friends, people I loved, who didn't manage the transition with me. Other people took their place remarkably quickly though, in what turned out to be a breakneck transition. Notice how little there is to say about it too when there's no trauma put there by others.

In most transition stories that is the end, of course. The heroine skips off into the sunset (preferably with a new love in tow), and we the audience are left to conclude that she lived happily ever after. Only that's not quite the case. For me, the completion of all the surgical paraphernalia of transition reminded me of the day I passed my driving test. From that point I was licensed to get in the car alone and choose where I wanted to go. I knew the rudiments of how to steer, how to start, accelerate, and stop. I could begin having an independent experience in a car. But I wasn't a driver, merely a trained operator of a motor vehicle. Passing your test simply allows you to start learning to drive, and I soon came to realize that the same applies to becoming a complete, integrated person too.

As a newly licensed woman, however, I was a bit of a mess, and I'm telling this tale because it may come as a surprise to those who know only the modern-day Christine Burns, a successful IT consultant, one of the key public faces of trans political activism in the United Kingdom through the most exciting period in our history, a woman whose face and words cover the hundreds of pages of that campaign's website and literature. But back then I was having difficulty accepting myself, let alone expecting others to do so.

On the face of it, all those years ago, nobody could quite see my problem. It was best summed up by the wife of a man whom I met at an early stage in my transition. She had met a few transvestite men before, and I'd been warned that she was likely to be challenging toward this more threatening person labeled "transsexual." The instant we first met, however, her jaw dropped, she paused for a second, and then flung her arms around me in a warm sisterly greeting. "My God dear, you *are* a woman!" The consensus among others was, "We've sensed it for years, what took you so long?"

My family saw it, much to my amazement. True, my parents had some questions to ask before they understood in their own terms, but strangely they never doubted or challenged the idea that my transition was right. Instead, they embraced their new daughter and bade farewell to their son. Business clients seemed to see it too. As a self-employed consultant I was entirely dependent upon acceptance by them to survive in transition and fund private treatment for myself. Paradoxically, however, my income and workload actually increased on starting the transition and continued to grow healthily afterwards. I was awash in acceptance, yet couldn't fully accept myself. Something didn't *feel* right still.

With hindsight (and to save you skipping to the end of this tale for the answer) the "something" that didn't feel right was the way in which I had learned to "know" myself through a medical label. I'd come to think of myself as a product of a condition, not an expression of a person. I had learned the art of denial, first as a way of trying to evade something inside that frightened me. But now that it was out for all the world to see, I'd continued the learned habit and was still trying to deny the full extent of the reality to myself. Being a trans person was still "wrong" in some way, a personal failure for which I ought to feel some guilt, especially for succumbing to it. Worse, of course, was conventional wisdom that says the trans person is supposed to conceal their past, which just compounded the problem. And I knew there was a problem, because every day I was greeted by people with a warm, affectionate, and unquestioning acceptance, which somehow eluded me. The fact that those people clearly couldn't even comprehend the difficulties I was having only contributed to the sense of being in some way "apart" still. In one sense I'd not changed the basic condition I'd known as a child: the sense of being different and separated from normality. At the same time I wasn't expected to have these feelings. I'd obtained the outward trappings of the thing I'd sought. The physical barrier to personal expression was removed, so why wasn't I yet free?

The "Wrong" Model

Like the wretched soul in the short story, I was trying to see around the very thing that was there before my eyes, rather than taking it out and examining it. The "model" I was using to explain myself just wasn't right. It couldn't explain my reality in ways that concurred with everything else I knew about myself. In the model I'd been taught, the unstoppable pursuit of the essential had to be interpreted as sick or bizarre, or deliberately and dangerously radical. I knew myself to be none of these things. Everything else about me was reasoned and planned. I tended to be conservative, if anything, rather than radical. Relationship-centered, yes, attention seeking or extrovert, no. Having allowed my big secret out into the open, all the force that had brought it out was dissipated too. There had never been any other "compulsion" or imperative like it. In that sense "need" and "solution" seemed to have been completely matched, like drinking when you're thirsty.

I was cured of the original "disease." Now I was suffering from the residual stigma of it being dubbed a "disease" in the first place. It's not just drugs that have side effects. Psychiatric classification is just as damaging. The "wrongness" didn't stop there, either. There seemed to be a schism in society too, between how people would describe me and how they would describe the label for people like me. If what I'd learned to date was supposed to be a scientific hypothesis to explain people of my kind, then it wasn't very good at predicting things in the way that a decent theory ought to be able to do! Things just didn't add up. No wonder I couldn't get comfortable. I was a bit slow realizing that scientists replace their hypotheses when they don't match the data.

A Conservative Lady

At first I sought peace in the pursuit of acceptance and assimilation. I became a Samaritan, learned the art of "active listening," and helped others find some answers from within themselves by asking remarkably little myself. I learned that dissonance comes in many wrappers, and that nobody was seemingly immune from anguish at some point or other in their life. It didn't solve my own dilemma, but at least I was rebuilding a new set of foundations for an ego that depended on being needed. There was something rather curious too in the sense of exploring, for the very first time, the sense of being "the one who's got it all together." I could see it in my fellow Samaritan volunteers too. Scratch the surface and everyone, every single one of them, seemed to be looking for some sort of answer. Perhaps learning to be professional and switch off our own feelings to listen to others was a means of temporary escape from questions that we couldn't answer for ourselves.

Now that I had a place and recognition among "nice people," the next stop on my journey was to seek out more mainstream forms of approval too. It was the time of the 1992 general election in the United Kingdom. My boyfriend at that time never missed a chance to poke fun at my "Conservative-voting" upbringing, so, in a rebellion of sorts, I volunteered to help my local party's campaign. A week after the election, however, the local branch secretary died suddenly from a heart attack and, before I knew it, I was suddenly stepping into his shoes. There it was again, that schism. These were people who later went on to prove that they had absorbed the same tabloid-trained ideas about transsexual people as I'd been taught from childhood. Yet without question they were pushing, *yes pushing* me to take up one of the most vital organizing roles at the center of their grassroots political activity. It was inexplicable. Flattering too, so I went along for the ride. After all, if these people instinctively liked me at first sight, then maybe I could find a way, through that, to like myself in the same way.

Other social acceptance roles followed—all thrust my way—never sought. A year later I had my arm twisted into becoming the chair of the Young Women's Supper Club. Three years of being branch secretary led to taking on the role of treasurer, then vice-chair. I cooked for fundraising events and canvassed on doorsteps as Conservative ladies do. Now and then people would ask if I'd like to stand for local government elections.

People seemed to see a very different person than the one I knew in the mirror, and the difference troubled me. Clearly they weren't wrong in what they saw and accepted, so what was wrong with me? What fueled my fear of completely letting go and accepting myself? Maybe I'd still be troubling myself over these questions, were it not for the fact that other activities began to take off at the same time . . .

Less Conservative Ideas

My very first piece of transgender activism dated back to mid-1990, a time when another trans woman, Caroline Cossey, came to general attention as the second of our kind to seek resolution for trans people's ambiguous legal position in the courts. Caroline's career as the model Tula had come unstuck in the way that was all too familiar—tabloid exposure. Her attempt to settle down as a married woman was undermined too by her

legal status in the United Kingdom as a male. Her position was the epitome of all trans people in the United Kingdom at that time: unable to
marry, no job security if "found out," vulnerable to blackmail and violence, no recourse when it happened, guaranteed a rough ride in the press
from the moment someone sold your "secret." And if all this could happen to such a beautiful woman as Caroline, these things clearly had nothing to do with looks or any other aspect of individual social acceptability.
If it could happen to her, then everything I had was presumably on limited lease from society too. I could never really feel safe in society until
society was made safe for me.

In 1990 I wrote a brief but poignant letter of support for Caroline to the
Guardian newspaper. As I said, it was my first campaigning act, but a timid
and limited one. I asked for my name to be withheld, otherwise I feared the
same experience as the woman I wanted to defend. It felt shameful to have
to hide this way. Still, what was the evidence in favor of doing otherwise?
This was the catch-22 situation. As trans people, we suffered from a whole
set of misconceptions about us. If one beautiful Caroline couldn't change
perceptions, what hope did the rest of us have? By coming out, we undermined what little basis we had for security and credibility. Whether I was a
Conservative association secretary or an IT consultant, people listened to
my ideas. Once known as "a transsexual" I was seemingly doomed to lose
those things, and then nobody would be able to hear what I had to say.

But by not coming out we simply colluded in our own oppression. How
could trans people be capable of holding serious places in society if you
never saw any of them doing so? And how credible is it to argue that you
are deserving of equality of opportunity if you're afraid to have that argument attached to your name? People in democracies like to see who and
what they are letting in. Change would not occur on its own—some sort
of activism was necessary to bring about that advance. Activists need
some sort of consensual power base from which to draw their authority,
and organized movements need visible leaders. But what happens if those
leaders then immediately lose their job, their financial security and tenuous
place in society? Was there a flaw in that feared argument? If not, it
seemed a hopelessly circular one, and timid anonymous letters of support
to mainstream newspapers (themselves one of the instruments of continued oppression) were going to achieve absolutely nothing.

So, at the same time as I was busy getting myself assimilated into mainstream society in pursuit of a slice of my own acceptance, the reasoning
through of these issues was also telling me that the thing I was building
had no foundations. An acceptance based on avoiding the fundamental
weakness of my legal position was no security at all.

Knowledge Is Power

I started getting interested in learning more about my legal position and attended the special medical and legal colloquy organized by the Council of Europe in Amsterdam in 1993. There I learned two things. First I discovered that there was knowledge and research about my situation, which was notably absent from the narratives I'd seen before. I'd learned how to view myself principally from the muddled half-truths and blatant misinformation peddled by a mainstream press with a social agenda of its own to pursue. If better and more accurate knowledge changed my thinking, therefore, what could it do for others? This later became one of my guiding aims when I began setting the ambitious goals for the website of the U.K. campaign group Press for Change.

The second revelation was that there were other trans people around the world asking similar questions, revisiting our history, relating our position and struggle to the examples of other excluded groups, applying basic theories of philosophy and human rights, and projecting our experiences and insights into the further evolution of dialogues in feminism and gender theory. I discovered a literature I'd never known about, and a basic consensus of thinking that was all the more remarkable because it had emerged along parallel lines around the world without all that much collaboration. It was all there for the taking. This was knowledge with the power to transform not only a trans person's view of themselves but also other people's perceptions of trans people. If the conventional medical model was like a drug with damaging side effects, this was the "alternative" herbal equivalent. What's more there were nontrans people in numbers who evidently understood some of this too. These were people who cared simply because they could see that something was wrong about the status quo. There were intellectuals worked up by the same basic wrong that I perceived too. The only difference was that I'd been scared of it. They saw it as a challenge.

Later that same year I flew over to America to see whether I could learn some more. I visited people I'd met in Amsterdam and stood in awe of the incredible achievements of some of them. I'd never met high-achieving trans people before. That wasn't in the script I'd been taught. At a conference held by the Harry Benjamin International Gender Dysphoria Association, which represents professionals working in the area of gender dysphoria, in New York that October, I saw how the intellectual equals of the psychiatrists were not prepared to simply sit and be patronized as delusional weirdos. I saw how another hugely feared and powerful edifice in the lives of trans people could be challenged if you simply stood up and said the philosophical equivalent of "boo" to it. This was starting to take shape.

Accepting the ghetto role we were given by society was the only thing that allowed the system to perpetuate. Our treatment was fundamentally wrong, simply on the basis of the facts, let alone any philosophical considerations. Challenging the oppression required people prepared to stand up and do so, yet people wouldn't do this until the fear of doing it was destroyed by others doing it first.

Press for Change

On returning to the United Kingdom I was invited to join Press for Change, an organization which at that point was so young and tiny that the first planning meeting I attended took place in someone's front room, over a shop in London's Golders Green.

I had the feeling that even those other campaigners looked on me a bit quizzically at first. What? A Conservative? The idea that I could be a trans person and actually work with and for the people at the center of our oppression was, admittedly, an odd contradiction. Still, if transsexuality doesn't define your sexuality, why should it define your politics? A few years later I did leave the Conservative party—another transition, another wrench involving the severing of personal relationships. But I moved on because both that party and I had evolved in different directions, on a whole range of economic and social issues.

At first I didn't have a specific brief in Press for Change, except perhaps to try to use my contacts in the Conservative party to lobby ministers. In this I was fortunate that my own member of Parliament (MP) was a privy councillor and about to become the chief whip in the government. This meant that top-ranking ministers very often came to our fundraising events, and I could catch them face-to-face over the smoked salmon sandwiches. It also meant that any issues raised through my MP would automatically get answered by the actual minister of state, rather than one of his juniors. That's the protocol. The first obstacle I had to come to terms with was "coming out" to my own MP, though. In the event this turned out to be far less traumatic than I expected, and Alastair and his wife Cecilia turned out to be extremely sympathetic (one might almost say "energetic") supporters.

So it was that I gradually began to break down my own fear of being "out," the fear that held the catch-22 cycle of oppression together for me. But coming out to a handful of well-educated politicians sworn to discretion is not the same as "being out" in the broadest sense. Getting to that stage took almost another eighteen months of confidence building.

The event that finally marked that stage came in the late summer of 1995, when Press for Change set out to organize so-called fringe meetings alongside the Labour and Conservative party annual conference events. By this point I accepted the notion that representatives of political lobbies have to be "out" in their dealings with the world, even if I felt scared stiff of the possible consequences. The idea of a "fringe" meeting is to get attention for the subject. You want the press. You want an audience. You want debate about the topics raised. To obtain those things, you also have to advertise in advance too. You have to issue press releases explaining the importance of the issues. You also have to explain who is going to be representing those points. In short, there is no ducking the connection between yourself and the subject matter!

Coming Out

Looking back now, it seems remarkable that, just seven years ago, such a prospect was still really terrifying. The night before the press release that would initiate that massive change in my life, I remember being physically sick. I'd already briefed key people in the local Conservative party about the event and myself. There was shock and surprise, but also something I hadn't expected: admiration and respect. It was stupid of me to think otherwise in hindsight, of course. Real politicians all need to face moments when their convictions are put on the line. I was simply another politician of sorts. The admiration was professional.

As the news spread and tabloids came looking for a reaction, I was quite unprepared for what followed. There was fear and concern among local party workers, of course. I was debated in my absence, and people were clearly grappling to resolve the difference between the nice woman they knew, and their stereotypes. They closed ranks in my defense, though. Even now I'm crying at the recollection of that experience. The newspapers had no story. And mysteriously, when it came to the actual fringe meetings themselves, those reporters who turned up expecting a laugh went away to write very little. It may have been years too early to write positively about the concept of trans people getting politically organized—even now most U.K. editors still prefer us as victims—but the next best thing is to write nothing at all. Just because you're not on the front page doesn't mean the important people haven't noticed you are there.

There were many political milestones that year, 1995. The groundbreaking case of *P* v. *S and Cornwall County Council* was heard in the European Court of Justice. The Liberal Democrat Home Affairs spokesman Alex (now Lord) Carlisle used his place in a private members' ballot to announce his plan to debate a possible bill in Parliament to change our legal status. The first exploratory meetings of a new Parliamentary Forum on Transsexuality were held. Things were changing. In fact, a barely reported meeting on the far edge of the annual political conferences may seem the least significant of these events. Nevertheless, on a personal level a line was crossed, from which there could be no turning back.

In case of misunderstandings, I need to say that this was not the first "coming out" of its kind. It wasn't even the first voluntary one. The subjects of high-profile court cases, people like Mark Rees and Caroline Cossey, had never had a choice. People like Press for Change founder Stephen Whittle had voluntarily appeared in television programs as a legal expert and trans man for some time. So had other trailblazers, like the immensely brave Julia Grant, more than ten years previously. Long before her, there was Jan Morris too. Although it was still a very rare thing to do, these pioneering people left me no excuse, had I thought of backsliding.

Having "come out" and found that the world did not fall in on me, the only way forward was onward and upward. The weak link in the catch-22 of trans activism was broken. It was no longer socially suicidal to thoroughly own my own condition and rejoice in a pride about it. People sometimes ask how I can talk of being trans and proud in the same breath. And, of course, there's no pride to be had simply in being who or what you are. I can't be proud that I've got blue eyes! The pride is in what you do with the cards you've been dealt. The achievement is in finding your way through the maze and turning the gypsy's curse into a gift.

Making Legal History

The rest, as they say, is history. It's a history you can read and research for yourself, because everything about the trans rights campaign in the United Kingdom has been proudly and publicly documented from that point forward on the website I started to create in 1996. The vision was simple: I wanted to facilitate the process of learning for others. Campaign-based websites of any kind were a rarity in those days. In practice, they contained little of any practical use. Once you'd read the contents, they ceased to be of value because they were rarely seen as a living, tangible embodiment of a movement. Trans-related websites were worse still. Those that existed in 1995 were mostly personal and essentially apologetic: "Here, look at me . . . I'm done up as best I can. Please say I'm acceptable and like me." There was nothing much on offer to reflect the things I'd seen on my travels. There was nothing to communicate the insights that were out there and were already firing up my own imagination to think about our position in a different way. If that information had so transformed my own thinking, what would happen if someone organized it for hundreds and thousands of trans people to read?

There was by now plenty coming out of the growing legally based campaign to provide news copy, analysis, and reference material. In 1996 "P" won her case in the European Court of Justice and brought employment protection to every trans person in Europe, via a new interpretation of the Equal Treatment Directive. Before long, other high-profile court cases in Europe (and later in the United Kingdom itself) were to be reported, each one requiring someone to be "out" to some extent to press a case for reform, and each one requiring journalists, lawmakers, and everyday people to think that bit harder about what we had to say.

In 1997 the landslide election of a Labour government opened new doors and led to the start of the first efforts at consultation between the U.K. government and its trans population. Where just two years previously we were a curiosity on the "fringe" of the Labour party conference, now we were suddenly invited to be an exhibitor within the heart of it. When high-profile cabinet ministers (even the prime minister's wife) stop by and pose with you for photos, something definitely has to alter in your perception of yourself and the world.

Things were hotting up all round. In 1998 two more trans women followed Caroline Cossey and Mark Rees to the European Court of Human Rights (ECHR), and came closer than ever before to an acknowledgment of the validity of their case to be legally recognized as their new gender. If just *one* judge had voted the other way . . .

In 1999 new law was enacted in Britain to formally incorporate the European judgment on employment protection into U.K. law. A new interdepartmental working group was set up by the then home secretary to start looking at the rest of trans people's complaints more seriously, and in early 2000 a handful of us sat and gave a presentation to officials from no fewer than twelve government departments in a meeting that, fittingly, seemed to mark the start of a new era. Six months later, those same officials published virtually every word we had said and written as the results of their research. This wasn't a snigger topic any more. This was serious review on a serious matter, the most significant advance for trans people in thirty years, and all because people were jumping up in increasing numbers from every direction and demanding that their position be looked at in terms of basic legal and social principles.

In June 2002, the ECHR in Strasbourg issued a unanimous verdict by no fewer than seventeen national judges that the treatment of trans citizens by the United Kingdom contravened two key articles of the European

Convention on Human Rights: Article 8—the right to privacy, and Article 12—the right to marry. It was such a landmark decision that the ramifications will be felt around the world for years to come and will affect far more groups than trans people alone.

Personal Transformation

I can't say that the rest of the personal transformation came overnight. Complete and fully integrated people take a lifetime to make, and I, like many, had some site clearance to undertake before building on new, rock-solid foundations. Each public advance has added something private too, and a lot of what I've learned and grown from stems from seeking out the shadows I fear and turning on the lights. As I've campaigned at higher and higher levels for change in the legal circumstances of the United Kingdom's trans people, as I've taught others new ways of seeing their position, and as I've recognized the regard that strangers have for our combined achievement, I grow and find myself wanting to own my part of that.

In case you think otherwise, this isn't a treatise about the need for every trans person to come out to the world, though. Press for Change has always believed in the rights of people to have their privacy and to choose if, when, and in what manner to "come out" to others. Court cases like that of the famous "P" have fought to retain anonymity for people when they wish for it, if only to create the means for others to use the law without losing their privacy in the process. Coming out to the world is far from obligatory. The only mandatory part is to come out to yourself.

There are parts of my own life where it would be superfluous to come out. Few people in my career as an IT consultant know anything these days about my past. Those who've learned about it tend to forget quite quickly too. The information isn't appropriate for the circumstances, and in that setting I continue to grow by seeking out other kinds of challenges, the things that scare me. I tackled new and difficult consultancy assignments, got promoted, ran for election to represent over eight thousand of my colleagues at board level in the company, criticized the chief executive's policies to his face, made enemies as well as friends, let go of the childish need to be approved of by everyone all the time. It seems that personal growth always involves some element of risk and overcoming your fears.

When people at work have seen me on the television or heard me on the radio or simply found my face and name all over the Internet's search engines, I learned to meet them with a smile. I gave them some reading material if they were at all interested, and I explained that I didn't take the campaign life to work, and vice versa. And that's the end of it. If they've gone on to say anything to others, then so what? Fear of that kind of exposure belongs with the outmoded belief that there was something "bad" about being who we are. The important thing is that I know I've done enough with my life to expect what people say to be a compliment.

A few days after the ECHR decision, a colleague remarked how different she felt walking down the road in her village. She said that she felt more confident, more of an accepted part of her community, and more able to see the friendly support of other people as something she deserved to receive. For me too, I already sense another shift in my language and self-awareness.

Two Transitions

This is why, looking back, I've come to realize, therefore, that there are those two transitions for people like ourselves to navigate on the road to completeness and peace. The first is not actually hard for some of us. All the difficulties in the physical transition (if you encounter them) tend to come from others. Nevertheless, the most that first transition could make of me on its own was a little girl in a big girl's body.

The second, more spiritual transition into maturity as a new woman or man is the harder one and is the least documented, because so many biographies seem to stop shortly after the subject's surgical transformation, as though there were no life from this point worth writing about. For that spiritual journey toward completeness, you first need to overcome your own fears and preconceptions. It's like a long-delayed process of maturing from a form of childhood into being a complete adult at last. Becoming a trans politician was my own way of making that journey. The milestones in my personal voyage are inextricably tied with the milestones we've achieved collectively. Every new advance in public and official understanding still provides me with a new aspect on my own self. And I'm genuinely amazed at times by the things I've found I could do.

So in the end I came to realize that the secret to seeing myself as others see me lies in altering a bit of both. I've set out to teach people what I see. I've grown from seeing them change, and in turn I've evolved that a bit more as well. Like the character in the short story, I had to learn to see the curse as a gift, and use the insights being offered. Maybe in this way the world and I will one day truly find ourselves seeing the same thing— I because that's what I see, and *they* because you and I transcribed it for them to read and understand.

AN OTHER-GENDERED BOY

Joe Samson

I MOVE IN THE SPACE BETWEEN GENDER. I have been "the other" for as long as I can remember. Looking back to my early days I can see the other-genderedness of me, but I couldn't really feel it until I was in my early twenties. I always felt different, but it wasn't clear to me what that difference was. I was born female and socialized as a girl. I grew up in a women's world of girls, schools, mothers, and aunts, but I never felt like a woman. I am in my late twenties now, and I identify as third gender and choose male pronouns over female ones. I have crafted myself a new name: Joseph Gerald Samson. My middle name honors my father, my last name honors my mother and grandmother, and my first name is all my own. What follows is some of my journey to becoming an other-gendered boy.

I was born in Vancouver, Canada, in 1973. I grew up with my mom and my older brothers. I loved to play piano, ride my bike, and read. If I remember correctly, I was a pretty happy kid most of the time. In retrospect I can see that I was often on the outside of the in crowd, but it didn't seem to bother me too much. I went to an all-girls private school until I was fourteen.

If there was one thing I understood about the people I was socialized with, it was that I was not like them on some fundamental level. I knew I wasn't a girl/woman as surely as I knew I couldn't be a boy. You know how sometimes you can know something on a cellular level, even if it is not articulated at the surface? That's how it was for me. I was not gender dysphoric exactly—I was just different, other. There was no strength in that, for me, not then. There was only doubt, a lack of self-confidence, and sadness. There was only an empty space where I thought I was supposed to be.

Are You a Boy or a Girl?

I remember being about six or so, in a restaurant, asking a waiter to take me to the bathroom. I followed him, and he opened the door to the men's room, and I was shocked because I'd never seen men peeing before. What I don't remember is what I said or did next. Just that moment flash-frozen. I remember being fourteen and working at the baseball stadium as one of those kids who goes around selling peanuts and popcorn and crackerjack. Someone in the stands called out as I walked by, "Hey, are you a boy or a girl?" And I was embarrassed and scared and I couldn't say anything. Couldn't find the strength to defend myself, to say I am what I am, no matter how confusing that might be. And I was the only girl working there that summer, and they told me the customers expected to see boys selling peanuts and popcorn, so I wouldn't be doing that anymore. They gave me hot dogs and soda instead, which required much more strength and endurance but made less money. Fuckers.

Aged fifteen, I had pictures of handsome, stylish boys at home on my walls. They were so appealing in so many ways. I wanted to be them and fuck them at the same time. Those boys on my wall were the only image I could find of what I wanted to become. But I knew I couldn't ever be that GQ magazine cover boy, because no GQ boy ever used to be a fat girl.

At the time I wanted to be with those boys as a woman. Later I would want to be with them as a boy—later still, as a woman again. Now I think of being with boys as a boy, and that sounds really hot, but so intimidating because it will never just be two guys fucking. I think of being with a guy as a woman, and I know that will never be easy because there will always be memory . . .

So, at seventeen I left home, came out angry, and became a dyke. I thought, well, at least I know now why I felt so different. I tried to manifest strength by putting the dyke identity on like an outfit. Tried to look tough, be tough. For a while my boy self was submerged. I had sex with boys then, too, but I never really connected with them. I was sexually wounded at sixteen, and I don't think I ever quite healed. I had been so much a girl then—let this guy lead me toward his ends, no power, no strength, no control. I think that somewhere I thought that being a woman was connected with being hurt like that. And it still has a hold on me. I felt none of that womanly pride in my body. This body was not sexy, not easy, not beautiful. Not even as a dyke.

It wasn't until I discovered my cock, my astral penis, that I could really own my sexiness. Discovering that I could actually feel my cock and balls and use them sexually was so liberating. I can fuck with that cock, beat off with it, own it, know it, and love it. And I came to love my cunt and my clit too. I have come to accept my breasts as best I can, even though they elicit stares and comments. For a while, though, I let people touch me in ways that were degrading. I did it because I didn't love or respect my body. I did it because being a fat girl, you take what you can get, even if it hurts.

Fat Power

Being fat was a kind of otherness too. Being fat shaped my life and my body. Developing into a woman-bodied person meant taking the visible form of woman. At thirteen, fatness and femaleness collided, squishing "me-ness" right out of the picture. Being fat meant having curves and hips and breasts, all of which were so visibly marking me as a woman even though I had never felt like one before. Now, even if I wanted to bind my breasts I can't because they don't make binders in my size. And top surgery for big boys is not as easy or pretty as it is for my smaller brothers. I have found other fat trannie boys, and we work on owning our fat boyness together. I was walking with my friend "T" back to the hotel and someone yelled, "Lose some weight, you fat faggots!" I was angry about the fat oppression piece of that comment, but I was also secretly proud to have been read as a fag and a fat fag at that. We joked about it later, about our fat faggot power . . . we owned it.

In my thinking I sometimes separate boyness and girlness, especially in my past, even though I know now that they are more connected than not. So up until my early twenties, the boyness was submerged and I passed as a girl, as a dyke. I passed and was unaware of this real, whole me that was just waiting to surface.

Since adolescence I have hesitated to dress in girl clothes because I feel distinctly uncomfortable in a skirt or dress. Sometimes I try that kind of femaleness on to see how it feels. Like going to a Halloween party in a tight black dress and big boots. This one woman could not get over the sight of me in this dress. She had to laugh and laugh and laugh. Many years later, I was wearing my girlfriend's beautiful long flowing blue skirt, so lovely. And the guy at the flea market says to her, "You should really buy your boyfriend some jeans!" We laughed about it together, laughing at what he didn't understand. I think of the girl clothes stashed in a box—lacy panties, black dress, black pumps . . . hidden away like a secret fetish.

My girlness is a secret sometimes, if only to me. The kind of femaleness that can move easily through the world is unreachable to me, just as the kind of easy confident maleness is beyond my grasp. And so I have stopped trying to stretch myself to fit into something. I don't expect to wake up one morning and step into femaleness like an outfit. I don't contort myself to fit into maleness either. Instead I am moving into that empty space; I am becoming the emergent me.

I grew up by becoming a part of dyke culture in Montreal. It was within that context that I began to really find myself and find my strength. Though I do not identify as a dyke or lesbian now, I do love women sexually and emotionally. There is something very unique about being with a person who is whole in her own identity as a woman. I feel most free in that context to be all of myself—my maleness and femaleness both present. What is also really nice about being with women is feeling like my own femaleness is validated and safe without having to lose any of my maleness. But what I really like are fat girls, girls with style for miles and a look that just commands my attention. I am so full of respect and admiration for all of the fat girls that are fighting really hard every day against size discrimination and fat oppression. There is a strong and vital link between trannie boys and fat girls, and it is powerful. We are all fighting for freedom together, and for what it is worth I throw my lot in with them; I stand beside them and behind them for all time. Truth be told, I think those fat girls who have come into their own are by far the hottest girls out there.

I am a fat, big-breasted boy. I have baby-carrying hips and a nice round belly. I have a handsome goatee but no sideburns (sigh). I am not currently on testosterone, though I do think about it from time to time. I see friends of mine who are on it, and I am envious of their deeper voices and sideburns. I have felt some pressure from within the trans community to be on testosterone and have surgery. Even among gender nonconformists there is a drive to conform to the still binary female-to-male continuum. Many people use hormones as a means to an end, to achieve passing maleness or femaleness. If I could, I'd rather use testosterone like an accessory. Even though its effects are not spontaneous, it might be interesting to be involved in that process. I'd like to see what kind of difference it would make to my gender presentation and my mind-set.

A Third Gender

I define myself as third gender, which for me means that I am between the poles of the spectrum. I am third because I am both male and female. Most of the time, I am content to be in between. I am not interested in becoming male, and I don't want to be on a conveyor belt in the trannie factory, moving from female to male. I don't want my differences to become invisible. When I went to my first trans conference, I did feel like an FTM. I felt like I had to get surgery and go on testosterone to be a real trans person. I know now that this is not true, though I think there are plenty of guys out there who think that way. There is a surprising number of folks in the trans community who have transgressed gender, but still want to fit into the box on the other side. Which is not to say all trans folk are like that—I know a few guys who have had surgery and been on testosterone but are not in the strictly male box. In order to have access to hormones and surgery, trans folks have to jump through a lot of hoops. They must be able to convince a therapist that they are on the track to living and being male. I think this bureaucracy makes it difficult to think of maleness as anything other than a goal. This paradigm of progression from female to male presents a view of gender that is like a river—flowing in one direction only. I propose that gender is much more like the ocean—large enough to contain many currents, channels, tides, and rhythms.

I don't think of testosterone or surgery as things that would change my gender, as much as they might alter my gender presentation. It would be easier sometimes to pass as male and move through the world that way, but I think I'd be missing out on a lot. It is a life-shaping experience to be between genders, and I wouldn't trade that for the world. I am other and I am a transgressor of the boundaries of preconceived gender.

I think this makes me well suited to work with children, which I hope to do professionally in the future. I will be attending school in the fall to complete my B.A. and teacher's certification, as I plan on being an elementary school teacher. I think it is really important for children to be in contact with positive and diverse role models, especially those who do gender in a subversive or transgressive way. Children need to see that there are people in the world who feel safe enough to be their true selves, even if those selves are not easily defined. The obstacles in my path are societal biases. I don't know yet how I will present myself in order to be hired. I know the kids won't care nearly as much as their parents. Kids can see more clearly sometimes than their adult counterparts and with less malice. Kids ask, "Are you a boy or a girl? A mommy or a daddy?" When I tell them that I am both or in between, they say "OK," and move on with acceptance.

When grown folk say, "Can I ask you a question?" I already know the shape of their inquiry . . . it will inevitably focus on my facial hair and from there onto my gender. It has been my policy that if they approach me with respect, I will answer and educate with respect. This has been mostly positive. People sure are curious though; I mean it seems to happen so frequently. Being other can mean being subject to stares, comments, and questions, and because of the status of other as outside the norms, people feel like there is no problem with asking pointed and sometimes inappropriate questions of me. Part of my process involves learning how to own my whole self and be strong. I am still learning to love and respect myself enough to get out of negative encounters. This part is still coming, still being forged. But I am so much closer now than I ever was before.

Bumper sticker: "The universe is much more expansive than our understanding of it." It's the same for gender. There is much more to gender than meets the eye or the mind. There is no point in compressing yourself into one box, or to confining yourself to one gender expression. Though it will certainly be difficult, you will ultimately be so much happier if you focus on just being yourself. Though this is not really talked about except in the context of anthropology, the truth is that there have been other differently gendered people across all cultures and across all times. The world needs people who can move in the space between, people who can bridge the gaps of understanding, bring evolved thinking into consciousness, bring being into reality. There is no shame in being different. If someone tries to tell you that there is, they're full of shit. They believe this because they don't understand how anyone could want to be different, because they are afraid of not conforming. But don't you be afraid—plant your feet, square your shoulders, look them straight in the eye, and tell them: "I am what I am."

MASKS AND REDEMPTIVE TRANSFORMATION

Jennifer Fraser

MY EXPERIENCE OF BEING TRANSGENDERED is of a constant tension between how I feel as a person and would like to relate to others, and the way others see me as a person and engage with me by virtue of the physical presentation of my body. When I gaze upon my body in the mirror or experience it in a tactile way, I do so with mixed feelings. I enjoy the feeling and image of my long hair brushing against my shoulders, but when I look at my face I still see the shadow of my facial hair just below the skin, no matter how recently, assiduously, and vigorously I have shaved, and if I touch my face, this shadow is revealed through the roughness of my skin.

In general I prefer not to gaze upon my naked body, but rather to see it and feel it in feminine clothing that suggests and enhances the swelling of my small breasts, caresses my skin, and completely hides my male genitalia. I would like to see myself and to be seen by others as a woman, but I feel betrayed by my body because it won't allow me to do so in unambiguous terms, and the world has a problem with gender ambiguity. I can't relate to people as in between male and female, because within the world around me there are only two categories, so I have to adapt by presenting myself as a man or a woman. I have difficulty with this, since I lack the body of a woman but I do not comfortably relate to the world as a man.

I suppose most of us experience some discomfort with our bodies at times. It might be overweight, unfit, old and tired, incapacitated, intoxicated, or insufficiently glamorous to facilitate what we wish to do or how we wish to relate to the world. In some instances, as in the world of the anorexic, this disjuncture may have tragic consequences. Tragedy haunts the world of the transgendered person as well. Although I seem to have avoided a range of self-destructive impulses that, according to many reports, are associated with transsexualism, I can clearly relate to how they might arise. For most of us, we do what we can through grooming, diet, exercise, clothing, and medical interventions to "fit in" and be what we want or need to be. We also largely learn to live with the limitations of what is possible and socially acceptable, with more or less good grace.

We are also open, however, to the possibility or perhaps the fantasy of what may be called the redemptive transformation. For instance, in the movie *Cat Ballou* Lee Marvin plays with comic mastery the part of the shambling, lurching, pot-bellied, drunken gunfighter.. His redemptive transformation takes place toward the end of the film (don't they always) when he sobers up, dons a corset, clean clothes, and a gun belt, and emerges as the epitome of lean, menacing masculinity to save the heroine from the gallows. As a transsexual person I have no desire to be menacing or masculine (although I'll go for a touch of lean), but I live in hope of transformation into a person who can relate to the world in terms of her femininity.

Different from the Rest

I was born a little over fifty years ago into a Catholic family and grew up in suburban Brisbane. Australia was a conservative place, and Brisbane was a conservative backwater. My first memory of feeling "different" from my peers in relation to gender was in my early years of school in the mid-1950s. I went to a Catholic primary school run by nuns. One of the threats they used against recalcitrant boys was that they would make them sit in the corner of the classroom wearing a girl's school uniform. In retrospect, this was just one of a range of empty threats that they employed. It never happened to anyone in my experience. In practice they maintained discipline using the more conventional techniques of the time—verbal humiliation and corporal punishment.

However, I believed them at the time, and my feelings about the prospect were a contradictory combination of fear of humiliation and intense curiosity about how it would feel not just to wear a dress but also to be seen by others as a girl, even if only in a daggy school uniform. Unlike the other boys, I experienced no feelings of revulsion, but I could not admit this to my classmates—and possibly not too loudly to myself either.

It was a few years later that I actually got to wear a dress. One rainy day I was playing dress-ups with my younger brother and sister. A neighbor had sent some clothes her daughter had outgrown. They were still too large for my sister but, as I found out, fitted me perfectly. I actually tried on several dresses that day. I only vaguely remember what they were like—cotton floral prints, skirts to around my knees, buttons up the back, so I needed help in putting them on, and at least one had a sash that tied behind the back. My memory of how it felt to wear a dress for the first time is much more vivid. It was a moment of sheer magic. When the buttons were done up the back and the sash tied, it felt right. For the first time I could tentatively but still clearly portray myself as a girl. I had expressed something that could no longer stay completely buried. I felt transformed.

It was not something my parents wanted to see. Although they indulged us that day, it was clear that they were not impressed. Soon afterwards any feminine items in my size disappeared from the dress-up collection. As far as I can tell, it was the first and last time my brother engaged in crossdressing. For me it was different. I could not forget the magic, and I could not really understand why others, my parents in particular, had a problem, but I learned shame and guilt in any case, although the magic stayed with me. From then on my crossdressing became furtive and opportunistic. Whatever I could borrow from the laundry when nobody else was home or when others were asleep, and girls' underwear under my "boy drag" were special secrets I could not share with the world.

I'm not sure what my parents knew. I was nearly caught a number of times, but I was never openly confronted with the issue. However, I'm sure my mother knew more than she let on. One day, for instance, she produced some plain cotton women's briefs in pastel colors with the story that she had bought them for herself but that they were too small. Since they were about my size and in her words "not too girlish," she asked me if I would wear them. I accepted them somewhat dispassionately and wore them until they became rags. Nothing more was said, and I'm not sure whether I passed a test or failed one. I was never given any item of clothing that was remotely feminine after that.

Most of my schooling was at a Catholic boys' school. I was not the sort of boy who stood out academically, although I was good at science, history, and English. Neither was I good at sports, particularly the team sports that were valued by the school. I was the subject of some bullying, but I also had a small group of friends with interests in science, music, and photography. I was always on the periphery of the elite. I suppose

I was something of a "nerd," but I expect that my experience was no more traumatic than average.

Since I went to an all-male school, I didn't really have any girls as friends except for a couple of neighbors, and I was not really interested in having "girlfriends" except in terms of wanting to "fit in." I was really more interested in friendship than sex. I joined in the adolescent boasting about sexual encounters with little conviction and feigned enthusiasm for the way girls were rarely evaluated by any other standard than their presumed capacity and willingness to satisfy male lust.

The Mask of Femininity

I remained a virgin until after I finished school. At that time I had many women as friends, but few sexual partners. Although I wondered if I was gay, I felt no sexual attraction to men. I had gay friends, and it would not have bothered me if I were. The main reason I wondered was that the only other men I knew that engaged in crossdressing were gay. However, I had no interest in "doing drag." Drag, to me, seemed to be a caricature of femininity, and often a vicious one at that. It focused on the wrapping— elaborate dresses, stiletto heels, wigs, gloves, and thick layers of pancake makeup. To me, it was a form of performance whose ultimate punch line was to expose the man beneath the mask of femininity, thereby demonstrating how clever the performer was in fooling his audience. I was not interested in impersonation. I had never met another transgendered person, so I felt a bit of a freak at times. There was just nobody I could talk to. On the whole, the problem seemed best buried, so that's what I tried to do. I hid behind my own mask, a mask of masculinity.

The first transsexual person I met was a friend at university who was FTM and was taking male hormones by the time we graduated. At university I was introduced to a broad range of feminist perspectives on gender, much of which argued that the relationship between sex and gender was an entirely arbitrary outcome of socialization and patriarchy. One implication was of a utopian vision of androgyny, a world without gender, where people could relate to each other in terms of their common humanity, and one half of the population would not oppress the other half on the basis of their possession of an appendage between their legs.

Although utopian visions may serve a useful purpose in defining and clarifying how we would like the world to be, they rarely suggest how we can transform the world of the present in terms of our utopian vision. Some suggestions of how this might be achieved through radical forms of reproductive technology and child raising struck me as the sort of nightmare explored by Aldous Huxley in *Brave New World*. Nevertheless, I suppose I saw androgyny as a personal possibility, and I continued to see myself as a feminist. However, I also came to understand gender as a complex intersection of biology and social circumstances. It is possible that I might have more critically reflected on my own sense of gender if I had not also met my current partner at university and married just after I completed my undergraduate studies.

My partner and I are soul mates. We became friends before we became lovers, and for my part the qualities I admired and respected in her were her assertiveness, intelligence, and empathy. The qualities she seems to value in me are intelligence, empathy, and I suppose some level of assertiveness, although on the whole she is more assertive than me. In a sense, our relationship seems to be based on a number of qualities on my part, which are usually understood as androgynous or even feminine, and some qualities on her part that are often understood in masculine terms. Nevertheless, we lived together in what would appear to others, and for most of the time to us, as a "normal" heterosexual marital relationship. We went on to undertake further study and pursue professional careers and establish households. For my part, I completed a doctorate in the social sciences in an area almost completely unrelated to gender and took up a university appointment. We went on to bring two children into the world. We have remained deeply committed to each other through enduring ties of friendship and love.

During this time my feminine side remained hidden from all but myself, finding expression through occasional crossdressing and fantasies involving various combinations of forced feminization, castration, and magical transformation. These seemed to be expressions of an irrational hope that the "problem" could be solved through some form of redemptive transformation by an external agency and thus absolve me of any responsibility for my perverse desires. For most of the time, these tensions were not a pressing issue. There were an abundance of work and social activities to occupy our time and emotional energy, and I felt no contradictions between my sense of gender identity and my expressions of sexuality. I wore a mask of masculinity, but I didn't really like the image that stared back from the mirror. My partner interpreted this as an irritating lack of vanity. I preferred to avert my gaze and feel what was beneath the mask—a person who was romantic, sentimental, sensual, and noncompetitive. It was a mask that could easily slip. On countless occasions I quickly dried the tears from my eyes when watching a romantic movie or listening to a beautiful piece of music.

The End of Denial

The beginning of the end of the period of denial started a few years ago, a little after the birth of our second child, when I was involved in a car accident. I lost control at high speed on a wet road. As it happened I was not injured, and the car was not even badly damaged, but the eternity of utter terror when the car was out of control and I avoided hitting the guardrails and other cars through sheer luck left a lasting impression. I could so easily have been killed. After that I suppose something inside me said that life is too short and precious to deny something that was so much a part of me. So Jenny was conceived. Shortly after that, I bought my own female clothes for the first time, shaved off the beard I had worn since before I was married, and within a very short time "came out" to my wife. I had started to shed the mask.

It might be nice to say that she took it all in her stride and took me shopping for a dress or two the following day. But this did not happen in real life. To say she was upset was an understatement. The revelation had come at a time when we were experiencing difficulties in our relationship associated with moving, having children, her career, and the fact that I was too preoccupied with my own problems to offer her sufficient empathy and support. It was not a good time to load her with an extra piece of baggage, but I felt I had no choice because maintaining a deception gave me more grief than I could bear. Her feelings were of anger and betrayal that I had not told her long ago; she felt that it reflected negatively on her own femininity and sexuality and was concerned at the impact it would have on our lives and those of our children. There is no denying the legitimacy of these feelings.

To the extent that I have come to terms with my sense of gender identity, I have done so through reading and engaging in dialogue. The Internet has been a mixed blessing. There is a wealth of information out there, but of variable quality, and it's really no substitute for face-to-face dialogue. The main problem in this respect is that I live in a small regional center where opportunities to contact people within the gender community are hard to find. In the past I attended meetings of a crossdressers' support group. Unfortunately this just taught me that I had little in common with the others and left me more confused. More recently I have attended meetings of a transsexual support group. I felt I had a lot more in common here, but there are still a few problems. The first one is logistical. There is a two-hour drive there and back, and often I just don't have the time, even if I want to attend. The other issue is that my circumstances still seem to be quite distinctive. It seems that some transsexuals are unable to maintain their pretransition relationships, whereas my partner and I are deeply committed to maintaining our relationship.

The other members of the support group either don't have a partner or have separated or divorced from their partner. Generally they implied that I would need to choose between transition to my "authentic" gendered self and maintaining the relationships I have with my partner and children. My partner and I are in a committed relationship that is integral to who we are. It is obvious that this relationship would need to be reworked and renegotiated in the light of changing circumstances, but this applies to a broad range of changing circumstances. Abandonment, however, was never an option. To me, my relationships to my significant others are an integral part of my "authentic self," but we have not found a model of how maintaining these relationships while going through transition has been achieved by others.

The most important dialogue has been with my partner, but this has also been the most difficult because it does involve a renegotiation of our relationship. This has been possible, I believe, because we have never felt bound to conventional gendered roles, and such conventions are not at the core of our relationship. However, the nature of the changed circumstances around which this renegotiation is taking place has taken time to be understood by both of us. When I "came out" to my partner, I did so as a crossdresser because that's the model I drew upon in understanding my previous behavior, but since that time my understanding has shifted, and this has made the process of renegotiation more difficult and stressful. I had a long history of denial to unravel.

Denial doesn't just disappear, and the biggest part of the process of denial is that we lie to ourselves even more than to others, and it is built layer upon layer. It also abates layer by layer. It was easier to tell myself and my partner that I was a crossdresser than to admit the possibility that my core gender identity is feminine. As a consequence, she tends to still see my gender expression as a "hobby" to be tolerated, to be kept in its place, but not encouraged. The problem is that, although there may be a small element of truth here, particularly in the past, in that I have gone through a process of experimentation in finding the means of expressing my gendered self, it is a feminine gendered self that is finding expression as my own understanding has shifted and changed.

I believe that we have both come to the recognition that my gender identity is largely feminine. In coming to terms with this, my partner has gone through a process of grieving. Issues of my gender expression still cause her some discomfort, and her acceptance is still provisional and circumscribed. She still resents my buying female clothes. On the other hand, she still will tell me if something looks good on me, and she has assisted with hair styling and makeup. She has contributed immensely to the early stages of development of my own sense of style. However, her acceptance doesn't go to the point of buying me an overtly feminine item of clothing or jewelry. For my part, this is a form of recognition that I would value immensely, but at this stage she is not ready to make that step.

An additional concern she expresses is that I am too preoccupied with gender and that it would be better to put the issue behind me and move on. Again, I think there is a major element of truth in this. Perhaps such an obsession is in the very nature of being a transsexual. For a woman or a man whose sense of gender is congruent with their biological sex, most of the time their sense of gender identity is called into question by neither themselves nor others. For a transsexual, the relationship between sex and gender remains open to questioning. When I speak to a stranger on the telephone and am read as a woman, I feel good. When I am addressed as "sir," however, I understand that people are being polite, but I still feel a little sadness and a sharp reminder of the insecurity of my gender identity. Perhaps there is also the additional issue that many people have to deal with of going through a phase of self-consciousness about their expression of their gendered self during adolescence with a great deal of peer support. But for a transsexual this takes place during transition in a much less supportive set of circumstances. Even though I have a supportive spouse, my limited contact with other transsexuals makes things rather lonely at times. This makes it rather difficult to "move on."

At the moment, I express my feminine gender identity as much as possible short of irreversible transition. I already naturally have a somewhat feminine body, long hair, soft skin, and small breasts, which have perhaps been enhanced by taking low doses of herbal estrogens. I have taken an epilator to what little body hair I have. I get sore nipples in cold weather, so I usually wear a light bra or crop top to flatten my boobs and keep them warm. I wear dresses and skirts when the kids are out or asleep. At other times I wear androgynous women's clothes mostly—T-shirts, drawstring pants, fairly plain blouses, overshirts, overalls. I no longer wear any male underwear. My voice is soft, and I am usually "read" as a woman by strangers (and some acquaintances) on the phone. This has been an outcome of gradually shifting boundaries, not really in a deliberate way, but more in terms of seeking a comfort zone that masks or de-emphasizes the masculinity of my body and gives expression to my feminine spirit in a way that is still more or less acceptable to those around me. The evidence is obvious enough for those who want to see which side the buttons are on. On the other hand, if people don't want to know, they don't have to see.

A university is a fairly liberal workplace, particularly in the arts and social sciences departments. A number of my colleagues are bisexual or gay, and I suppose here I'm no more unconventional than average. One of my work colleagues remarked that I looked a bit like a "lesbian feminist." I took it as a compliment, even if that was not the intention. In the broader community, people either don't notice or don't care. I have no illusions that nobody notices, particularly the kids, but I suppose there's a sort of "plausible denial" going on.

What to Do Next?

It hasn't been easy, but my partner and I have stayed together and probably have a stronger relationship now than ever in the past. What to do is another matter entirely. There is no model to follow. The key problem is how all this will affect our children, particularly their relationships with their peers. In terms of gender identity, the major problem is that I am caught in the contradictory tension between two sets of imperatives—the need that I deeply feel to identify myself within the world in terms of a gender identity which is more feminine than masculine, and the similarly vital need for the love, respect, and companionship of my partner and my children. If I was in a position to deal with the first issue unencumbered by the second set of considerations, the path I would seek to pursue would involve having my ears pierced, removing my facial hair with electrolysis or laser treatment, taking hormones, and going on to live full-time as a woman. It would possibly but not necessarily involve sex reassignment surgery. If I were in a position to deal with relationships with my significant others unencumbered by the gender considerations, it would involve expressing a more masculine public persona.

However, both scenarios are entirely hypothetical because they do nothing toward resolving, or at least easing, the contradiction. To seek a resolution I need to consider the relationship between my sense of gender identity and how I see and experience my body. To me, the most glaring disjunctures are, in decreasing priority, facial hair, which, because of my combination of hair and skin tones, still leaves a fairly obvious shadow even after close shaving; although I have small breasts, I am still overweight and lack feminine waist and hips; and finally I possess male genitalia.

I am dealing with the issue of body weight through diet and exercise, although I am concerned that I may lose weight in the wrong place, particularly my breasts. To some extent I can deal with my body shape and bulge between the legs by the clothing I wear, such as dresses and skirts and underwear that does some judicious reshaping. Facial hair is rather more difficult because I dislike heavy makeup. It feels like "doing drag," and it's a temporary solution in any case. On the whole, the facial hair is more of a constant irritation than anything else because I see it every time I look in the mirror, feel it every time I touch my face, and find shaving an ongoing burden. To me it is a manifestation of the mask of masculinity that has brought me so much grief. The other things don't so constantly and obviously draw attention to themselves.

The strategy that this suggests is to deal with the facial hair as a first priority, possibly through laser treatment, and have my ears pierced as well. The former would certainly deal with the constant tedium of shaving and is, in itself, an androgynous rather than overtly feminine intervention. It would, however, mean that my gender presentation would be much more defined by hair, clothing, jewelry, makeup, and bodily expression. As a second priority, judicious use of hormones might be considered to soften my skin and redistribute some body fat in a more feminine way. The option of SRS would not be pursued. This is not, to me, the path to redemptive transformation. My transsexualism is not a disease to be subjected to surgical treatment, but an integral part of me and, as such, something I have to live with.

I expect that if the boundaries were thus pushed beyond androgynous, few people who matter would be particularly surprised, but I would still be in a position to present myself in an androgynous way. SRS would not suit my partner, and I don't think it's necessary to make me a woman. I already am one. In the future I would like to express this more obviously in public. But what's between my legs is private. Whatever I do, however, I do with my significant others.

I'm not sure what broader lessons can be learned from my experiences. My greatest fears and anxieties about how the world would treat me as a publicly transgendered person have not materialized so far. Perhaps I'm fortunate or a little unobservant, but I have not suffered humiliation or ostracism because I present myself in an unconventionally gendered way. Other issues seem more important to people. I suppose if someone dislikes me, my transgenderism may provide a convenient pretext for vilification, but I'm also a "hippie," a "greenie," and to the left politically, so this is just one of a range of available choices. If people like me, they like me for who I am. Of course, I don't seek confrontation, nor do I generally associate with people who are likely to be particularly hostile to alternative forms of gender expression, irrespective of my own gender identity.

Although I have altered the packaging somewhat, the person underneath has not changed very much. I can't judge whether I'm better, worse, or just different: that's up to others.

Perhaps we live in a more tolerant society, where alternative expressions of gender and sexuality have moved from the closet to at least the edge of the mainstream. It is certainly the case that the social world I live in now is very different from the one of my childhood or adolescence that spawned the fears and anxieties that I have found so difficult to overcome. However, sexuality and gender are different matters. Sexuality is not necessarily and constantly expressed in public. Gender is, and as long as it is understood as a binary divide, it will never be easy to live as a transgendered person. We will seek invisibility. The day when I fill out a census form and there are more than two boxes to tick when we are asked to identify our gender is the day when I might really believe that the most important form of redemptive transformation is beginning to take place. In the meantime I have a life to lead, so I'm not holding my breath.

RIKKI'S STORY

Rikki Arundel

NERVOUSLY I ENTERED THE MEETING ROOM. Around fifty people, all experienced members of Toastmasters International, were chatting in small groups. A few people glanced my way and smiled as I walked in, but said nothing. This was strange—nearly everyone in the room knew me, though they had not seen me for a year.

However, they knew me as a rather overweight middle-aged businessman in a suit, with short, graying hair. Now my hair was quite long and dark, I had lost thirty pounds, and my face looked more late thirties than early fifties. And I was definitely not wearing a business suit. I approached a couple of very familiar faces and said hi. They glanced at me and responded—then stopped—looked again, a slightly puzzled look on their faces as their memories searched to place this oddly familiar face—then— a stunned look of surprise as realization dawned.

I purposefully kept my introductions to a small number of people, to enhance the impact I would later make—this was the area final of the 2002 Toastmasters International speech contest, and I had a very special speech lined up. I drew first to speak in the contest and, introduced by my new name, Rikki, and dressed in bootleg jeans, a distinctly feminine top, denim jacket, high-heeled boots, and a faint but noticeable touch of makeup, I walked to the podium.

> Mr. Contest Chairman, Ladies, and Gentlemen,
> Some of you might be wondering about my appearance this evening.
> Odd isn't it, had you met me thirty years ago, I would have been
> dressed in a similar way, but I doubt if you would have noticed then,

because in the early seventies you would probably have been wearing much the same.

But this is not about me trying to recapture my youth. My androgynous appearance today is the result of me deciding that I no longer wish to hide who I am, because I am transgender . . .

For the next seven minutes, I told my story. It was not the scariest thing I had ever done in my life, but it was close. And most of the scary events of my life have all taken place since December 14, 2001, which had been my first public coming out, but let me go back and recount what brought me here.

I was born in Malta in 1950, the eldest of four children, but have lived in the United Kingdom most of my life. I'm of Yorkshire stock (I can trace my Arundel family name back to 1700 in Yorkshire), but until last year I lived in or near London. Then, on the breakup of a ten-year relationship, I moved to the north of England, and apart from the cold, I am really enjoying living here.

Discovering My "Secret"

My father was a man's man. When I was born, he was a chief petty officer in the Fleet Air Arm and had played an active role in the sinking of the *Bismarck* during the Second World War. Oddly he had wanted his firstborn to be a girl, partly because his older sister had pretty much looked after him as a child, and as he and my mother planned to have four children, he figured that an older daughter would act as his sister had. Though I never knew about this till much later, what I saw as his obvious preference for my two younger sisters was something I used to attribute as the reason for my secret.

It's difficult to remember the first event—I was probably about five or six playing dress-up with my brother and sisters—we had a huge attic and a dressing-up box. I recall being rebuked and humiliated for clonking around in a fox fur and a pair of my mother's high-heeled shoes, as my sisters so often did. The socialization process had begun in earnest. I had reached the age where it was odd or embarrassing for a boy to be effeminate, and I now needed to learn to be a man. Boys don't cry; boys are handsome not pretty; boys shake their dad's hand, they don't hug and kiss. Throughout my early life I became more and more bitter that the girls were treated better than me, and could not understand why they thought I got the better deal.

Then I discovered my secret—I was looking for a pair of underpants in my drawer when I came across something unexpected: white cotton panties with a nice pattern and delicate lace trim—what made me put them on I will never know—but the feeling I got from doing so was breathtaking. I knew this was wrong, but how could something so nice be wrong? I hid them, and so started the first of many wardrobes. Bit by bit I accumulated stockings, suspenders, skirts, jumpers, and eventually even a bra. I did not try to understand this—as I grew older, the erotic arousal from wearing these clothes increased, as did my guilt and fear of discovery.

The Terrifying Fear of Being Caught

Then one day it happened. I was not yet a teenager, and at the time we lived in a pub, so my parents were usually very busy at night. I used to get away from my siblings by shutting myself in a little-used sitting room listening to Radio Luxembourg—the only pop radio station available in the United Kingdom in the early 1960s. I could also wear some of my secret collection under my other clothes, and one day I found a skirt and tried it on over my jeans.

I had just put it on when my father came looking for me. I could not undo the button, so in panic I rolled up the skirt so that my long jumper covered it, but then I had to go outside with him. Then my brother saw a bit of the skirt hanging down at the back. I ran in panic, locked myself in a toilet and removed the skirt, throwing it out the window, but the little bastard would not give up—he had already rallied my sisters. They found the skirt and reported to my mother.

I stammered through some completely implausible excuse about wanting it as a duster, which seemed to be believed, and nothing more was ever said about the incident, but the fear—no, the terror—of that moment has never gone. It's difficult to explain to anyone who is not transgender what it feels like to face discovery. The social pressure for me to be masculine was so great that I lived my life in constant fear of any sign that might have given me away. And back then I had no idea that there were other people who felt the way I did.

It was not till my late teens that I discovered the term *transvestite* and saw a picture of someone who was very definitely a "bloke in frock." Now while that helped me to know I was not alone, it did not make me feel any better. The derogatory comments made by my friends who were with me at the time confirmed that this was something I could never reveal. And so I buried my secret deeper and deeper, often managing to deny the feelings for years.

A Lifelong Passion for the Performing Arts

Encouraged by my father, I began to pursue an educational program that would lead me to follow in his footsteps and become an engineer, as I was good at maths. It was a mistake—sciences and technology, though fascinating topics, were not subjects I enjoyed studying, and I flunked most of my exams. I persuaded my father to let me have one more year when I switched to social sciences. That year, 1968–1969, was one of the best years of my life. Now in my third year at college, I was quite well known, and with a friend plotted to bring the college up-to-date by holding its first ever rag week (a fund-raising program of stunts, parades, and entertainment organized by students). While sitting talking to him in the canteen about this, a stunningly beautiful girl I really fancied walked in.

I made a typically masculine comment about her breasts, to which he responded, "You should see her in her underwear." He explained that the college drama group put on a Shakespeare play every year and that she was in the group—and there was only one dressing room. I immediately auditioned for the play and discovered a talent. I got a big part in the play—Marc Anthony in *Julius Caesar*—but there was a catch. I had to take extra drama classes. In fact, I discovered that the entire drama course coincided with all my free periods, and so began my lifelong passion with performing, and a great cover for my secret. Now I could learn all about makeup without fear, and got to play dress-ups.

The previous summer vacation I had spent the season at a Butlin's holiday camp working the bars, so as my final year at college ended, I returned to Butlin's, but this time on the entertainment staff, known as Red Coats. I had applied for university and auditioned for drama college, but although I passed all my exams, I did not do well enough and found myself at a crossroads.

The First Disclosure of My Secret

I decided to pack my bags and head for London and, taking the advice of a friend, got a job to tide me over while I figured out what to do. I joined the insurance industry, and a new and completely unplanned phase of life began that would last for thirty years. Crossdressing was less of an issue at this time. It was 1969, and I was a bit of a hippie, dressed at weekends in flared trousers, gypsy and tie-dyed tops, and high heeled boots—an interesting contrast to the suited appearance in my job as a mortgages clerk, where they reluctantly accepted my shoulder-length hair as a sign of the times.

Living in a flat with a friend had also made it pretty much impossible to keep a femme wardrobe, so when I met and began living with the woman who would become my wife, I found myself for the first time with access to an Aladdin's Cave of feminine clothing, most of which fitted me. I could not resist and began crossdressing again in secret.

Then she disclosed a fantasy about dressing me up. I had never told anyone about my secret. A mixture of terror and excitement swept over me. Should I tell her? Would she reject me? I so wanted to play this fantasy, but did not want to appear too enthusiastic, so at first I resisted. That proved to be the right decision, as her fantasy required resistance. We had a lot of fun, but now I faced the agonizing decision that every trans person faces when they enter a long-term relationship. Do I tell her my secret?

We had entered the glam rock era with David Bowie's *Ziggy Stardust* and the *Rocky Horror Show,* and I should have been able to come out safely, but the fear was so deeply rooted from my childhood that I started to tell her I had a dark secret, but could not bring myself to tell her what. Fear of rejection and ridicule is a powerful fear. Now of course, she wanted to know what it was and kept on at me for weeks. She began to have visions of me as a secret ax murderer or worse. Knowing there was a secret was undermining the relationship, and so finally, and requiring more courage than anything I had done in my life, I told her. "Oh, is that all?" she said, almost disappointed. It was an anticlimax, but there was also no enthusiasm to repeat our dressing-up game. When we went to David Bowie concerts, there was no encouragement to glam up, and I still did not have the courage to do it.

Caught Again

My crossdressing remained in the closet, with me grabbing odd opportunities when I could—the best was a couple of days off work with flu or a gastric bug. It was on one such occasion that my partner unexpectedly came home from work early. Suddenly I was very glad I had told her, because although she was uncomfortable with it, it opened the door for me to dress at home more openly. It was tolerated, even though she had no desire to participate, and when I started to go out dressed, she became increasingly nervous about it and would not accompany me. Unfortunately it didn't last long. A new job with another insurance company demanded a more conservative look. In 1974 we married and soon were expecting the arrival of our first child. We moved from London to a nice middle-class area in a small market town, and crossdressing in front of our son was banned. I was firmly back in the closet.

Years Passed

Over the next ten years I rose to the position of head of marketing for a major financial services organization and rediscovered my performing skills through public speaking to become one of the best-known speakers in my industry. On the home front, our family expanded with the addition of another son and a daughter, and we steadily climbed the property ladder to find ourselves living in a beautiful village in a comfortable executive home.

But the price was high. Throughout that time, my crossdressing had followed the path of so many others. The desire to crossdress came in waves, then after a flurry of secret dressing, receded again. On more than one occasion, guilt and disgust with myself led to entire wardrobes finding their way to charity shops—thousands of pounds' worth of clothes and shoes literally thrown away in an attempt to purge myself of this "curse."

At the same time, the overwhelming pressure to succeed and be the stereotypical male provider was telling on my marriage. Men are fundamentally competitive and enjoy the cut and thrust of the business battle. I did not; I could not stand the boardroom and senior management politics. Was there something wrong with me? I had never played team sports or even watched them, and I was not comfortable in the jocular and sexist male camaraderie in the bars after work. I had always been drawn to creative work—writing, speaking, performing, and networking with people. Having to hire and fire, and spend all my time in competitive management was not fun.

The stress was burning me out, and I turned to crossdressing for relief. The combination of working late and then pretending I was working late when actually I was out in my car dressed or wandering around dark empty streets at night was too much for my marriage to bear, and it failed—slowly and painfully.

Cursed: Dealing with Feelings of Guilt and Disgust

I began to see a pattern with my crossdressing: when my life and relationships were not going well, the desire to crossdress increased. I began to associate crossdressing with being unhappy. It was like an antidepression drug—if I felt stressed, I could go away and dress as a woman, and that made me feel OK. But it was always an erotic experience. After I had masturbated, it culminated in my experiencing immense feelings of guilt and disgust, and I immediately had to divest myself of all the clothes and makeup. The desire to dress was at its greatest whenever I was alone, and

I could seldom spend a few days on my own without dressing. It was a curse that I could not rid myself of.

As my marriage failed, I began looking for new relationships to protect myself from this curse. There is a strange aspect here—I have always got on well with women, much better than I do with men. I can listen to them and talk for hours; I can chat over the phone forever. My interest in literary subjects and my ability to tell poems in an entertaining manner captivate them. I have a strong interest in alternative health and I was shifting toward vegetarianism. I had always been a fan of personal development courses and the esoteric. These are strong feminine interests, and attending the courses meant I would meet a lot of interesting women. But despite all those feminine qualities, I was an attractive, successful man and so appeared to be "a good catch," and I soon found myself in a new relationship in which I hoped I would find greater acceptance.

I Am Not a Man: Neither Am I a Woman

But being transgender is not just about clothes. We now know that male and female brains are biologically different, and I had a female brain in a male body. This is not easy for women to come to terms with. Most seem instinctively to want someone to take care of them. They love the idea of a man who is in touch with his feminine side, but most also want a man to protect and provide for them. It took me the next ten years and two more broken relationships to understand this, and to understand that I am not a man. But I am also not a woman.

More than anything else throughout the 1990s, I explored my feminine qualities, and although I disclosed my crossdressing, partners did not want me to openly dress in front of them or their children. I had another daughter with my first partner, and the second had two of her own daughters, so I stayed in the closet.

I got out of the rat race and became a self-employed marketing and public relations consultant, and developed my skills as a speaker and journalist. In 1999 with a few friends, I founded the Professional Speakers Association in Europe, becoming its first president and significantly raising my business profile within the global speaking industry. But because I put so much effort into voluntary work, I was a disaster financially. I proved not to be able to provide the essential security my partner was looking for. She had left her strong, dependable, and financially secure husband to be with me and felt she had wasted ten years, so during the painful separation, she threatened to tell the world my secret. I have never felt so much fear and panic.

Facing My Greatest Fear and Coming Out

That threat was, I believe, a final attempt to rescue the relationship and shock me into being the man she thought I should be. It didn't work, and I was now truly on my own for the first time in my life. But I could no longer live with that fear—I had to face it and come out.

The first step, I decided, was to visit some of the transgender clubs I had found on the Internet. So, on a trip to Manchester for work I decided to visit the Northern Concord Club in the gay village. I walked up and down the street outside the club for about an hour, but the sight of the burly security guy on the door scared me, and I bottled out. In September I decided to try the Way Out Club in London. My makeup skills had been improving, and I had a nice new outfit, but I still sat in the car outside for an hour before finally plucking up the courage to go in. I had a great night chatting with other trannies, and I discovered I really did need a new wardrobe, makeup lessons, and to lose a lot of weight.

December 2000 was the first significant turning point for me. I decided to go to the launch of a new club, the House of Drag in London, and booked a makeover that evening with a TG dressing service in London. This resulted in an important tool: a picture of me looking fabulous—a bit strongly made up, but good enough that most people seeing the picture saw a woman, and no one recognized it as me.

I work mostly from home, and because I was now dressed in female clothes most of the time at home, I was nearly caught a number of times by a friend who regularly popped in unannounced. Time to tell her. Over coffee I said, "I want you to see something." I pulled out the picture from my wallet and passed it to her.

"Who is she—a new lady in your life?" she said, her eyes lighting up.

"Sort of," I said. "It's me."

"Shit! You look stunning," she replied. She looked from me to the picture a few times, and then said, "You look better than me, you bitch!"

We laughed, my fear disappeared, and I explained everything. She thought it was great, and our friendship changed, there and then. She began to treat me differently, almost as if she were having coffee with a girlfriend. The male/female barrier had come down and I became more comfortable just being me for the first time in my life.

I had planned Christmas alone that year, happy to dress up and be a woman for the day, but my friend was having none of it. She insisted that she would pick me up after lunch—I still wanted my vegetarian meal—and I would spend the afternoon and evening with her and her husband—dressed. She had already told him. I started to panic again.

Though she had seen the picture and had seen me wearing some feminine clothes around the house, she was visibly impressed at my appearance when she arrived, and could not stop telling me how stunned her husband would be—I was in panic mode again. We walked out to get into her car. "Oh," she said. "I walked—I thought we could have a nice walk back through the village." I could not believe she had done this to me. I had never walked around near my home in broad daylight before. With a mixture of fear and excitement, off we went. She was right—her husband was stunned. The day was like a dream fantasy come true—I was being treated as a woman, as if it was the most normal thing in the world.

It's Not a Curse, It's a Blessing

Throughout 2001 I became more and more confident: shopping became easier as I became less and less concerned about what people thought, I went to clubs regularly and improved my appearance. I started wearing rather androgynous clothes out and about and letting my hair grow longer, and finally began to experiment with some color to hide the gray.

More important, I was allowing the woman inside free expression, and instead of fear, I was experiencing exhilaration. Women were opening up to me and sharing their feelings in a way they had never done before, and I was changing inside as a result—it was as if my inner instincts were overriding fifty years of male social conditioning. As my confidence grew, I decided to take an even bigger leap and come out in my business life.

Every December my biggest client, who had employed me every month as a professional speaker for ten years, held a fancy dress party. Lots of guys did this event in drag, but I was always too scared. In 2001 the company had been taken over, and lots of people were leaving. So it was the last party; past staff were invited back, and the theme was to be pantomime. I planned to go as Snow White's wicked stepmother. Then there was a change of plan—the party would not be fancy dress, it would be black tie.

My work for the company was very high profile as chairman of eight conferences a year and lots of other speaking and PR functions. I worked closely with the meeting planner and we had become good friends, so I decided to come out to her and tell her I was still planning to go dressed. "Great," she said. She had noticed traces of eyeliner and nail polish in the past, so was not surprised. And I had thought it was a secret. I agreed to perform a few humorous poems as entertainment for the evening—especially as I was not just going dressed—I was going to wear a dress that I knew stops traffic. This would be my official "Coming Out Party."

The Coming Out Party

Friday, December 14, arrived. I wanted this to be flawless—if the world was going to know I am transgender, they would also add, "And she/he looked fantastic." So, I added a makeup lesson, nail extensions, and new wig to complement my stunning black and silver sequined dress and diamante jewelry.

My arrival was announced, and when I entered there was a cheer and applause, but most people thought I was just another tall girl from the company. When I began to speak, I could see and hear the jaws hit the floor. When I finished my first poem there was a stunned silence. "You can applaud," I said, to get them out of the shock.

The rest of the night was one of the best I have ever experienced—the first time I had been at a straight event dressed, and with people I have known for years. I got lots of excited congratulations, especially from the women, including comments like "You make a better-looking woman than a man" or "You even dance like a woman."

The sequined dress was hot and heavy, and eventually I had to get changed. There were some disappointed appeals for me not to from some of the girls as I left, but when I returned in an off-the-shoulder floor-length glittering black evening dress, the jaws dropped for a second time. "When you said you were going to get changed, we thought you meant into a dinner jacket," people said. I realized now that not everyone could handle this, and for the rest of the evening a noticeable few—mostly men—were clearly uncomfortable and have never spoken to me again. Others, mostly women, were thrilled, and I danced the night away as one of the girls, simply accepted as one of them as the barriers came down and conversations became more personal, with lots of hugs, giggling, and laughter. I have seldom felt so good, and I never want to attend a black-tie function in a dinner jacket again as long as I live.

Living as a Woman

That day also had another significance. The nail extensions were not temporary—I had decided to take a month off work and live as a woman over the whole of Christmas and the New Year holiday. I had my ears pierced the next day and packed away all my male clothes. I had to know what this all meant to me—a month of facing the world every day, of having to go shopping as a woman, of being read and getting comments—even, as it turned out, having to attend a business meeting.

At the end of January, when I had to revert to male mode, I knew the truth—I hated going back. So although I still do work presenting a male image from time to time, I decided to become openly transgender: my hair has continued to grow and change color, and I am increasingly taking steps to feminize my appearance. I adopted an androgynous name, Rikki, which works however I present myself, and increasingly attend business functions presenting a female image, including an insurance industry gala dinner where I am considered a minor celebrity.

But there is a downside. Being transgender is not socially acceptable yet, and my business has slumped. I have to shift my focus completely. Writing is becoming more important as a source of income, as is entertaining, and I am developing a drag act. I am studying gender issues and capitalizing on the fact that as a trans person I have a unique understanding of male and female communications.

More important, there are very few openly trans people in business, or even the performing arts—I have found only a handful of openly transgender speakers, entertainers, and writers anywhere in the world. That indicates the huge challenge ahead. So few people have ever met someone knowing them to be transgender. And the people I meet every day just jump at the chance to ask questions and understand. In the two years now since I started coming out, I have not had one single unpleasant experience.

I have told all my friends and family and have even been clubbing with some of them. Some of my friends were almost hurt that I had never told them before. Financially, coming out has made this the worst time of my life, but emotionally it has been the happiest. My daughter summed up the way life is for me now when she said recently, "Dad, I have never seen you look so happy in all my life—and can I borrow this dress tonight?"

THE CONSTRUCTED LIFE

E. Tristan Booth

I NEVER HAD MY OWN CALF. OK, yes, I know this statement warrants explanation. When my elder brothers were children, my father owned forty acres of Illinois farmland in the United States, and his boys shared in that great farm family tradition of raising their own calves. The farm had served as the family business since the immigration of my German great-grandfather, and at the time of my birth in 1962, our house had already aged more than a century. With my auspicious arrival, however, the farm was transformed into an evergreen nursery, selling trees, plants, flowers, and the like. Come to think of it, I never had my own evergreen either. But I digress . . .

The nursery, like most, had what is commonly called a garden shop. This one was a long, rectangular building that housed not only the requisite cash register but also two specific categories of merchandise. Perusing the long, dark aisle on the left, you would find all manner of tools: the not-unexpected shovels, rakes, and saws, plus a few metal objects with no obvious discernible purpose. The aisle on the right, however, offered an alternate universe called Peggy's Gift Shop. Peggy, of course, was my mother—the woman who introduced my young impressionable mind to such cultural icons as Barbie dolls, the art of crochet, and the wonderful world of cheap knickknacks. These she would sell with aplomb to the otherwise apathetic wives, while their husbands roamed outside among the rows of saplings—roots encased in little burlap balls—in an effort to fulfill their dreams of landscaping nirvana, finally venturing into the tool aisle for a fix of manly reassurance. And between these two strictly gendered domains there sat a solid impenetrable wall. Thus, it was made clear through my early years that when it came to the masculine and the feminine, the twain were not intended to meet.

As for those Barbie dolls, I can't say that I ever really played with them. I did grasp the initial setup process, however. I don't know about today, but in those days, dormant Barbies were stored in large plastic boxes in a variety of attractive pastel colors. You would open the box, stand it up on its side, and thus create the walls of Barbie's provisional home. Employing a number of these boxes, I would create elaborate, if sparsely furnished, mansions for my anthropomorphic clients—the models of womanhood with which I was meant to identify. Having completed these structures, I would lean back in the pride of my accomplishment, paying scant attention to the dolls I'd tossed to one side. What exactly was I supposed to do with them? My mother had actually sewn entire wardrobes for these creatures. OK, so I'm supposed to change their clothes with alarming frequency. Then what?

So when it came to "girl toys," I couldn't make heads or tails of them (so to speak). But neither was I drawn to the cars, trucks, planes, and trains so favored by male children. Why should I wish to push a toy tractor around the floor when my father had a real one outside? I didn't want to pretend to be a doll, or assume a godlike presence over a fleet of miniature vehicles. I wanted to get behind the wheel of my father's tractor and drive the damn thing. And I don't think I've ever forgiven him for banning me from the riding lawn mower either.

So if I wasn't into gender-extreme toys, what did I like? Well, in keeping with my compulsion to shelter Barbie from the elements, I was drawn to all forms of construction. I loved nothing more than the creation of structures, preferably large enough for my own use. Legos, Tinker Toys, and simple wooden blocks figured prominently, as did blankets draped between pieces of furniture. And while the other children were building snowmen, I was carving out forts and caves. I spent my childhood building walls.

Sadly, however, I have not always been the best architect of my own life. I spent years following blueprints designed by others—in my case, the blueprint for femaleness. I learned from observation how to style my hair and put on makeup. I realized subconsciously that there were cultural rewards for smiling sweetly, obeying the rules, and getting good grades. I experienced my early childhood as a shy little girl at school and a daring, determined little boy at home, climbing onto the rafters of an old abandoned farm building to hang my own indoor tire swing. I lived a very schismatic existence, ever conscious of the fact that I was alternating roles—one authentic, mindless, and free; the other inhibited, practical, and cautious. And I instinctively knew that this conflict was not universal. I was not like the people around me; I was something else.

I remember once telling my mother, rather matter-of-factly, that if I chose to, I could be a famous actor one day. It was a casual statement, quite free of vanity or emotion. I knew it was true because I'd practiced this craft on a daily basis. Acting, I sensed at the time, was not so much a question of talent, but more a natural consequence of desperation. Anyone could do it if he had to. But there is a distinct difference between the acting we feel we must do, and the acting we willfully choose to do. As children, my friend Margie and I would put on little plays, purely for our own amusement and rarely for an audience. Invariably, she would be the princess, the housewife, or the chanteuse, while I would be the prince, the husband, or the affable male host of some variety show. This gender divergence was never discussed, but occurred naturally. On some level, we both knew who we were. And somewhere in Illinois today, she has become the happily married woman she expected to be. And I am becoming the affable male host of my own presentation.

A Double Life

Upon my parents' divorce in 1975, I moved with my mother to Scottsdale, Arizona—a world away from the rural place of my childhood. I entered high school still shy, but with an underlying impertinence and a heightened sense of self. Fortunately, my advanced placement English class offered its students some leeway for eccentricity (we were supposed to be fairly bright, after all, and they didn't want us getting bored). So on May 19, when I brought in homemade chocolate chip cookies to celebrate the day Oscar Wilde had been released from prison, the instructor simply smiled and allowed me to usurp half the class period. I was learning to follow the advice given so matter-of-factly by the Pet Shop Boys: "We were never being bored, 'cause we were never being boring." But this burgeoning personality was largely muffled, both by shyness and by my annoying tendency to follow the rules.

The guardians of society had taught me to be a lady on the outside, but had said not a word about where to hide my soul. Eventually, I managed to hide it in a novel, begun in my late teens. Ostensibly, this was a work of fiction, for its truth did not lie in its plot, and its characters never experienced an earthly existence. But it held a hidden truth. It was the one place I could go to wake up from the sleepwalking state of my daily life. Here, I could be a young, good-looking guy exchanging meaningful glances with a slightly older but equally attractive Englishman on the streets of 1970s London. (Note to self: not all gorgeous men are from the British Isles; it only seems that way.)

So the double life continued. Only now the free-spirited little boy of my childhood was no longer building clubhouses, no longer creating safe spaces for himself in the real world. I was now a young man living in a universe entirely of my own construction, relegated as it was to a mind housed in a woman's body. And when I looked out through this woman's eyes, I realized that the so-called real world could not see me at all. My only acknowledgment came from the fictional characters of my fantasy, so I spent a lot of time there.

In June of 1981, I turned on the news and saw coverage of the Phoenix gay pride event. My immediate reaction was one of great loss. Why hadn't I known about this? Why wasn't I there? I vowed to myself that I would find the pride committee and next year would be with my people. I don't remember how, but I did eventually locate them, and the following spring—at age twenty—I was sitting in a stranger's Phoenix apartment amid talk of permits, electrical outlets, T-shirt designs, and fund-raisers.

I lived this odyssey on and off for roughly thirteen years, working on eight pride events. I graduated to secretary and the board of directors, eventually finding my name—my female name—in the group's articles of incorporation. So here was this dedicated enigma in their midst, and they weren't sure what to make of me. Most must have assumed I was a lesbian, yet they never saw me dating a woman. When I gave some organizational assistance to a local bisexual group, the pride committee thought they had me figured out (although they still hadn't seen me dating a woman). It had also been observed that I had a crush on one of my friends, so a couple of guys decided I must be there to pick up gay men. They obviously thought I was foolishly unrealistic as well. But regardless of my perceived orientation, I did a good job, which was all that really mattered. Volunteers who show up on time and get the work done are a rare commodity. So I was appreciated, and I felt a sense of belonging, but something was still missing. And that something was visibility. I wanted to be seen. I wanted these people to be aware of my identity.

But addicted as I was to shyness and insecurity, I hadn't yet hit my rock bottom of desperation—that disquieting place that years later would propel me to speak my truth. Yes, I told a few close friends over the years, but it made little impact on my psyche, for while they were accepting on the surface, I don't think they really took me seriously. People seem to think with their eyeballs; not seeing doesn't allow for believing. Feeling invisible as I did, I found myself choosing my company very carefully. My best friends were gay men, and I spent little time with women. This was partly due to the fact that I identified with the men, but I was also very image conscious. It was a guilt-by-association thing. If you look like a duck and hang out with ducks, chances are you're just another duck. No one would guess that you might be hiding a peacock under there.

This social avoidance of women made for some interesting—and disturbing—misinterpretations. In my mid-twenties, I took a university course in small-group communication. When the class was initially subdivided, my working group consisted of two women, three men, and myself. We wrote our final paper in teams of two, and with its compilation, I made a shocking discovery. The two women had written that I was obviously prejudiced against minorities, since one of them was Asian and the other Mexican. I had never been rude to them, nor did I care about their racial backgrounds. I simply hadn't paid much attention to them, as I was working more closely with the guys. Stunned by this accusation, I wasn't sure how to defend myself. Had I given the honest explanation— that I wasn't going out of my way to associate with women—they probably wouldn't have believed me. After all, I was a woman too, wasn't I? And did I have the courage in the mid-1980s to tell a bunch of presumably straight college students that I was transgendered? I'm sorry to say that I didn't. So, as I had never disabused them of their assumptions, these people probably left the course believing that I was prejudiced—a nagging suspicion that troubles me to this day.

Acting Like a Woman

My personal life, meanwhile, could be summed up in one word: settling. And settling can be a decidedly unsettling experience. I married the wrong people just because they asked. I saw no hope of ever being myself, so I settled for less. (Note to readers: *never* do this.)

Acting as a woman, I followed the rules I'd learned in childhood: smile a lot, don't speak your mind if you think it might annoy people, and pretend that you're not sure how to do stuff. What's more, I had the irritating habit of marrying people who felt sure that they did know how to do stuff (and I certainly didn't want to embarrass them by pointing out their failings).

Like everyone else, I craved intimacy, but lacked trust. How could I allow myself to be vulnerable with a partner who believed I was simply the woman he could see with his eyes? How could I be physically expressive when my variant soul was restricted to a female body? Naturally, my inhibitions were taken for indifference. Consequently, there are several people out there who, if asked, would swear that sex doesn't appeal to me. But given the privilege of trotting through the streets of my inner universe, they'd undoubtedly encounter a few frightened horses.

My first two marriages were mercifully brief and unencumbered. There were no children, and we possessed little wealth to divide. The third proved much more complicated. Yet it was this complication—the serious nature of having babies and owning property—that clearly revealed for me the contrast between what was, and what should have been. It was not that I hadn't known this before; it was the stark emptiness of my life and the realization, as I entered middle age, that this state of affairs might be permanent.

What the hell was I doing in a rural neighborhood, married to a very traditional husband, washing two loads of laundry per day and racing to have dinner prepared early enough to take the children outside to play before their father arrived home to complain that they'd been spending too much time in front of the television? Why had I chosen (settled for) such a controlling man who told me (for my own good) not only what to eat, but *how* to eat it and how to sit while I ate it? Why was I tolerating the shouting, the swearing, the slamming of doors, the throwing of objects, and the accusations of selfishness when I craved a few minutes of privacy?

Because I'd been raised by a mother who taught me, both verbally and illustratively, that women need men to survive. Because this particular man offered a degree of financial security that I doubted I could achieve on my own. Because I convinced myself that children might afford me a sustenance level of happiness. Why did I give up my dreams and lose my sense of identity? Because, in this culture, generally speaking, that's what women do. Because I knew the world would always see me as a woman. Because I thought I had to do what women do. Because I didn't think I had any choice.

My epiphany came late one evening as I sat alone at the dining room table. I was supposed to be a writer. Why was I not writing? I had the soul of an activist. Why was I not agitating? I had brought myself to a place that couldn't have been much further from my nature. Instead of meetings and marches, my life revolved around preschool and potty training. Absent of rainbows and lavender, my days were painted in shades of blue dog and purple dinosaur. I did, of course, love my children, but I no longer loved myself. Because my self was no longer there. I had somehow abandoned him in my novel, now hidden away in a filing cabinet. So I decided, late that evening in January of 2001, to dive back into those pages and attempt a rescue. I reread everything I'd written some twenty years before and found, to my relief, that the characters were still clinging to life. I spent the next year on the resuscitative work of editing, rewriting, and furthering the story lines.

And it was this effort that kept me alive through the first half of 2001. For as I gradually began to reveal myself—purchasing men's shirts and cutting my hair progressively shorter—my husband became increasingly hostile. I consequently moved into a separate bedroom, escaping the tension by inhabiting the fictional characters of my work, living their lives each night before falling asleep. I write very realistic dialogue, not because I learned the skill in a classroom, but because I have performed every word of it in advance. So I was back to the double life. But this time, reality had real possibilities.

Finding Support

More than anything else at this point, I craved support. Books and websites were useful, but I wanted to meet people. I combed the Phoenix gay press, but could find no organizations relating to gender identity. Finally, my friend Beth—former chair of the pride committee—remembered that a current pride board member was also involved with a local transgender group. With great relief, I called someone named Mallere. She described the organization—Transgendered Harmony—and offered to escort me to my first meeting because, she said, it would be scary to walk through those doors for the first time. I was touched by this concern, but if the truth be told, I couldn't bloody wait to walk through those doors.

An hour before the meeting, we met at a nearby coffee house to get acquainted. She was tall, black, and funny with an attitude. I liked her immediately. And arriving at the meeting, I honestly don't remember what it felt like to walk through the doors, but I do remember sitting next to Mallere in the front row and being introduced to those in attendance as an FTM. And I remember feeling male in a room full of females. The group was diverse, in that it ranged from crossdressers to transitioned women, yet there was no one else presenting as male. There used to be one, I was told, but he had moved away. And Tucson was fairly crawling with them, apparently. But in Phoenix, well, I was it.

I knew this couldn't be true, of course, but I didn't know how to find any others like myself. So I formed friendships within the group and attended meetings whenever I was able to leave the house without too much harassment. I also sought out counselors, spending hours with well-meaning professionals who encouraged me to talk about my husband but offered little expertise on gender identity issues. They did seem to agree that I should leave the marriage, however.

The deterioration of that relationship became increasingly obvious through the second half of 2001. I looked forward to Christmas, when my brother from out of state would spend a week at my mother's home nearby. But upon his arrival, as I was approaching our car for a planned visit with him, my husband began another tirade about my selfishness, throwing various objects through the garage. His tone was a death knell for the marriage, but I found that while his behavior still unnerved me, the finality was a welcome relief. I spoke to an attorney in January of 2002 and moved out exactly one month later, just days before my fortieth birthday. The old adage that life begins at forty could hardly have produced a more striking example. For this was both a renewal of life for me as a single person striving toward independence, and the beginning of a public life for Tristan, fighting at last for visibility.

My First Suit

Living alone, I was free to attend Transgendered Harmony meetings twice a month, weekly transgender coffee socials on Thursday evenings, and various other special events. The group produces an annual workshop and dinner called Puttin' on the Glitz in late February or early March. In making plans to attend, I was told that while the day of seminars was relaxed and casual, the evening's festivities had a decidedly more formal atmosphere. Yes, it was time for a suit. Some had suggested a tuxedo, but frankly, I never have liked them. I had developed a passion for Perry Ellis shirts, so I contemplated renting one, but when I checked on the rental prices, it seemed more cost efficient to simply purchase one for unlimited future use.

I first took a stroll through Dillards, a moderately high-end department store. They had racks and racks of men's suits, all guarded by a conservative-looking middle-aged man who eyed me suspiciously. Did I really want this guy measuring my inseam? I thought not. So I headed to Robinsons-May at the other end of the mall. Spotting the suit racks in one corner of the men's department, I decided to stop first in the center section of the floor, home to DKNY and the like. Instantly, my eyes fell upon a rack of lightweight woolen suits in black, with flecks of white. It was a modern design and I loved it. Examining the labels, I found that it was on sale at a very reasonable price. But even better, it was Perry Ellis. I looked around to see who the salesman was for this section. Unlike the stuffy older man at Dillards, this guy was about my age. He did look awfully straight, unfortunately, but you can't have everything.

It was one of those moments in life when you simply and gleefully have to just go for it. So I walked up to the guy and asked how open-minded he was. He responded politely in the affirmative, so I declared that

I needed to buy a suit. He treated the situation quite matter-of-factly . . . until he had to take the measurements. At this point, he was out of his element as a salesman, and clearly unsure of himself as he wrapped a tape measure around my waist. He also made nervous jokes about how his work was not typically this much fun. But I never took his remarks as crude or inappropriate. We were both on a curious new journey here, and it didn't seem relevant to me that he had a male body while I had a female one. When it was time for the dreaded inseam, he knelt on the floor before me and explained, "I usually do this to guys" (like I didn't already know that).

The measurements taken, we went about the business of trying on suits. Jackets were no problem out on the floor, but pants required a dressing room. You hear so often about male-to-female transsexuals and cross-dressers getting kicked out of women's restrooms or fearing the repercussions if they try on "women's" clothing. But women aren't viewed as a threat in male territory. At worst, they may be seen as impudent radicals; at best, as jokes. My suit salesman thought nothing of ushering me into the men's dressing rooms and waiting outside as I tried on pants. He did seem to feel awkward, however, each time I opened the door and invited him in to see how they fit. And nothing seemed to fit quite right. If the legs were loose enough to accommodate female hips, the waist was too wide, puckering the material beneath a fastened belt. Jackets posed a similar problem. Those large enough for the hips ran too wide in the shoulders. After roughly an hour, it became clear that no matter what I chose, some tailoring would be needed. So I went with my first love, the Perry Ellis. And, as one might expect, the alterations cost almost as much as the suit.

In the months after this purchase, I went back in to visit the salesman several times, answering his questions and explaining my identity. He has since moved away, taking with him some knowledge and understanding of transgender issues. This is education at its most basic: meeting people one-on-one and putting a human face on a mysterious subject.

Living Outside the Gender Box

Along these lines, I have also participated in what our organization calls outreach. Outreach presentations are opportunities for the members of our speakers' bureau to tell their personal stories to nontransgendered groups, such as university classes. At my first, I could literally see my hands shaking in front of me, yet despite my background of shyness, I wanted to do it. I felt a sense of mission—that education on this and related subjects was what I was meant to do with my life (although, frankly, I do it better on paper). But I have found that the more I am myself, the more easily people can relate to me. As the persona I present to others becomes more authentic, much of the shyness falls away. And without the constraints of shyness, I am actually able to make people laugh. Laughter, in turn, garners attention, allowing me to get some real information through to a largely bewildered audience.

So what do I tell these groups of unsuspecting college students? Needless to say, I've not yet perfected the quintessential five-minute autobiography. At first, I said too little. Hearing this criticism, I then said too much. But there are certain points I go out of my way to include. One example is the fact that not all FTMs are attracted to women. I have been amazed to find that I must delineate the difference between gender identity and affectional orientation. Yet without this explanation, such aspects of my personal life are actually taken for granted. The reason for this is what I like to call heterocentrism. If heterosexism refers to a prejudice against nonheterosexuals, then heterocentrism relates to the inherent assumption that one either is heterosexual or would certainly wish to be. In other words, if I was born into a female body and I am attracted to males, I am already in the privileged heterosexual class. Why on earth would I want to become a gay male? The simple answer—which most of society has trouble grasping—is that I already am one.

But I also venture into more esoteric territory, such as the philosophies of TG writers Kate Bornstein and Riki Anne Wilchins about gender—that it is a socially constructed concept in the first place. While I may use the dualistic language, I recognize that *male* and *female* are not static terms with clearly defined boundaries. When you get right down to it, words like *masculine* and *feminine* have no definitions at all, since every ascribed characteristic is a stereotype. For the sake of simplicity, I often tell people that I feel "mostly male" or "male most of the time," and that, once in a while under certain circumstances, I also feel "female." But can I define these states of mind to someone else's satisfaction? Probably not.

I label my identity as "gay male" because, most of the time, I feel like a male attracted to males. I've not really been attracted to genetic females, yet in the past year I've made an interesting discovery. Through the acquaintance of several transgendered individuals, I've found that I can also be attracted to genetic males who present as female. When they are in this "female" mode, I never feel that I am in the company of men, nor does it feel exactly the same as interacting with genetic women. It's a "third" thing that I sometimes find very appealing. Of all the gender-related categories, I've always been the most attracted to androgynous or feminine men. And as one might expect, most of the androgynous men

I've met have been gay. Consequently, as someone who appears to be female, my experience has always been that the people I've longed for the most have been unavailable to me. And while it may sound pathetic to some, I haven't blamed them. Because I am them.

The transgendered community has far more fluidity to it. I am free to be myself (whatever that is at any given moment) while in the company of those who are doing the same. I didn't get involved with this community in search of romance—nor have I actually found it yet—but I must admit that I'm enjoying the possibilities. The boundaries here are less rigid, although there are exceptions, such as some transsexual women whose heartfelt desire is to exemplify the female stereotypes. To be somewhere in between is, for them, a degree of failure. And while I fully support their efforts to present themselves as they wish, I can't help but grieve for us all in this mass of rules and regulations.

Will I ever transition? I have no idea. Apart from the fact that I still have young children with a hostile father, I also believe that to make this most life-altering decision without absolute certainty would be, quite frankly, stupid. My mother had an amusing comment on this subject during the process of my divorce. She said to me, "I wouldn't mind if you were gay, I could handle that. But I don't want you coming back as some hairy man." (Apparently, it's the hair that she finds particularly troubling.) Well, Mom, you'll be pleased to know that I'm not too keen on facial hair myself. And FTMs are, in fact, allowed to shave.

Can I find happiness by simply looking androgynous while communicating to others about the male side of my identity? While it may be possible (and certainly cheaper), I'm still in the midst of that determination. I do not write this story at the conclusion of a lifetime, and there is no tidy ending. We are here in this world, I believe, for two reasons: to learn and to teach. I am currently engaged in both. But I do know that whatever my body may experience in the future, I will always be transgendered. And strange as it may seem to some, I will always be proud of—not embarrassed by—that label.

Finding myself trapped in one gender box, I have gazed longingly at the other, finally realizing that boxes and structures are not so much shelters as prisons. Yet quite often it's a voluntary incarceration. After all, if most of society remains safely behind the cell doors, it can be a lonely experience for the few who roam the hallways of freedom.

MY PURPLE AURA

A JOURNEY TO SELF-ACCEPTANCE

Andy Colson

MONDAY, JANUARY 24, 2000: the day my life was changed forever. The day I told my wife, Fiona, that I liked to dress in women's clothes and had done so for as long as I could remember. And now, for the first time ever, I wasn't the only one in the world who knew. I was thirty-six years old and had kept it secret for almost thirty years. I have lived with gender dysphoria for most, if not all, my life, although it is only recently that I became aware of the term. And now my secret was out. I was wondering where my life and our life together were going to head from here. Naturally I was hoping that things might turn out for the better, but I really had no idea. In many ways, it was now out of my hands.

I had been crossdressing for such a long time, but probably like most transgendered people, I had no understanding of why I did it. I liked the feelings associated with being dressed femininely, but there was more to it, I suspected. I really didn't know. I had never met another crossdresser, or any transgendered person for that matter—not knowingly, anyway. I just liked to feel feminine in any way I could. Now I had told my wife that I sometimes wore her clothes when she wasn't home, but had I been truly honest, there was more.

I don't know exactly when my female dressing actually began, but I suspect I was about eight. The memories are all quite vague; I don't even remember the first time I became intrigued by an article of clothing, so I may have been younger. As far as I'm concerned, those feelings have basically always been there. Did I think of myself as a girl? No. I was old enough to recognize that I had been born male. My body was male, I was treated as a male, and even my hobbies, toys, and interests confirmed my conclusion that I was male. So I never believed that I was actually a girl. I simply knew that it was vital for me to be able to express my female feelings. Because I never came to a conclusion that I was actually a girl, I never felt any connection to the description of "a girl trapped in a boy's body"—a phrase often bandied about in the popular media and also in most literature on transsexualism. I have never used that phrase to describe myself to this day.

Throughout the years I had never identified with the term *wrong body*. For better or worse, this was my body. I had male genitals, so I was a boy, and always had been. As I got older I therefore concluded I couldn't be transsexual. Certainly I dressed in female clothes, so I presumed that qualified me as a crossdresser. For years it never bothered me; labels didn't matter and I rarely gave them a thought. I was too embarrassed to even open a book on transgender issues anyway. So terms and definitions remained unclear. I was just me. Pretty normal really. I just happened to have a big female part in my head. Possibly bigger than my male part. I didn't know.

To say that this need to express a female side only involved clothes would be misleading, however. I was jealous of girls. I wanted to pretend to be like them, even if I wasn't one. I wanted to experience things like them. I may have accepted that I was a boy, but I so desperately wanted to know what it was like to be a girl. I don't remember ever feeling ashamed of what I did. I don't think I ever thought of what I did as wrong, so this probably helped me avoid a lot of the negative feelings that many transgendered kids can develop. Having said that, I did know that what I did was not normal. I figured out at that very young age that it was best kept as my secret and not for anyone else to know. I felt extreme embarrassment for my feelings and behavior, and the threat of humiliation was always present. So I went to extraordinary lengths to ensure no one ever found out. For this reason, I never wanted to develop any outwardly feminine characteristics. This was about feeling female, not about being an effeminate male.

Although I felt little serious distress over who I was, I always felt very confused. Why did I do this? Why did I have this unrelenting drive to look for opportunities to crossdress? It was totally confusing. But there was more to it than simply having additional needs than other boys. There were aspects to being a boy that caused me much distress, to which, at the time, I made no direct connection with my crossdressing. I spent huge amounts of time and energy avoiding typical boy social situations. I never felt like one of the boys. The more masculine a situation got, the more I felt the need to flee. But in general I couldn't. I didn't want to be seen as a wimp, but I hated being with large groups of guys. I felt threatened. I hated male competition and dearly wished I could be included in the girls' groups. But I didn't fit in there either, and felt just as out of place within their ranks because I wasn't one of them. I was a boy and had no social skills in how girls interacted anyway. So I didn't feel at home in either camp. I had friends, but liked to keep the interactions to one-on-one so that the male dynamic could never take over. Sure, I could do quite well with the more practical things that are generally associated with the male role, but socially I knew I didn't fit in.

In many ways I consider myself to have grown up as a very typical Anglo-Saxon kid living in suburban Melbourne, Australia. I completed high school, went to technical college, and studied electronics and audio, finding myself a good job in the broadcasting media on completion of my studies. Forming relationships had always been difficult for me, as I felt extreme anxiety in playing the male role. In time, I realized I only saw myself sexually as female. It wasn't until I was twenty-seven that I met Fiona, my first real girlfriend. Within eighteen months we were married. If I thought settling into a happy relationship was going to be the end of my transgendered desires, I was sadly mistaken. The fact that we both had differing work hours each week meant it wasn't long before I found increasing opportunities to spend more time crossdressing. I soon came to the conclusion that this was a part of me that I should accept and let be. This worked for a good period of time and I felt reasonably comfortable, although a little guilty for hiding it.

New Year: New Me

As the years went on, I increasingly craved information on why I was who I was. At work I started to search on the Internet for texts on transsexualism, but the paranoia of being caught made me a nervous wreck. Eventually I got an Internet connection at home and could finally read up privately on all sorts of related issues. Now the seed of curiosity was growing. I read lots but still couldn't particularly identify with any one group. I was just me—a "me" that nobody really knew, and I felt like a bit of a fake. I wondered if people would still like me if they knew the real me. It was starting to cause significant distress. After nearly seven years of marriage, a major turning point came with the celebrations of New Years Eve, 1999: the start of the new millennium. I stood out in the back

yard with Fiona, looking at the blue-tinged light of an approaching sun-
rise. As the sun came up on a new century, I was thinking, "I can't go on
hiding myself like this, denying who I am." With this new era, and the
feeling of a counter being reset, it was time to tell. It was now or never. It
took me another twenty-four days to do it.

Lying in bed on that Monday night, the opportunity came up. The
lights were out, so I felt I could hide my embarrassment. I had been looking for an opportunity for days. I don't remember how, but ultimately the
topic of some of Fiona's clothes came up. There's my chance: go! With a
trembling voice, I said that I liked to wear some of her clothes. I was shaking and so afraid. But the words had just come out. For the first time in
nearly thirty years, I had said it out loud. I kept my words to few, not
wanting to overly stress her, thinking she might interpret what I was saying as not of major significance. In hindsight this may not have been a
good approach, but it's the only way I could handle the situation. Lying
there, we didn't say much to each other. Feeling very awkward, I tried to
sleep but was awake nearly all night. The next day, I headed off to work
feeling very strange and something of an outcast. Luckily, and to my wife's
credit, the situation resolved a few days later as we sat and talked. I found
myself to be blessed with a totally supportive and understanding partner.
In a few short hours my life was changed forever.

It was late January, midsummer, and I had just found someone who
accepted me for who I was. I was on cloud nine. I felt that at last my
"femme" side was accepted as valid and real. Now we could shop
together, and for the first time in my life I bought clothes that fitted. We
had a lot of fun shopping, and I started to put together my own wardrobe.
At last I could give my female side her own identity and not "borrow" it
off others. She was part of me and no longer banished to feeling hidden
or ashamed. Later that year I finally found the courage to let Fiona see me
dressed. I was nervous, but for me the moment was a beautiful one. A
huge milestone had been reached, and it felt nice—not humiliating or
embarrassing, but filled with feelings that were overwhelming, peaceful,
and serene. That year was filled with the most exciting times of my life. I
was on a constant high, even though I could not let anyone outside our
marriage know. Unfortunately, it was a high that would last for only a
few brief months.

By the latter part of 2000 I found my feelings further evolving. I was
getting increasingly anxious about my situation. In terms of my gender
issues, I had been isolated all my life and had never met another person
in a similar position. I was growing ever keen to meet with someone else
who crossdressed. It would be a relief simply to meet and chat openly

about our situation. I had no desire to go out dressed as a woman, even though I fantasized about it often. I knew I wasn't the only one in the world who did this, but I had no idea how others coped. I wanted to learn about myself. It was at this point that I started to keep a diary of how I felt and where my life was going. The isolation was getting to me. The urgency to meet someone else in a similar situation was becoming a priority. To understand myself was becoming a priority. In retrospect I now recognize that subconsciously I knew major things were brewing within and had to resolve all the built-up tension that had become such a part of me.

I had read an article in a weekend newspaper a few years before on crossdressing and had kept it secretly hidden away. I called the number and made arrangements to meet for an induction meeting. So after work one Thursday evening, I headed for a cafe not far away for a meeting with the first transgendered person I had ever met. I was extremely nervous, but on sitting down and chatting I surprised myself at the ease with which I could open up and talk about such personal issues with a total stranger. I felt a connection right from the start, and really didn't want the interview to end. But ultimately, after about a forty-five-minute chat, it was time to go, and I left with the details for an upcoming Seahorse club meeting. I could go dressed as I chose. I left wondering what was about to become of all this. I sensed things were starting to change.

For my first Seahorse meeting I opted to go dressed as a male. Naturally I was incredibly nervous, but happily my wife attended with me, easing my nervousness immensely. My heart was pounding as I entered, and my conversation was probably stifled, but I did it. And I actually enjoyed the experience. We met many new friends, and by the end of the evening I felt the odd one out dressed in jeans and a shirt. I agreed next time I would go dressed en femme. I got home finding myself counting the days until I could go out into the world presenting myself as female for the first time.

Crossdresser or Transsexual?

There was, however, one growing question that wasn't so exciting. In fact, it was outright scary. The more people I spoke with—or, more appropriately, observed—at the meetings, the less I began to feel I could relate to them. Of a great many members present, I was bewildered by the way they spoke and the things they spoke about. The male in them seemed to shine through, and they almost seemed to revel in the knowledge that they were male, even though most presented quite well as females. I could glance around the room and almost just by looking know who I might identify with. Something in these members told me we had a connection. As time went on, and I attended more meetings, now dressed en femme, it became glaringly apparent that those who I identified with most were, in fact, transitioning transsexuals. None of them identified themselves as crossdressers. Alarm bells started to ring within. I felt severe anxiety coming on, although I still maintained that this was purely coincidence. Was it that I was just a little less threatened by them for some reason? But the more I heard their stories, the more I could stand there nodding in agreement. These weren't the stories of being trapped in men's bodies or switching off their female side as soon as they settled back into their week at work. Nor were they necessarily attracted to men, as I assumed transsexuals to be, and most were about my age.

Even at this stage, I never consciously thought, "I want to be a girl." I just wanted to be like them and experience some of what they experienced. I kept telling myself, "I'm a guy," even if I have a big female component to who I am. Like it or not, for better or worse, I am male. My body proves what nature meant me to be. But my head would not buy it—not that simply. I would go every week to the shopping center, as I had done for years, spend twenty minutes looking at books or CDs, but then be looking in women's clothing shops, makeup counters, and more particularly, how women behaved together. I realized I had been doing this for nearly twenty years. I felt intense jealousy watching women out shopping together and enjoying being women. I felt distress seeing a woman out with her adult daughter, having a coffee together, and I kept thinking how I wished I could do that with my mum. I'd see a mum go past with her baby and wish that was me. I'd see teenage girls having fun at the makeup counter and wish I was with them. The simplest of things were now causing me extreme anxiety.

I lost count of the number of times I went home from those shopping centers in tears. I had become totally absorbed in trying to feel female all the time without outwardly showing it. I was thinking about my gender continuously. It was totally taking over all my waking moments. Everything I did, I said, I gestured, I was comparing with if I had been born a girl. I began to hate how I walked, how I spoke, how I picked things up. I was crucifying myself. And I felt like something of a fraud to all my family and friends who saw me as being so normal. They didn't know the real me. I hid what was the largest component of my sense of who I was. The need to come out and be honest to my family and closest friends was getting more and more pressing.

The hardest people to tell were going to be my parents. As in telling my wife, I battled with it for weeks. In reality I had contemplated it for years, but now the time was nearing, and I wasn't going to get any peace until the deed was done. The stress was building to the point where it was all I could think about twenty-four hours a day. Ultimately the timing was taken out of my hands. My body took over physically. At a family birthday celebration, I walked in to find my sister wearing a top almost identical to one I had. My stress levels went through the roof. Tears were welling in my eyes, but I hid them. My hands were shaking so much I had trouble putting sugar into my coffee, and I couldn't eat a thing. But a restaurant with everyone around was not the appropriate occasion. On getting back to the car I felt physically ill, struggling not to vomit. I burst into tears. That was it. The next day I had to tell them, and by the following evening, they knew. A huge wave of exhilaration, ecstasy, shame, and fear washed through me. My secret of thirty years was out.

Happily I had their full support. Their biggest concern was that I had to struggle with all these feelings for so long and couldn't talk to them or anyone else about it. And naturally they were shocked. But we talked for hours and agreed to catch up again in a few days, once all the emotional trauma had settled a little. We did, and I now feel so much closer to them. I thank them with all my heart for being so warm and accepting of who I am. I wish I had found the courage to tell them earlier, but that was not a reflection on them, rather an indication of my readiness to face my situation head-on. It took me that long.

As more people got to know about the real me, I was being increasingly told how I must feel so much better now that I didn't have to hide. In a way I did, but there was a big "but." My anxiety was now only growing in a more chronic way. Who was I? I didn't know anymore. My sense of "male, female, crossdresser, trannie" was now completely shot. I didn't know how I wanted people to treat me. As which one of these? All of them? None of them? My sense of identity felt totally fluid and almost varied from one minute to the next. How am I supposed to behave? Like the old Andrew? That felt safe, but all this seemed pointless; it felt like I was still hiding myself, even though most people knew, if somewhat academically, about me. I had put so much of myself on the line, yet nothing practical had changed.

A common response from the majority of people I had told was along the lines of "That's fine, you're so brave for telling me this; I'm touched you've confided in me, but it really doesn't change anything. You're still the same old Andy." For me, that last statement was upsetting. This does change things. It changes a lot. It changes everything. I couldn't clearly identify it at the time, but in fact I didn't want people to think of all this as "nothing's changed" or "the same old Andy." I wasn't going out with them dressed as a female, nor had I changed my mannerisms, yet I wanted things to be different. I was very frustrated. I had put so much of myself up for scrutiny, yet I still felt trapped. Now everybody was aware of my situation and free to talk about me, yet nothing tangible had altered. And so my anxiety went up another notch.

Crisis Point

It was now April 2001, and I hit crisis point. I was now struggling to get through a day at work and seriously doubted my ability to function. My weight had dropped 15 kilograms (33 pounds), and I had completely lost interest in all my old pastimes. I no longer played my guitar, holidays seemed a waste of time, and I lost my interest in seeing friends. If I listened to music I tried to find a transgendered interpretation to it or switched it off. I sought out movies on transsexualism. All I could think about was my gender issues. I realized I hadn't stepped into a men's clothing shop in three years because it threatened me. That would be a step backwards. And now I was increasingly waking up during the night drenched in sweat from nightmares related to gender. I would dream of images of female figures beckoning me and of male figures that threatened me and left me trying to escape. I was struggling to cope. My defenses were crumbling and I was thinking about my situation constantly. To go ten minutes without thinking of it was rare, and the anxiety was leaving me exhausted. My weight was plummeting. I didn't feel like eating. All my thoughts revolved around wanting to be more like a girl. Not to be a girl, but to be like one.

In my mind, there was a big difference. At work I was now using pliers to pull the hair from my arms, causing bad skin irritation. Not only was I jealous of the girls, but also getting angry with the guys for being able to feel "normal." The situation had hit a crisis point, and my world was collapsing around me. The previously strong me now felt very frail. One afternoon, while eating lunch, I hit my breaking point. I couldn't eat and felt I was about to vomit. I had to run in a panic. I went downstairs, and in desperation called a friend from Seahorse pleading for someone who could help me. I was referred to a psychologist who deals exclusively with gender issues. I made an appointment for the following afternoon, and rather than feeling apprehensive, I was literally counting the minutes until I could see her and get the help I needed.

I left my first session with Linda already feeling happier. We had a lot of work to do, and she made it clear this wasn't going to be resolved in weeks, or even months. I was in for the long haul. It then dawned on me how I remembered saying to Fiona about a year prior, when I couldn't stop myself constantly talking about gender issues, that this was going to take two or three years to work out of my system. At the time I felt perplexed about why I had said it, but it felt honest, not melodramatic. I had subconsciously known all along there was a lot buried in there. Linda also explained how, as there were no formal tests to diagnose my situation, it was basically up to me, with her guidance, to work it out. She did say, however, that what I was describing was a condition called gender dysphoria. I had heard the term and thought it was a more recent term used for a diagnosis for what used to be called transsexualism. "Oh, they must have broadened out its definition," I thought. I was still in absolute denial, because as far as I was concerned, I was a crossdresser.

My counseling continued. Around my third visit, things were starting to dawn on me. After an early morning session I returned to work with an intense feeling of "I feel like I've just been diagnosed as transsexual." But it still didn't feel real. Purely academic. True self-acceptance took almost another six months. We talked about my fantasies and various coping techniques. It was only after a particularly confronting session where I questioned Linda, wanting some outright answers, that the truth finally hit home. Hard. "So, of all the clients you see who describe similar things to the ones I've described to you, how many would you say are transsexual?" She said she thought I already knew the answer. I shrugged my shoulders. The answer: "All of them." So there it was in black and white: I was transsexual, and it had hit home.

I burst into tears and cried all the way home. It had taken thirty years to admit it to myself, truly within my heart. Not just academically, but with a true sense of knowing. I couldn't go to work the next day, and just sat around the house in shock. The world was surreal. Nothing seemed real anymore. I described the feelings at the time as extreme happiness mixed with extreme sadness, totally canceling each other out and leaving a big void of nothingness. I was sad for what might happen to me, to my lovely wife and our relationship, but I also felt overjoyed to know at last what I was dealing with. It was threatening, but now tangible. I had denied my transsexualism all my life, but not anymore. All my anxiety and fear lifted that day. The black monster was no longer a monster that lived in my head, but was now there for me to see. I was no longer being driven by some hidden, mysterious force that I had zero control of, but by me. I still didn't understand it, but it was a part of me. And now that made it feel beautiful. My own unique sense of being. I described this force within me as a beautiful purple aura, rather than the previous ominous black. And now I was back in control—for the first time in years.

Choices

I now also saw that with this came a vast number of choices. Not a single choice, but many hundreds of little (and some not so little) choices. Not only were they available, but they were now mine to make, not someone else's. I also accepted that gender transition is not a fantasy, but something that is real. Some people do it. It is a real option, a choice in life. A difficult one, but nevertheless a real choice, and it comprises many other choices within it.

In an absolute sense I still haven't made a firm commitment to where I am going. I take it one day at a time, making the choices that I feel comfortable to make. And it is from this position that I see so many patterns that have been repeating themselves over and over in my life, yet I hadn't recognized them. Simple ones—like I would never go to the toilet standing up and avoided the toilets at work if I saw a male colleague go in ahead of me. I'd look at my hands as I got a coffee and wonder if they'd ever pass as a woman's hands. If the guys at work were clowning around with a tennis ball in the corridor I'd go around another way to make sure they wouldn't summon me—a total avoidance of being seen as one of the guys.

But there were also the more insidious patterns that would force me to take "the next step." I'd get a thought in my head of something I'd like to do, but I'd consider it threatening and scary. So the idea would start to play on my mind. If I didn't respond to it, it would take over all my thought patterns. Still no action—I would start to have bad dreams and not sleep. But still I would hold out, and so the physical reactions would come into play. I'd start to feel anxiety, to feel sick, and eventually not be able to eat. I had to solve this dilemma that I had created.

Ultimately, it was less traumatic to deal with the issue than put up with the extreme anxiety and so I would carry out what I set myself to do. Only then would a wave of euphoria come over me, and I would feel relieved of the stress. Initially this period of well-being could last months, but over time, the euphoric period became shorter and shorter before the next objective became apparent. In the end I had several challenges running at once in any given week. And so an intense emotional roller-coaster was set in motion—one I couldn't get off. It was this cycle that had taken me through my first episodes of crossdressing, buying clothes, coming out to my wife and family, joining Seahorse, and going out dressed for the first time. I could go on. There are hundreds of examples. And it is this same pattern that I can only assume might see me through complete gender transition. Only time will tell. The only difference is that I now recognize the patterns and feel a sense of control. I am back in control of my destiny, but have to work within the framework of who I know me to be: transgendered, trans-sexual.

And so it is that I have already made many decisions about where I am going. I recognize that I am already on the road to at least partial transition to an androgynous way of life. For most of 2001, well before I had accepted my transsexuality, I had been making changes—probably as a result of my frustration in people still relating to me as the "same old Andrew." I was frustrated with how little had changed with my coming out nearly a year earlier, and in August, with my psychologist's support, I started hormones. I had fantasized about it for years. Now it was true. I felt ecstatic as I went to work knowing I had estrogen in my body, just as the other girls did. I started growing my hair and reveled when people noticed differences in me. Being one who absolutely hated attention, I had always been sure I would freak out at the thought of people noticing something about me that may even vaguely imply a feminine nature, but instead I now loved it.

Although my interests and personality remain very much intact, I am not the same old Andrew anymore. But even so, it is a case of steady-as-you-go. I still find it incredible that right up until last year I had denied that I was actually transsexual. For years I fantasized about being a girl and maybe one day growing to be a woman, and this in turn became a wish. What I had for so long been calling fantasies were actually deep-seated wishes. They have always been there and affected every part of my life. I now feel that I probably should have been born a girl. Certainly my life would have been easier, if that is what nature had blessed me with. But it didn't, and although I might have called myself a boy, I could never bring myself to call myself a man. Ever. In a gender sense, I have been waiting to grow up. I don't claim to be anyone other than me. It is only now that I come to a point of true self-acceptance of who I am, and this is where my sense of self now lies.

THE NEVER ENDING TANGO

Katrina C. Rose

THIS IS THE STORY of how I transitioned from male to female while also transitioning from human to lawyer. So, it should go without saying that *The Paper Chase* this is not. Even now, after snagging several pieces of paper—the combination of which allows me to practice law in the states of Texas and Minnesota—I am neither a typical Texas lawyer nor a typical Minnesota lawyer. And a typical lawyer I will never be.

I've attempted to write this story on numerous occasions, but to no avail; I've always hit a snag. I've never had a problem with how to begin it, or even where to begin it. No, my nagging problem has been how and where to end it. Perhaps all writers have a problem with knowing precisely when to stop (the late, great Douglas Adams, after all, never saw the need to stop the *Hitchhiker's Guide to the Galaxy* trilogy after the close of the third part), but my problem with this story partially stems from my having, on my first attempt to commit the story of my law school days to paper, begun it at the end—or, as I've come to characterize it in the years since, *an* end.

On Sunday, May 17, 1998, I graduated from law school. And I did it as the real me—after having started law school as a version of the me that I'd always been told I should be. What better place to begin, eh? An end that was a beginning? Well, to put that day in perspective, I need to go back a bit to a beginning—a beginning that was, to a great degree, an end.

I knew that there was a part of me that I had never allowed to truly exist. I knew it back in 1993 when I first began considering going to law school. Despite being an artist at heart, I'd also always had a strong interest in how the law is used by certain elements of society to keep other elements of society down; so I thought it might be a good idea to actually learn the law so I could use it to help people and, hopefully, make a living. I knew about that part of me in 1995 when I actually began the process of applying to law schools. I knew about it when I made the decision to give up a well-paid job as a structural designer to head off to South Texas College of Law. I knew it all throughout the treacherous first semester, in the fall of that year.

And, for the record, I'd known about it as far back as I can recall. Insert obligatory anecdote here about at age four or five asking Mom for a dress and being told that boys don't wear dresses. I'm sure everyone has heard plenty of these tales, some far more compelling than mine, so I won't take up a great deal of space elaborating on mine except to date myself by saying that it involved the old television series *I Dream of Jeannie,* which, for those unfamiliar with it, was a late 1960s series starring a young, pre-liver-transplant, pre-*Dallas* Larry Hagman as an astronaut who crash-lands on a desert island and finds a beautiful genie, played by Barbara Eden. I identified a good bit more with Eden's character than with Hagman's, and not simply because Jeannie had all of the cool, magical powers.

I survived the first semester, and somewhat respectably so, ending up around the top third in my class of two hundred or so. It was a grueling experience, though, as anyone who has done the law school thing can attest (whether all are honest enough to do so is another matter entirely).

After semester one, gender issues or no gender issues, I had to chill out afterwards, so I went on a road trip. While driving around parts of Texas where even uttering the word *transsexual* might well get a person shot, a realization hit me: despite being in law school, and despite being booze-free for over two years, I was feeling my emotions taking the same negative turn that they often had during most of my adult life.

Yes, I was happy that I'd managed to avoid failure—at least the immediate failure of flunking out after the first semester—on the big law school gamble. But I was failing in another way—overall, I was not happy. Moreover, I was "not happy" in almost exactly the same way that I was "not happy" during my days as an undergraduate at Texas A&M University almost a decade before: I was not happy because I was trying to be a heterosexual male.

Realization

Finally, over two decades, after realizing I wasn't a "typical" male, after learning the word *transsexual,* after figuring out what my father's opinion of transsexuals was (I was in the room with him on several occasions when stories about the male-to-female tennis player Renee Richards appeared on television, and I shan't even paraphrase what was said) and realizing that there was no way I would ever be able to transition while dependent on my parents for survival, after dealing with the seemingly impossible dichotomy of being attracted to women yet knowing that, deep down, I was a woman . . . finally, beneath a cobalt blue sky, while speeding along a lonely, yet scenic, relic of a west Texas highway, I finally admitted to myself why there had never been a real heterosexual relationship—and why there would never be one. I was not male. I was female—a lesbian female. And I had to do something about it.

I had to do something about it, otherwise I was going to crater, and then where would I be? No $40,000 a year job. No law degree. No reason to stay sober (which I'd been since 1993, after spending a decade or so keeping several breweries in business).

The final decision to go to law school resulted from my brilliant conclusion that I wasn't getting any younger. The same was true for bringing the real me into being. I had to go for it while I was in school—with no employer to pacify regarding any changes in appearance that might occur. Strangely enough though, one of the first people I ever came out to in person, as opposed to online, was my first employer in the legal field. Over that Christmas break I'd also taken time to volunteer at the local office of the American Civil Liberties Union, and during the spring semester I came out to my supervisor there. Well, if you can't come out to the ACLU, who can you come out to?

Although mine might have seemed like a well-organized plan, and was to a point, there were a lot of things I didn't know. Luckily, however, when I was younger (sometime between *I Dream of Jeannie* and sinking into the denial of alcoholism), I heard of sex reassignment surgery, so, unlike far too many people who find themselves coming to terms with their innately legitimate feelings of gender variance, there were some things I did know: I knew there was hope, but I didn't know how exactly to get from point A to point SRS.

Fortunately, this was 1996 rather than 1976. I was able to find the Gazebo, a transgender chatroom. There I met people who pointed me to the Texas Association for Transsexual Support (TATS), a Houston-based resource and support group, as well as to the Texas T Party (which, for lack of a better description, was a Texas trannie convention, and, somewhat bizarrely, in 1996 it was held at the same hotel in Dallas where I first sold a piece of artwork a decade prior). The latter of those two is where I did my first bit of actual de-closeting. The former became my well of non-loneliness. Soon I started venturing out on my own, doing the bar thing while wearing the most femme stuff possible and makeup thick enough that it could have deflected bullets had I ever been unfortunate enough to be bashed.

And all of this was during my second semester of law school, when I could still have easily blown things completely by flunking out. Funny, huh? First I worry about failing because I'm not doing anything about my gender issues, then I worry that I might fail because I did address them. And, as finals approached, I did begin to worry that, just maybe, I had spent a bit too much time bringing Katrina out of her shell that semester. As I sat down to my first final that spring, Contracts II, I found myself staring at the exam paper and getting the horrible feeling that there was no "maybe" about it—I *had* spent too much more time on me than on studying. But after the exam I saw similar looks of bewilderment, pain, and confusion on everyone's face. I knew that everyone couldn't have been beginning gender transition that semester, so maybe it wasn't me; maybe it was just a truly bizarre exam.

I guess it was. I ended up with a B- on it; not great, but not bad for someone who had spent the semester cultivating the biggest decision of her life. I survived that semester—not without a slight dip in my grade-point average, but I survived nonetheless. I started venturing out even more, and I began seeing a therapist in preparation for a referral for a hormone prescription. However, as spring turned to summer in 1996, I looked like crap. Yes, far better than I thought I would look in the light of day before I ever got the courage to venture out, but I looked like crap nevertheless. Strangely, though, I felt better than I had in my entire life. Some people may disagree, but sometimes it really is better to feel good than to look good. Of course, I would never stop trying to look good, and although it took me a while, I finally did get good at that part as well.

After the entirety of that first year, I prepared for a trip to England for a study-abroad program conducted jointly by my law school and one from Alabama. Of course, at this point I hadn't come to understand the pivotal role that U.K. law (one U.K. case in particular, *Corbett* v. *Corbett*) had played in transgender law all over the world by not recognizing trans woman April Ashley as female; perhaps this was a good thing, as I might have been tempted to grill the professor of my British law class, a practicing barrister, about both the decision and the judge who authored it. Similarly, I deliberately did no research on a professor from the other school who was going to be teaching another one of my courses that summer. He was a former governor of Alabama. In the years since, I've read that he was a civil rights moderate, and I've also had people tell me that he wasn't as much of a moderate as some other people think. No matter which is true, I can say that he and his wife were two of the nicest old folks I've ever met. And if you're keeping score: no, I did not come out to either of them.

The Real Me

While in England, I met up with a wonderful transsexual called Miranda whom I had developed a friendship with via the Gazebo. She guided me to some trans-friendly clothing and wig outlets in London, guided me away from some horrifically overpriced transvestite makeover shops (places whose business methodology of overcharging closeted cross-dressers she described as "preying on the afflicted"), and ultimately showed me a wild trans-friendly London nightspot: the Way Out Club.

There, on a steamy July evening, I realized that I'd come about as far from Houston, Texas, as I could come. I was out as the real me in London, England. This was a year before the first Austin Powers movie, so, thankfully, it didn't occur to me at the time to think in terms of "swinging shagadelic London." Besides, this wasn't about shagging or anything of the like; one drunk had tried to pick both me and Miranda up at the club, and I was repulsed on sheer principle. (It did not help that the guy was almost a dead ringer for Homer Simpson.) Despite being firmly lesbian, during some times of sexual confusion and despair in my past (translated: before I sobered up) I might have said yes, but once I began to transition, I began to feel good about being me—sex or no sex. After that night in London I started feeling even better and better.

"Maybe this will happen," I began to think, referring both to the gender transition as well as to getting through law school. You see, much to my surprise, I received three incredibly good grades in those classes I took while in England. The trend continued over the next two semesters, but it hiccuped a bit during my final year, and I ended up being percentage points below the top-half/lower-half demarcation line.

And yet, however much it may have affected my job prospects—which, given the total lack of willingness of the legal profession, including that portion of it that should know better than to discriminate against sexual minorities, to embrace openly male-to-female transsexual attorneys, is probably not at all—I have no regrets regarding the source of that final year hiccup: a really cool research assistantship with a really cool straight professor; a really wild, not to mention successful, Houston City Council campaign for a really cool lesbian, and a really fantastic (though, sadly, not fantastically paying) gig contributing written distillations of my thoughts to a really cool newspaper, the *Texas Triangle* (which was, for much of the time I wrote it, the only queer newspaper in the United States to allow a transgendered person to speak for herself on a regular basis about the realities of transgender life, law, and politics).

Now, despite feeling better about myself than I ever had, my confidence fluctuated wildly over those last two years of law school. The folks I met during that time—folks in the Houston gender community like Dee McKellar (who, sadly, did not live to see me graduate), Marie Gallagher, Vanessa Edwards-Foster, Phyllis Frye, and so many others who I don't have room to list here, and cyber-icons like California's Gwen Smith (now the author of one of the only other regular transgender issue columns, in the *Bay Area Reporter*)—helped keep me sane, even while I was intermittently driving them equally insane with my fear of the unknown.

The help of those folks and others paid off when a happy woman named Katrina C. Rose, rather than a perpetually depressed, emotionally unfulfilled alcoholic male, walked across the stage at the George R. Brown Convention Center in Houston and received a law degree.

Graduation Day

And so we've returned to Sunday, May 17, 1998—the end that is also the beginning. That afternoon began with more fear than I'd known in a long while. Prior to the ceremony, all the graduates-to-be lined up backstage, and there I was in a rather small room with more than two hundred people, all but a half-dozen or so having no idea that one particular female in their midst had started out with them three years earlier as a male. I was so nervous that I had to make at least a dozen trips to the ladies' room.

My trip across the stage was fairly uneventful. My name was announced, which resulted in cheering from my supporters, including, most importantly, my mother (long divorced from my father and who, only a few weeks before, had learned and accepted that she had two daughters instead of one son and one daughter), and I received a doctoral hood. I did, however, get a hearty handshake (no laurel, though) from the school's registrar, who had bent over backwards to ensure that I was able to officially appear at the ceremony as the real me. (Her only "demand," so to speak, had been that I get my name- and gender-change court order in time for the graduation programs to be printed—a quite reasonable demand, though, sadly, something that is far more difficult to accomplish in many parts of the country than it was for me in Houston and, even sadder, something that only a year later became all but impossible even there.) That handshake apparently made me stand out, though; someone later mentioned to me that I was the only one to whom she extended one. And, of course, I was also the only one to get a big bear hug from a transgendered lawyer as I was returning to my seat. And it felt good—as did the whole day.

So good, in fact, that late that evening I first began attempting to write the tale you now find yourself reading—it began as a simple few paragraphs of thank-you's to people who supported me, some of whom I'm still close friends with, some of whom, after growing tired of the perpetual financial pain of being out, retreated to closets of success (or at least survivability), and some who, in the years since, have died. That "thank you" letter grew, of course.

I am, after all, a lawyer (then a lawyer-to-be, but you get the idea). Does anyone really think a lawyer capable of stopping after but a few paragraphs? No, I couldn't stop with a few paragraphs. It grew so long that my e-mail handler almost choked on it when I'd refined it enough to feel comfortable hitting the "send" button. Some of the recipients e-mailed back saying they found it inspiring and asked if they could pass it along to others. I was flattered and told all who wished to do so to proceed. Some did, so, before you even ask: yes, if you find yourself with a strange sense of déjà vu while reading this, it is indeed possible that, back in 1998, the earliest, crude form of this story may have found its way into your inbox. Then, I called it simply *The Graduation Tango*.

One friend from the West Coast wrote, "Lovely . . . made me cry for you." Others told me they cried, and cheered, and were proud of me. Inspirational well-wishes from friends, both near and far, at a pivotal moment in my life. A great spot to end the tale, perhaps?

Well, in a better world, perhaps it would have been. In a better world the bar exam would have been . . . OK, forget that; transgender equality or not, the bar exam is still excruciating and will always be so, as is the wait to find out whether you have passed. To put things in a bit of historical context, as it turns out, I learned I'd passed the Texas bar exam two days after one of the darkest days in the state's history: the 1998 statewide elections. Those elections were on Tuesday, November 3. The bar exam results were officially released on Friday, November 6. Do the math. That's three days rather than two. The significance? I can't count the number of times that persons officially connected with the administering of the bar exam assured the examinees that, under no circumstances, did anyone ever get exam results earlier than the official release date and time. Uh huh. And, I bet that they don't inhale either.

Granted, I thought that I'd been inhaling something on Thursday evening when I checked my e-mail and saw a message from a friend of mine, a nontransgendered friend who works in the legal field, with the subject heading "Wahoo." Being a curious Kat, I looked at that message first—which turned out to be a message of congratulations followed by what seemed to be text copied from an Internet site—text that listed me among those who had passed the July 1998 Texas bar exam. Thursday, 8:03 P.M.—and I had the bar results.

I was ecstatic—so much so that I immediately sent instant messages to everyone I knew who was logged onto the Internet at the time. Of course, then, just to be cute, I went to the official website to see the text for myself. But I couldn't access the "successful examinees" section, and so I began to freak out. No, actually, that's not true. I began getting really paranoid. What if my friend lied to me? What if someone lied to him and then he told me?

Now, four years down the line, four years that have included watching various inaccurate bits of transgender-related information traverse the globe on the Net, that second flash of paranoia doesn't seem so paranoid. I know that my friend wouldn't lie to me, but what if he had somehow accessed bad information?

Despite the paranoia, I did manage to fall asleep. Of course, I woke up excessively early and, of course, began playing around on the Net, and when I accessed the site around the official information release time of 7:00 A.M., all the names were there, including mine.

Rejection

Yes, this would be a good spot to end the tale as well. And in a perfect world it might have been. In a perfect world there would have been a job offer at some point—either in the weeks after May 17 or surely after I became licensed to practice law. But there wasn't.

Several months went by. Hundreds of résumés mailed. Intermittent answers. Even less frequent interviews—some involving driving halfway (or more) across Texas—all to no avail. An occasional client from the TG community and one legal writing gig as an independent contractor, but no real job, and even less hope, it seemed. After one particularly long journey for an interview, I returned home in total despair to but one message on my answering machine, about a law clerk position in Minnesota.

Tired of rejection, I almost didn't even return the call. But I did. The employer had seen my résumé and was impressed that I was so dedicated to research and writing—even the transgender-related items that were on the résumé—and, most amazingly, he expressed dismay that people would refuse to hire me solely because I'm transsexual. He didn't refuse. Based solely on the telephone interview, he hired me. Though not an attorney position and only temporary (years rather than months), it was a real job—as the real me, where I've been ever since, though it is a position that is not scheduled to last more than another two years at most.

I look back and find myself unsure of whether I've fulfilled any of my promise and potential. My greatest accomplishments thus far have not been in the courtroom—where transsexuals all across the nation are in dire need of competent representation from qualified transsexual attorneys—but in dusty books-to-be, likely already lost to most in the law library aisles of academia. And even this success has been not as a law professor, but simply as one unknown transsexual sitting in an apartment in rural Minnesota, spending all of her free time distilling far-flung bits of transgender law into law review articles—sorely needed guidance for a legal profession that is almost as incapable of properly dealing with transgender legal issues as it is with male-to-female transsexual attorneys—whose very presence as accomplishments when listed on my résumé all but ensure that the résumé and I will never be taken seriously.

Yes, lightning struck once, but, in spite of civil rights rhetoric about "progress," truly fair-minded people (of any sexual orientation—my boss, whose sense of decency and fairness came from growing up poor on a farm, is heterosexual) are the rarest of commodities. Pessimistic as it may sound, I often feel as though it will never happen again.

Four years after I began *The Graduation Tango,* do I regret transitioning? Not in the slightest. The me of today is the real me, and always was. Had I tried to remain male, I'd now be either off the wagon, or off the planet entirely.

Do I regret coming out? I now no longer know. Yes, I look at my scholarly achievements and think it has been worth it, and may become more so if courts ever see fit to utilize any of my legal analyses in cases involving transgendered people. But, more often, I look into the sad eyes of my lover—eyes filled with sadness far too often because she sees my despair over the continual rejections by law firms and universities and she feels helpless—and I feel as though it has not been worth it. I think I deserve better. But I *know* she does.

And I know that the GLBT rights movement deserves better than the continual loss of transsexual attorneys, who could be bringing a new vitality to the movement the likes of which has never been seen, but who, instead, are forced either into the closet or out of the legal profession because they cannot find employment.

My lover (who, ironically, had it not been for the discrimination that drove me out of Texas, I'd likely never have met) has faith in me, even though, as a nonlawyer and a nonactivist, she is often perplexed by my research work and, at times, a bit dismayed at my devotion to it (especially on cool fall Minnesota days, when the sky is as cobalt blue as it was in west Texas in December of 1995 when I made my transition decision, and we'd both be a lot happier if I dropped my research and headed up to the north shore of Lake Superior). She and others have enough faith in me to harangue me into backing away from the logical conclusion to dark thoughts I've occasionally expressed. I think there's still enough of that hope and energy that I felt on May 17, 1998, to keep me going.

So it looks as though, after four years, I am indeed right back to the ending that I used for my beginning; and rightly so for a story such as this. It was one of the happiest moments of my life—never to be repeated, but also never to be forgotten. *The Graduation Tango?* Nah—I'll try to muster a positive note and call it *The Never Ending Tango*—with the hope that the only thing that comes to an end anytime soon is the discrimination that hurts all of us.

○

BUTCH

A WORK IN PROGRESS

Jay Copestake

I SIT AT THE COMPUTER wondering to myself what I'm going to tell you about how my gender fits or doesn't fit, as the case may be, with the sum of my experiences on this planet—my politics, my desires, my fetishes, my angst, my expectations, my high points and low points, my hopes and dreams, my friends and lovers, my childhood, my career, and so on. And how all of this adds up to me today—thirty-four years old, a butch woman in the inner city of Sydney, Australia, semi-self-employed working a variety of jobs, living in community housing, single, and with a small network of friends.

I've always wondered if my life would have been far less confusing if only I had listened harder when at twelve years of age, my older brother accused me of "being butch." His comment perhaps said as much about his own search for his masculinity as it did about mine. Few could have anticipated his masculinity being threatened by his sister's, could they?

I'm getting a dog—a puppy actually. Tomorrow, I'm getting a puppy. Will I be her mummy or daddy? To a zillion people, this question would not even be considered; the answer, after all, would be self-evident. Up until about three years ago, and free from internal gender confusion, I too would have found the question moot. I would have been the dog's mummy. "Come to Mummy, little one," I would have cooed, without hesitation. But today I'm becoming increasingly uncomfortable referring to myself as Mummy. When the hell did that happen? For years I was butch;

it felt right, it felt comfortable, I sat right, and knowing myself as a butch woman silenced the confusion of my teenage years. "When did this slight waver over my gender identity emerge?" I ask myself. As a butch dyke into power games, and a sex-positive feminist with anarcho and separatist leanings, how do I reconcile my own slowly emerging affinity with male pronouns?

I identify as a big butch dyke. A bear. I'm into butch-on-butch and butch-femme sex. Sexually I'm a top—I'm a Dom. Nearly eight years ago, as I departed the London SM scene and returned to Australia to go to university, I had some exposure to women who identified as "daddy," "sir," and "master," but I wasn't into it myself. In some ways I didn't get it. At twenty-six, I didn't understand how some dykes' use of male pronouns was anything other than a light-hearted adoption of the male during a role-play scene. Could it be an accurate self-description that was deeply felt, and out of the simple A or B choices that society offered us, the male most closely matched what they were about? At thirty-four, I'm beginning to understand where some of those butches and queer girls were coming from, but I'm jumping ahead a bit; let me go back to when I was younger.

A Work in Progress

I have believed for many years now that being butch is a "work in progress." I've watched myself change and get more butch as the years go by. It took me until I was about twenty-three or twenty-four to accept my own butchness. From that point onward, my life made more sense. As a butch dyke I found my place in the world, one that I was comfortable with, and one that no longer felt like I was inhibiting or disguising a part of myself. Every year that passes I am surprised that I get a little bit more butch in appearance, manner, and probably in a million other ways that I am not able to recognize. It's not a conscious thing. Somehow it just happens. Could it be simply that the older I get, the more confidence I have to do my own thing and break social conventions on how a woman is supposed to look? Whatever the reasons, now I have an entire wardrobe of male attire.

> *When I turn the corner and encounter a predatory pack of boys,*
> *I know one false move will ensure that I am marked,*
> *targeted, and vulnerable to their fists and jeers.*

I cannot remember when it became clear to me that no wedding, job interview, family gathering, or bar mitzvah was going to convince me that putting on a frock or feminine attire was a viable option. And certainly it didn't feel right! In my early twenties, on the rare occasion that I wore a frock or a skirt, I felt like a fraud; somehow it seemed inauthentic, like I was playing dress-ups. Back then I didn't look completely like I was cross-dressing—I even sometimes elicited wolf-whistles from men—these were both incredibly unwelcome and perhaps made me feel even more like I was playing dress-ups. Maybe it was something about the way I strode along in heels, but I felt like I was crossdressing. If I did it today, I would look more like an MTF crossdresser than a woman.

Those days are long gone, and now when I pass a butch woman in the street wearing a skirt, a dress, and heels I think to myself, "Who are you try-ing to kid?" Does the gender disparity come through so clearly because she feels so uncomfortable in the skirt? A discomfort so deep that you can read it in how she carries her body? Or is she so used to carrying her body in a butch way that she forgets or is unable to carry her body in a more feminine way, even if she wants to pass as feminine? When you get down to it, is it about the difference between the body and equipment you were born with and how you present to the world? Or is there more to it than that?

How will my friends react when I tell them I'm this little pup's daddy? Will their jaws drop open in shock? Will their minds reel and spin to make sense of this new information? Recount the numerous feminist discussions we've shared, trying to count the number of times I've dismissed, ridiculed, scoffed with cold anger at men, and considered most anything male with contempt and as irrelevant to my world? Will they think these thoughts in a desperate attempt to collect evidence, to de-confuse the sit-uation, to remind themselves and seek comfort, knowing the words com-ing out of my mouth are not the sort of thing I would usually say?

As a teenager, I was told repeatedly, when not in words, then through people's eyes and actions, that I was undesirable. I failed to be thin, I failed to be feminine, I failed to be amused by boys or interested in them. I was confused and lonely during high school. I didn't understand why I didn't like any of the boys at school, why I spurned the few boys who showed interest in me. I had been wanking since the age of twelve and desperately wanted to have sex—just not with any of the boys I knew. I wanted sex, wanted to be sexual, but no one interested me, and this con-fused the hell out of me. I felt undesirable, yet horny as all hell. So I wanked!

During my teens I had few friends, but always one best friend, and I never spoke about any of this with them. I don't know why I felt unable to; maybe I knew the risk was too high and I was scared of losing the few friends I had, so I shut up. And to this day I've never talked about any of this with my parents or brothers. I may never know if a part of me knew that I was a dyke and another part of me was desperately denying it to myself. I knew I didn't really click with many people at school or in my neighborhood.

Feeling Different

Some of the girls at school were as unforgiving of my difference as the boys were. Those girls made me feel inadequate because they pulled off the feminine girl thing without a hitch and I couldn't. Mostly I didn't even want to, but on a gut level I knew I was breaching the rules about how girls were supposed to look, and I knew I was meant to want to be feminine. Somehow I was too different—my femininity was clumsy and it just didn't work. I didn't convince anyone, least of all myself. Somehow in that era, in that part of town, lesbianism as an option didn't even get a look in.

Writing this reminds me of how powerful social conditioning, social codes, and ideas about normality that surround us are, and just how strict they really are. Those strict social codes came through loud and clear to me. My parents were liberal with a small *l*, which in Australia at that time meant fairly relaxed and tolerant of difference, but believing everyone can make it if they just get off their arse and try. Whereas I think that's bullshit. There is no level playing field. Some people have it stacked in their direction and others have it stacked up against them. This is not to say that some people are eternal and inescapable victims, but rather they have to work a lot harder, make more adjustments to fit in and pull it off. And goddamn it, some people just run out of energy, and to me that's understandable. It's tiring getting it from all sides.

My father was almost, but not quite, a "leftie." My mother, on the other hand, was raised in the outback, generally racist and much more "right" politically. It's almost like they evened each other out. I think my mother, for the most part, kept her more right-wing views to herself, and I wonder if she inhibited them because her patriarch/husband would not approve. Dad tried hard to be democratic with us kids and in family life in general, but the patriarchal power he was born with sometimes raised its ugly head. As a young child, I was onto it quick smart and told him so straight out, and if needed, I was ready to vocally fight it out, so I don't doubt that I kept them on their toes.

My dad coped with my up-front style, with my dominant ways, my outspokenness, my determination to get whatever I wanted despite being female, for I knew in my gut that, regardless of the rhetoric, some doors were meant to be closed to me. I don't quite know how I got to be so aware that women were not meant to have it all, at such a young age;

maybe it was simply that I picked up on subtle nuances in the differences in how us kids were treated. I was not a rough-and-tumble tomboy, but I always gave as good as I got. Fighting stuff out physically rarely happened in my world as a kid, and never happens as an adult.

I remember I'd stopped communicating with my family by the age of twelve, in relation to anything to do with me, my inner thoughts, the loneliness, the ostracism I faced at school—all the important stuff that went on inside my head, and I escaped into the land of books and depression. To this day I still struggle to remember to share my inner thoughts and feelings with friends and lovers that I trust. I'm so used to having an inner dialogue with "me, myself, and I" as a solitary person that it's hard for me to even imagine saying really personal stuff out loud as a normal way of operating in the world.

Over the past five years I have become practiced at articulating my inner thoughts, and I plan to keep working on this. At the moment I live alone, so once again I have conversations with myself, but now it's because no one else is around, and when I need to talk, I pick up the phone. I talk all day; I have great conversations, heated and intricate conversations about politics, sex, intimacy, and interpersonal dynamics. Sometimes the really personal stuff (immediate feelings) remains lost in silence. That's probably true for lots of people.

Mothers and Daughters

My mother and I have little in common. We are both passionate about our politics, yet sit at either extreme of the system. I call her a neo-Nazi, she calls me a troublemaker (who just won't lie down and take it like a woman?). In a weird way I think she respects me being a rogue. Perhaps a part of her is happy that I am outspoken and sure of myself and destined to live a life free from the restraints and limitations her era of heterosexuality ensured.

At thirty-four, I can see that it was no small feat for Mum to get her head around what I had become: a big butch dyke who is unapologetically out for the world to see and sneer at. I guess she has had to confront the homophobic ideas that she was surely raised with. Dad's best friend of thirty years was a poofter, but a very closeted one, and he never talked about it. That's so much easier to deal with—after all, you can just ignore it—but me, I was a different kind of queer: I talked about it, wore it openly (do butches really have a choice?), and celebrated it.

Mum must have concluded to herself that it was more than "a phase I was going through" because once, she even tried to get me back together with one of my ex-girlfriends: a woman who clearly fell into Mum's definition of "nice and acceptable" (read: a femme who passed as a respectably straight, middle-class girl). But I digress. Mum and I have a rapport, which is dependent upon its superficiality—if either of us delves beneath the surface, huge ruptures are immediately evident and our conversations break down. Occasional and unexpected moments of connectedness do occur, though.

We had a moment such as this the other day. I was talking to Mum on the phone and she told me she had bought me a half-price calendar at the shops.

My mind spun. What on earth did she find in the shops and think I might appreciate? Maybe she stumbled upon one of those arty African women calendars—after all, she knows I like black women.

"Oh," I said. "What type of calendar is it, Mum?"

"It's of women," she responded.

"Black women?" I asked excitedly.

"No," she said. "They didn't have any black women—they're white women."

"Oh," I said dejectedly, and continued, "Are they naked?"

"Yes," she said.

"Really?" I responded. "You went to the shops and bought your daughter a calendar of naked women?"

"Yes," she replied. "I told the man at the cash register that the calendar wasn't for me."

Sniggering, I quipped, "Did you tell him you were buying it for your daughter?"

"No," she said, laughing.

"Mum," I started. "I worry about you sometimes—first you offered to get me sex toys next time you were in San Francisco, and now you're buying me erotica."

"It's not erotica—it's pornographic!" she jumped in.

"Pornographic? These women are totally naked with their legs spread apart?" I questioned incredulously.

My interest is sinking at the thought of this calendar; the image forming in my mind is of anorexic white Barbie dolls with long blonde hair, silicon implants, and a false tan that fools no one. "Now that might be a male fantasy, but it sure doesn't do anything for me," I thought to myself.

Mum interrupted my thoughts and said, "I think they're totally naked—I'll have a look. Yes, the calendar's called Bikie Sluts."

"Bikie Sluts," I say out loud, slowly. My interest is renewed, thinking I can get off on white trash. "Yeah, Mum, it might be OK, I might like it."

At the other end of the phone, my mother proceeded to flick though the calendar in question in an attempt to accurately describe it for me.

"No," she said. "Some of them are wearing clothes." She proceeded to describe to me the positions of each woman's body and the amount of clothing they were not wearing.

I said, as gently as I could, trying to not appear ungrateful for her efforts to get me a gift (read: masturbation material): "Well, if I don't like it, Mum, can I give it to my brother?"

"No," she immediately jumped in. "I'll use it."

"You'll use it?" I questioned. "Mum, you cannot put a calendar like that up in the family room for all your friends to see."

"No," she said, without hesitation. "I'll put it up in my study!"

Not Seeing the Wood for the Trees

In an underlying way, out of my conscious thoughts, I think a part of me knew about the existence of lesbianism when I was a kid, but at that time I consciously had no idea that it was to be my path. I knew that being a gay man was a viable option—they were weird and sick, but they existed. Somehow in my narrow world it didn't follow that if gay men exist, then lesbians exist also, and therefore it wouldn't matter that few boys were interested in me and, more important, that I was not interested in them. As I saw it, at least until I left school—and by God I couldn't get out of there quick enough—you either liked boys or you were celibate, so I stayed celibate. I wasn't happy about it! As it turned out, it took more than leaving school to expand my options in any meaningful way beyond heterosexuality.

Today I'd call it a medical scene. Back then, aged four or five, Melinda and I played doctors. Why was the doctor always the boy and the patient always the girl? And how come breasts, nipples, and cunts were the focus of this play?

At sixteen I left school and started a hairdressing apprenticeship, where I developed a first-hand insight into, as I saw it, exploitation. I was politically left before that, but I'm sure doing an apprenticeship furthered me along that path. My first boss was a poofter. He was also a misogynist arsehole. Through him, I got my first insights into how gay men can be antiwomen, and the next eighteen years proved that point, again and again. I haven't had anything to do with gay men socially since I was twenty-four, when I completely gave up on them having anything in common with women's issues or lesbianism. To a degree, that boss was fairly "out" at work—he owned his own salon so I guess that made it more viable. He dressed as a woman for gay drag nights and competitions and had a number of gay and lesbian clients.

Looking back now, I have to wonder: "Did the gaydar of those lesbian clients prick up as they met me?" Did they think to themselves, "Check out the baby butch?" I will never know. I didn't immediately feel any particular affinity with those lesbians, but then I wouldn't today either—my memory of them is that they were quite conservative and probably even identified as "gay women" (as opposed to using more in-your-face terms like "lesbian" or "dyke" to refer to themselves). I used to think`that the reason why I didn't think these women were sick, perverted, or abnormal was that I was tolerant and open to diversity. Yet when I came out at twenty-two and first slept with a woman—who was to be my girlfriend of two years—it dawned on me that the most likely reason why I accepted those lesbian clients was that a part of me knew that I was one myself. Funny how life makes sense when you look back at it, but as you are living it, you cannot see the connections.

Mostly, when I played with my harem of Barbie dolls as a kid, I kept on forgetting to include Ken in their adventures. Poor old Ken, with his plastic mound so badly in need of a good packing, just seemed to luck out.

My First Girlfriend

That first girlfriend and I played butch-femme. She was high femme, so that meant I was supposed to be the butch, right? In the years that followed, my desire for high femme women was to be repeated again and again. We met each other through work and gradually got more and more intimate with each other. I remember so clearly, one night we met at an intimate bar after work. We were in London. I was working at a dodgy car rental company as assistant manager and she worked at another branch of the same company. I'm not much of a drinker; in fact, I hardly drink at all, although I am a chocoholic. I remember that night we had one drink together. Dutch courage? It must have been about 7:00 P.M., and I can still see in my mind's eye how I pointedly put my empty glass down on the table, with false bravado or a pretense of confidence, and told her something like: "It's time to go to bed," took her arm and led her away. I didn't have a plan, and when I look back, I didn't have a clue about what I was going to do once we got into bed, but for some strange reason that didn't faze me. Little did I know then, but this was the first of many encounters in bars, where I would bang my empty glass down on the table, a little too harshly, and announce it was time to go "get it on." My vocabulary got more explicit, my confidence increased, my need to lead the fuck was realized, and over time I knew exactly what I was going to do once I got the woman home.

The first time we had sex, it just felt right. I knew at that moment that nothing would ever be the same again. I'd finally found my path. It was the same kind of knowing—a deep down in the gut kind of knowing that defies rationality—that I have experienced since: when I embraced being butch, and when I knew the time was right to leave my last major relationship. But I digress. We both came out together as bisexuals to most of our friends, because the "bisexual" label was easier to face than overcoming a lifetime of "lesophobia" overnight. At least that's what I said two weeks later when I declared I was not bisexual, but a lesbian. I knew then that the two isolated and very drunk times I'd gone to bed with men were it. I realized so completely where I belonged and who my crew were. I felt calm and at peace, perhaps for the first time. Her journey, on the other hand, was not as peaceful as mine.

We had a tumultuous relationship for two years. Along the way, her inner demons emerged. I was too young and inexperienced to deal with her internalized lesophobia—she seemed to have a greater need to fit in with society's rules than I did. She was raised a strict Catholic and struggled with a sense of being deviant, sick, abnormal in the eyes of the church and her conservative family, fearing how they would react. I neither shared these concerns nor knew how to support her to work through them. Six months before we broke up, our sex life died. She kept holding out a carrot that went nowhere. I've since learned that this strategy is a common one among heterosexual women—it's a site of power! Perhaps it was easier for her to deal with us if we shared a puritan form of love, a sexless love. I'd read about the Boston Marriage phenomenon and didn't want to live it. I knew a sexual relationship was what I needed after all those celibate teen years. So eventually, after trying to reinvigorate our sex life, we broke up.

I was devastated, but determined to spend my adult years fucking. I pledged to myself then and there never to stay in a sexless relationship ever again, and I never have. OK, I haven't had many "real" relationships, but I've had my share of casual flings and one night stands to feel like I've made up for the drought that was my teens. I've often wondered if the strong need for sex is hard-wired into my character or if it was environmentally driven. Regardless of why or how, it's still true today: I would rather be single than in a sexless relationship.

Sometimes, when I'm out at a club, a butch in the distance
piques my interest and I have an overpowering urge to bark at him:
"Hey boy, get over here and get on your knees."

Learning to Take Up Space

I have explored how my teen years did nothing for my sense of sexual self. That first relationship barely helped, and there I was at twenty-four hitting the dyke scene. Over the next two years I began to reread my body as not so much undesirable but as taking up space—something women aren't supposed to do—and I liked that about myself. Size can be powerful, and power can be positive. I began to realize that I didn't have to be a size twelve to be desired. Over time, I met other big butch women, and they were accepted within the lesbian subculture. The more comfortable I got with my body taking up space, the more I allowed myself to reject whatever femininity I was wearing on my body, and slowly I began accepting myself as butch—like it was a good thing. From this self-acceptance, I began to realize that I had the right to be sexual and get laid, despite being big and butch.

I was insecure about my sexed body. Hell, what woman raised in the West isn't? I didn't relate well to my body. I didn't feel comfortable in my female body. I didn't feel that I was a man trapped in a woman's body; it was less specific, more intangible than that. It was more a sense of being different and not being comfortable in my own skin. I had always put my clumsiness at "doing femininity" down to being fat and being told that I was undesirable. In my early teens I didn't get that the reason why I had no interest in carrying or showing my body off the way teenage girls do was an indication of my not being comfortable doing female gender as society prescribed it, rather than signifying an inner disinterest in sex. There was a conflation going on in my head between being sexual and doing gender, and that took a long time to sort through.

Being a top or bottom has nothing to do with being butch or femme.

However, I did have a disinterested relationship with my breasts. I would have been just as happy had they never taken shape. I hated having to put a top on in the summer heat, just because of my breasts, and I felt it damn unfair that the social codes dictated that boys and men were allowed to go topless without punishment, but that freedom was never open to women. I don't recall being conscious of overtly hating my breasts, but I always felt, and still do, that they looked wrong on me and that they didn't fit with my body. Through the years I have suggested to lovers that I would be happy to have them removed, and without fail, these women have responded that they love them. This is clearly something I am unable to do. Ironically, I love the women I fuck—both butch and femme—to have large breasts. Go figure! I can get an erotic charge out of my nipples, but my breasts never make me feel sexual.

Did the need to present myself as more sexually experienced than I actually was come from a weird pride thing, or an intuitive understanding that women liked or needed me, the butch, to be the experienced one, or was it a desperate attempt of denial—to write away the pain of my younger years? Have most people, at some point, buried their performance anxiety deep within themselves, like I did? I wonder what is the percentage of bluff that all of us use?

Sex and Power

My sexual insecurity began to die down as I began to recognize that I was OK in bed. I also started to realize that some dykes liked me. Not despite of, but because I was big and butch and took up space. In addition, I discovered some women liked different things in bed, and I began to recognize that most of my sexual interests were more adventurous than most.

During those teenage years I could never see heterosexual sex free from a power imbalance, and, in fact, I still can't. At the time this made me very uncomfortable. I guess being a woman, as I saw it, meant that I was destined to be dominated by men, and the thought of that was abhorrent to me. Looking at it now, it makes total sense that I would be repulsed by the idea of being dominated by a man when I was destined to find dominating women a fantastic turn-on.

In my mid-twenties I was sorting through where I stood on sex and power. I discovered that my fantasies and some of my sexual activities were both adventurous and not shared by all dykes, but also had a name. The labels that still fit me best are dominant and sadistic in that order. I discovered that there are whole subcultures of perverts like myself out there. There were books written on this terrain. There were theoretical and instructional books out there that explicitly attended to issues of consent and to the variety of perverted acts, and some even explored the ethics of power play between different people and touched upon the cultural power bodies carried with them into the bedroom, so to speak. I was hooked. The tension around how playing with power and sex sat within my own strand of cultural feminism took about four years to sort through.

Along the way I readily fell into the dyke SM scene. They were my crew. They will always be my crew. I could talk dirty without worrying about offending anyone. I could talk about sexual techniques and turn-ons with a freedom to be up-front and honest, and, freed from political correctness, I could objectify women without being flagged ignorant or misogynist. As my confidence grew, so did my comfort with wielding power—for the first time I realized I had a sexual currency of my own. By the age of twenty-six I knew I was desired for my size and butchness and the way I owned my space. I was powerful because I was becoming centered and knew what I was about and where I was headed. That confidence was almost tangible, and somehow others picked up on the fact that I had my shit together. I was no longer faking it—I was an out butch dyke without apology. Social conventions became all but irrelevant to my world. I had grown to reject most of them, not because I was unable to fit into them, but because I didn't respect them and how they limited and inhibited so many people and kept us unhappy.

> Now I can see that I wear my butch gender atop a female-sexed body, and I wear my gender explicitly. Butch gender to me is intricately caught up with masculinity, desire, and sex: being desired and desiring other dykes. When I put on a certain pair of black boots that I've had for years, I am transformed within minutes into a predatory butch. I carry a strong sexual presence and it's one that plays with and on power, and I know exactly what I am about. And it's all about sex! And good sex is all about power. When I'm packing a prosthetic penis, it matters not whether I am wearing those boots or not, I instantly feel an additional layer of sexuality emerging and merging with my sense of self. I can almost feel surges of testosterone running through my body.

I walked away from my last deep relationship over a year ago, licking my wounds. This relationship honored many of my sexual fetishes and had an erotic charge that is hard to do justice to on paper. For a while it worked and we were happy. I played the butch and she played the femme, except that I wasn't playing anymore, and I don't think she got that. Since then, I've had a few casual affairs, but no one who has really rocked my world. I have a small but fabulous group of friends who I connect with and love dearly. And today, were it not for the occasional lonely moments, my life would be good. I'm getting a dog tomorrow, a puppy actually. Will I be her mummy or daddy?

RESOURCES

THE FOLLOWING IS A LIST of contact details for some of the organizations and websites mentioned in this book.

Australia

FTM Australia
P.O. Box 488
Glebe, NSW 2037
Australia
Telephone: +61 (0) 2 9571 9245
Web: www.ftmaustralia.org
Support group for female-to-male transsexuals and transgenders.

Gender Center
P.O. Box 266
Petersham, NSW 2049
Australia
Telephone: +61 (0) 2 9569 2366
Web: www.gendercentre.org.au
Support services for sex and gender diverse people.

Seahorse Club of Victoria
P.O. Box 86
St Kilda, VIC 3182
Australia
Telephone: +61 (0) 3 9513 8222
Web: http://home.vicnet.net.au/~seahorse
Support group for crossdressers, trans people, and their families.

Sex and Gender Education (SAGE)
P.O. Box 879
Randwick, NSW 2031
Australia
Web: www.sage-australia.org
Campaign and education group whose aim is to achieve equality for sex and gender diverse people.

South Australian Transsexual Support Group (SATS)
P.O. Box 907
Kent Town, SA 5071
Australia

Japan

FTM Nippon Newsletter
E-mail: ftmjapan@mve.biglobe.ne.jp
Publishes a quarterly newsletter for trans people.

Trans Net Japan
Web: www.geocities.com/tnjapan
Support group for trans people in Tokyo.

The Netherlands

Het Jongensuur (the Boys' Hour)
Binnenkadijk 176
1018 ZH, Amsterdam
The Netherlands
Female-to-male transgender support group.

Humanitas
Postbus 71
1000 AB, Amsterdam
The Netherlands
Web: www.wgtrans.nl
Support group for trans people.

Nederlands Transgender Film Festival (NTGF)
c/o T-Image Foundation
P.O. Box 15650
1001 ND, Amsterdam
The Netherlands
E-mail: ntgf@cs.com
Web: www.transgenderfilmfestival.com

T-Image Foundation
P.O. Box 15650
1001 ND, Amsterdam
The Netherlands
E-mail: t4image@cs.com
Nonprofit organization that aims to improve representations of transgender people by organizing cultural events.

United Kingdom

Beaumont Trust
BM CHARITY
London WC1N 3XX
United Kingdom
Web: http://hometown.aol.com/bmonttrust
Educational organization providing information on transsexualism and transvestism.

Gender Trust
P.O. Box 3192
Brighton BN1 3WR
United Kingdom
Web: www.gendertrust.org
Support and services for trans people.

Gendys Network
BM GENDYS
London WC1N 3XX
United Kingdom
Web: www.gender.org.uk/gendys
Support and services for trans people.

Northern Concord Club
P.O. Box 258
Manchester M60 1LN
United Kingdom
Web: www.northernconcord.org.uk
Social and self-help group for crossdressers, transsexuals, and their
wives or partners.

Press for Change (PFC)
BM NETWORK
London WC1N 3XX
United Kingdom
Web: www.pfc.org.uk
Campaign group dedicated to achieving equal rights for trans people.

Transgender UK
Web: www.transgender-uk.info
Contact and information website for sex and gender diverse people.

TransLiving International
P.O. Box 3
Basildon
Essex SS13 3WA
United Kingdom
Telephone: +44 (0)1268 583761
Web: www.transliving.co.uk
Self-help network, run by volunteers, serving the needs of crossdressers,
transsexuals, and their families, partners, and friends.

The Way Out Club and Guide
P.O. Box 70
Enfield EN1 2AE
United Kingdom
Telephone: +44 (0) 7778 157290
Web: www.thewayoutclub.com
Publishes an annual guide for trans people, holds regular club nights,
and provides links to other resources.

United States

FTM International
160 14th Street
San Francisco, CA 94103
USA
Telephone: (415) 553-5987
Web: www.ftmi.org
Support group for female-to-male transsexuals and transgenders.

The Gazebo
Web: http://content.gay.com/people/trans_gazebo
Transgender chatroom.

Harry Benjamin International Association for Gender Dysphoria
South Second Street, Suite 180
Minneapolis, MN 55454
USA
Telephone: (612) 625-1500; Fax: (612) 626-8311
Web: www.hbigda.org

International Foundation for Gender Education (IFGE)
P.O. Box 54022
Waltham, MA 02454-0229
USA
Telephone: (781) 899-2212
Web: www.ifge.org
Educational organization for promoting the self-definition and free
expression of individual gender identity; publishes magazine
Transgender Tapestry and has a bookstore.

Intersex Society of North America
P.O. Box 301
Petaluma, CA 94953
USA
Telephone: (707) 636-0420
Web: www.isna.org
Provides education and resources on intersex issues.

National Transgender Advocacy Coalition
14252 Culver Drive, #904
Irvine, CA 92604-0326
USA

Web: www.ntac.org
Campaign group striving for equal rights for sex and gender diverse
people.

PFLAG (Parents, Families, & Friends of Lesbians & Gays)
1726 M St., NW Suite 400
Washington, DC 20036
USA
Telephone: (202) 467-8180; Fax: (202) 467-8194
Web: www.pflag.org

Southern Arizona Gender Alliance
300 East Sixth St.
Tucson, AZ 85705
USA
Telephone: (520) 624-1779
Web: www.sagatucson.org
Support group for southern Arizona's transsexual and transgendered
community.

Texas Association for Transsexual Support (TATS)
Telephone: (281) 437-2975
Web: www.genderweb.org/~tats

Transgender Aging Network (TAN)
6990 N. Rockledge Avenue
Glendale, WI 53209
USA
Telephone: (414) 540-6456; Fax: (414) 540-6489
Web: www.forge-forward.org/TAN
International network of people interested in transgender aging issues.

Transgendered Harmony
P.O. Box 8028
Tempe, AZ 85281
USA
Telephone: (602) 954-7553
Web: www.tgharmony.org
Education, social events, and support services for transsexual and
transgender people in Arizona.

THE EDITORS

DR. TRACIE O'KEEFE DCH is a clinical hypnotherapist, psychotherapist, and counselor originally from the United Kingdom, where she practiced in London's Harley Street, who now lives and practices in Sydney, Australia. She gained her degree and doctorate in clinical hypnotherapy at the American Institute of Hypnotherapy (now the American Pacific University) and took postgraduate diplomas in hypnosis and psychotherapy at the National School of Hypnosis and Advanced Psychotherapy in London, as well as studying at the Open University and various other educational institutions.

Part of her clinical work involves helping people with many forms of sex and gender identity, and she is a member of the Harry Benjamin International Gender Dysphoria Association. Tracie is also a patron of Gendys Network and TransLiving in the United Kingdom, as well as international adviser to the T-Image Foundation in the Netherlands and one of the founding members of the campaign group Sex and Gender Education (SAGE) in Australia.

In addition to operating a busy clinic, Tracie runs a school of hypnosis and psychotherapy and lectures internationally on sex, gender, and sexuality. She is the author of two books on these subjects, *Trans-X-U-All* and *Sex, Gender & Sexuality*, and many articles, and is professor of sex, gender, and sexuality at the Calamus International University. She has also written two books on hypnosis, *Investigating Stage Hypnosis* and *Self-Hypnosis for Life*.

Tracie is also an active human and animal rights campaigner. For more information, visit www.tracieokeefe.com.

KATRINA FOX is a freelance journalist and editor also originally from the United Kingdom, where she worked for four years as a reporter and features writer on various publications before moving to Sydney in 2001 with her partner and coeditor, Tracie O'Keefe. Her specialist subjects include social justice; human and animal rights; environmental issues;

complementary health; women's issues; and sex, gender, and sexuality. Katrina is the coauthor of the book *Trans-X-U-All* and the editor of three other titles. She has written articles for the United Kingdom's national lesbian magazine, *Diva,* and currently writes for Sydney's *Lesbians on the Loose.*

Katrina has a bachelor's degree in performance art and worked for many years as a dancer and actress in London. She is currently looking forward to pursuing her interest in creative writing and fiction.

In addition to supporting human rights campaigns, Katrina actively promotes veganism and campaigns to end animal abuse. For more information, visit www.katrinafox.com.

THE AUTHORS

RIKKI ARUNDEL has built a successful career as a sales and marketing executive, with a strong emphasis on using technology, particularly the Internet. Throughout his twenty-five-year career, he used his acting training and talent as an entertaining speaker to sell his message to clients and resellers.

Now as a successful international keynote speaker and presentations skills coach, he helps clients do the same by speaking at their conferences and trade shows and coaching them in advanced presentation skills. But there is another side to Rikki: he is transgender. While most men with this condition keep it a secret, he has chosen to openly use his gift of understanding both men and women. Because Rikki is a master communicator and entertainer with a unique ability to cross the gender divide, the audience members don't just listen to him, they participate in an exciting motivational event.

The founder and first president of the Professional Speakers Association of Europe, Rikki will become British chair of the International Federation for Professional Speaking in 2003. He is the author of two successful books, *Sell Your Way to Success* and *The ABC of the WWW*, and more than five hundred articles, and is the world's first openly transgender professional speaker. For more information, visit www.professionalspeakers.org/members/RikkiArundel.

PHILLIP ANDREW BERNHARDT-HOUSE is a bisexual metagender, post-Christian theologian, pagan spiritualist, and lycanthrope. Originally from western Washington State in the United States, Phil currently lives in Cork, Ireland, and is a Ph.D. student studying at University College Cork, having previously studied at Sarah Lawrence College (Bronxville, New York); Wadham College, Oxford University; and Gonzaga University (Spokane, Washington). Phil's dissertation title is *Cú Chulainn and the Celtic Werewolf: Warriors, Shapeshifting and Sex from Celtiberia to the Kennels of Camelot*.

If you have ever read the *White Crane Journal* (although it's a journal of gay men's spirituality, and Phil is a bisexual metagender, it is somewhat close enough), you may have seen a poem by Phil called *Dionysius in the Labyrinth* or an article called *Life in Liminality Land*. Phil has presented internationally on bisexuality and theology, and hopes to publish on this topic as well, having produced a thesis for an M.A. in religious studies titled *Serving Two Masters: Bisexual Theological Foundations*. In addition to his student activism and community-based activism on queer issues, Phil is involved in BDSM and is an ordained minister in the Universal Life Church. If you wish to contact Phil and talk about anything under the sun, please do so by e-mailing alfrecht@hotmail.com

E. TRISTAN BOOTH (formerly E. Young) earned a B.A. in broadcasting production from the Walter Cronkite School of Journalism and Telecommunications at Arizona State University (ASU) in 1987, and is currently pursuing a master's degree in rhetoric from ASU's Hugh Downs School of Human Communication. As an undergraduate, Tristan wrote a weekly editorial column for the *State Press* student newspaper and served as an intern for the late congressman Morris K. Udall in his Washington, D.C., office. From 1989 to 1992, Tristan was a freelance writer for the *Phoenix Resource*, a local GLBT publication.

Formerly an officer for Desert Pride in Phoenix, Arizona, Tristan now serves on the board of directors for Transgendered Harmony in Phoenix, acts as liaison to the Southern Arizona Gender Alliance (SAGA) in Tucson, and sits on the GLBT Community Advisory Board for the Phoenix Police Department.

Tristan's current and archived newsletter articles for Transgendered Harmony are available at the website www.tgharmony.org. Personal e-mail should be addressed to tris@mediakingX.com.

CYNTHYA BRIANKATE is twenty-six years old, lives on eastern Long Island, New York, and does not identify as a man, a woman, or any known gender, for that matter. Cynthya is a writer and poet. S/he will soon have a bachelor's degree in English from Stony Brook University. S/he is also a performance artist, an actor/actress, and an aspiring filmmaker/documentarian. S/he has written a short film, *Dealing With It*. Cynthya starred in the film *Love, Neutered* and acted in the radio play *The XX, XY Files*. S/he has been published in *Cogar* magazine, *DamselZine*, and *Anything That Moves*, and is currently writing for Gauntlet Press.

Though not connected to any groups right now, Cynthya is involved in animal rights and has helped rescue several hundred animals. S/he has cared for many different kinds of animals and even helped breed pigs at one time. S/he presently lives with a Pomeranian, some hamsters and rabbits, and a magenta tarantula. Cynthya does website design. S/he has learned HTML programming and has built and maintains hir homepage entirely by hirself. S/he has also become involved in digital activism and has recently joined a campaign against Internet censorship. Cynthya can be reached at Barbieboy01@aol.com or atdarkkate@yahoo.com; hir homepage Fluidity can be found at www.angelfire.com/ny/BrianKate/

CHRISTINE BURNS has been a trans community campaigner for many years. Before starting out with Press for Change (PFC) in 1993, she worked as a Samaritan volunteer and was elected secretary, treasurer, and vice chair of her local Conservative party in the rural county of Cheshire in the United Kingdom, where she lived. Prior to becoming a vice president of PFC, she established herself as an active lobbyist with the support of her local member of Parliament and was already a familiar face at international conferences. Later her work shifted gear when she "came out" to become one of the public faces of the PFC campaign, appearing on over a dozen local and national television features and performing countless radio interviews. She also set up the campaign's first official website and then concentrated on writing consciousness-raising content for the community, with the website and PFC's subsequent e-mail-based news services as her main channels for dozens of articles covering every conceivable campaign issue.

Christine believes in the importance of knowledge as a catalyst for change on both sides of any social divide and was quick to see the opportunity to accelerate the process of knowledge sharing via the Internet. In August 2001 she retired from frontline work as a campaign leader, although she continues as a member of the Parliamentary Forum on Transsexualism, represents PFC in the human rights group Liberty, and remains part of PFC's government negotiating team. Christine now lives in Manchester and recently left a high-profile job with a major consultancy firm to explore ways of sharing what she has learned with other groups. Christine's personal writings can be found on her website at http://ourworld.compuserve.com/homepages/christine_burns, and her political writing can be found on PFC's website, www.pfc.org.uk.

ANDY COLSON was born in Melbourne, Australia, thirty-eight years ago, the eldest of three children. He studied electronics after leaving high school, being keen to find a career in sound and music. On completion of his studies he found a job in the broadcasting media, where he is still employed today. Andy plays guitar, loves camping and the outdoors, along with reading, listening to music, and generally enjoying life. Having crossdressed from a young age, Andy finds himself now emerging from something of a gender crisis of the past twelve months and has only recently found self-acceptance in the fact that he is transgendered. Finally now feeling more at ease with his situation, he sees himself at a critical juncture in his life. Only time will tell which path his journey will see him travel. Andy is married with a very supportive wife of nearly ten years and has no children.

Throughout the past two years, writing has been a very important component to Andy's learning to better understand himself. It is this writing that inspired the story in this book, in the hope that it might assist others in working through the many issues that bring people to accept that they are transgendered.

JAY COPESTAKE is a thirty-four-year-old butch woman who lives in the inner city of Sydney, Australia. Jay is semi-self-employed, working a variety of jobs. Having previously been involved with lesbian feminism and considering most anything male with contempt and irrelevant to her world, Jay is now exploring issues around gender.

TRACY DEICHMANN has always known that she is female, but unfortunately she was born with a male body—she is transsexual. She tried to live as a male for the first forty-seven years of her life, until finally she could take it no more. She overcame her fear of rejection and transitioned into the woman that she had always known she was. Three years after starting transition, Tracy now lives quietly in a small Australian country town with her transsexual partner, Andrea, and is enjoying a life that she thought would be forever denied her. Her interests include computers and reading, and she dreams of a world where people with gender dysphoria are treated no differently than anybody else with a birth defect.

REBECCA J. DITTMAN is a fifty-six-year-old transgendered individual living in Liverpool, in the north of England. It is only in the past nine years that she has lived in her chosen gender role, a period that has had profound effects on her personality and outlook. Working for twenty-three years as a registered nurse, she is now employed as a personal adviser to a government program assisting long-term unemployed people back to work, something she knows much about from her periods of extended unemployment during transition.

Through her own experiences of transition, she has become active in supporting others with gender identity issues, maintaining a Web-based service, Transgender UK (see Resources), and she is happy to take calls from anybody on trans issues. In the past two years she has become an independent external adviser to her local police force on matters relating to the trans community. She has made a number of appearances on local and national radio and television, and believes strongly that the portrayal of the trans community in society can be positively changed only by being open about our beginnings.

Rebecca also practices as a three-dimensional artist using a variety of materials, most recently stained glass, and her work can be seen at www.mercurialspirit.freeserve.co.uk/index.html. As a complete radiophile who has had radio production training, she is currently exploring another outlet for her creativity by setting herself up as an independent radio producer, and has plans for future documentary packages, one of which will concern the lives and experiences of trans people. Rebecca can be contacted at +44 (0)151 1432.

JENNIFER FRASER was born in Brisbane, Australia. She is currently exploring issues of transsexualism and is determined to stay with her partner throughout any transition. She does not, however, see sex reassignment surgery as necessary to her living in the gender role she chooses. Jennifer now lives in New South Wales where she works in a university.

PETER HÄBERLE is a thirty-three-year-old man from the Czech Republic who was born physically intersex. Having been brought up as a girl, he struggled with issues of being different. Peter trained as a chef and left his country for the West in 1989. He lived in Austria and Germany before settling in the Netherlands where he had corrective genital surgery and continues to live today.

KAM WAI KUI is thirty-three years old, was born in Hong Kong, and now lives in the Netherlands. He studied art history and film and television studies. He has organized events at the Third International Transgender Film and Video Festival in London (1999, codirector) and the Gendebende Transgender Film Festival in Amsterdam (2000, programmer and organizer). He is the founder of the T-Image Foundation in Amsterdam, a nonprofit organization set up in 2000 that aims to improve representations of transgender people by organizing cultural events. Kam Wai is now the festival director of the Nederlands Transgender Film Festival (NTGF), a production of the T-Image Foundation. The first NTGF took place October 3–7, 2001, in Amsterdam, and is held regularly. For contact details, see the Resources section.

TUCKER LIEBERMAN graduated from Brown University in the United States in 2002 with a B.A. in philosophy. His first novel, *The Insatiable*

Adventures of the Eunuch Monks of Krat, was published by XLibris. A sequel is forthcoming. He lives in Providence, Rhode Island.

NORRIE MAy-WELBY is a person of both sex and gender diversity, being physically neuter and multigendered in behavior and identity. Over the past decade, both locally and internationally, zie has presented workshops and lectures on sex and gender that include performances and audience participation. Zie has enjoyed putting the audiences through some transgender experiences, such as holding public discussions of their genitalia and having to fit into ill-fitting labels. *The Cartoon Guide to Gender & Transgender* is zir favorite print-format piece on the topic, and is available on norrie's homepage at www.cat.org.au/ultra/sex.html

Since 1989 zie has been on the management committee of the world's first transsexual refuge, in Sydney, Australia (now catering to all people of sex or gender diversity). Zie has been employed as the transgender project worker for the Sex Workers Outreach Project of New South Wales for the past five years, where zie is also currently the acting outreach team coordinator. Zie was a founding member of the Transgender Lobby Coalition, and serves on the steering committee of the campaign group SAGE (Sex and Gender Education) in Australia.

Born in Scotland in 1961, norrie grew up in Perth, Western Australia, and now lives in Redfern, Sydney, with zir gay-identifying boyfriend and a human-identifying cat. Every Sunday, zie visits zir eighteen-month-old godson. Every New Year and Easter holiday, zie runs around naked in the bush at a gathering of like-minded souls. Zie enjoys yoga, comic books, news, radio, *New Scientist,* and being a fairy godmother.

MELANIE MCMULLAN is a person with many jobs and interests in both genders, including being a bank official, a university lecturer in law and in finance, and an author of several books on various aspects of finance and law. She also writes for television. She is the secretary of the Gender Trust in the United Kingdom, which is a charity that provides help to transsexuals, transgenderists, and intersexuals who are gender dysphoric. She is also a patron of another U.K. group, TransLiving, and is a member of the Intersex Society of North America (ISNA). (See Resources.)

Melanie believes passionately in the pastoral care and support of anyone who has Gender Identity Disorder, be they transsexual, transgendered, or intersex. It is through her involvement with the Gender Trust, TransLiving, and ISNA that she is able to make a contribution to the welfare of others who may be less fortunate. She has written many articles on gender-related topics in the Gender Trust's *Gems News* and TransLiving's *Translife* magazine over many years and is noted for writing, along with Stephen Whittle, the book *Transvestism, Transsexualism and the Law.* She is also coauthor with Rosemary Turner of the *Gender Trust Guide to Transsexualism, Transgenderism and Gender Identity Disorder.*

NATALIE MURPHY is a transgendered woman who lives in Southampton, England, with Karen, her married partner of fifteen years, and their two children, Andrew and Aaron. Natalie was born into a struggling family in postwar Britain in 1952, but the midwife who gleefully announced, "It's a boy" to the happy parents didn't realize that what you see is not necessarily what you are going to get. It became apparent to his family that all was not going according to plan when at six years old, their son Shaun had more girlfriends than the average boy, and playing with other boys was out of the question most of the time.

After decades of abuse and rejection by his blood family and those who thought of themselves as friends, a failed marriage, and a lot of introspection, Shaun took his first steps to put right what had been dreadfully wrong, changed his name to Natalie, and set about the painful and traumatic journey into womanhood. Natalie now lives contented and happy in the knowledge that the life-changing decision that she took in 1994 to "change her sex" was the right one for her. Although the odds that their marriage would survive were considered to be slim, Natalie and her partner Karen have shown that love is far more powerful than the prejudice and bigotry that the rest of society thinks the couple should be subject to because they have dared to be different and reject the accepted view of gender stereotypes.

NERO is an eighteen-year-old bisexual trans man living in Ireland with his mother and his boyfriend. Originally from the United States, Nero is a writer, web designer, and actor.

JACK POWELL is a trans man who lives in a small terrace house in Sydney, Australia, with his partner, Michael, his dog, Talaska, and cat, Cleo. He sees himself as a masculine being with an interesting story. Jack has worked in several areas of the community sector and has a passion for mental health and gay, lesbian, bisexual, and transgender issues. Recently Jack presented at several conferences in Australia on transgender and mental health issues. Currently he is working with GLBT youth and their families. He also provides training to service providers throughout New South Wales on working with GLBT people. To enhance these practical skills, Jack is also studying adult education and community development at the University of Technology Sydney.

Jack is the cofounder and current president of FTM Australia. FTM Australia is a peer support network for trans men and those affirming their masculine identity. It provides information, support, social events, and a bimonthly newsletter, *Torque* (see Resources).

Any given weekend you will find him in the garden, pottering with his plants and animals; at the moment his garden is full of succulents and bromeliads. Jack also loves to create things with wood. Several items of furniture in his home are one-of-a-kind works of art. He has a bed that is six feet off the ground with an entire study underneath.

KATRINA C. ROSE holds a law degree from South Texas College of Law and a B.A. in environmental design from Texas A&M University. She is an attorney and currently lives and works in rural Minnesota (though still licensed to practice law in Texas as well), but spends copious amounts of time with her life partner, noted St. Paul–based photographer Tanith Rattazzi, and a bevy of four-legged, furry, friendly creatures (too numerous to name here) who keep them both company. Katrina is the author of numerous law review articles on transgender issues, notably *Sign of a Wave? The Kansas Court of Appeals Rejects Texas Simplicity in Favor of Transsexual Reality*, published in the University of Missouri-Kansas City *Law Review* in 2001, and *The Transsexual and the Damage Done—The Fourth Court of Appeals Opens PanDOMA's Box While Closing the Door on Transsexuals' Right to Marry*, published in Tulane University's *Law and Sexuality* in 2000.

From 1998 to 2001, Katrina was a weekly columnist for the *Texas Triangle*, and still contributes to the paper intermittently as its resident transgender legal historian. She anticipates returning to school in the near future to seek a Ph.D. in history, focusing on transgender legal history. And, despite all of her research endeavors, she still finds time to indulge in her artistic passion—photography—occasionally exhibiting and selling some of her work.

SARAH J. RUTHERFORD is from Adelaide, South Australia. She is the coordinator of the South Australian Transsexual Support Group and a writer with over thirty years' experience; her work includes books, short stories, poetry, and nonfiction. Sarah is also an artist, though by no means a professional one. Art is purely for fun, and her favorite genre is abstract.

She is currently studying for an arts degree in Australian studies at the University of South Australia, and graduated in English literature at Adelaide University in 2002. Sarah likes soccer, reading, writing, history, art, classical and jazz music, good conversation, animals, old solid timber furniture, and chess. Her dislikes include unjust and unwarranted abuse or discrimination of any kind, physical, mental, or spiritual, in any time, or at any age. Also politicians, smelly and moldy blue cheese, rap music, and her youngest son's abandoned socks . . . oh, and supposedly user-friendly computers and related software.

Sarah's aim in life is to live to see the day when being transsexual will be no different than being supposedly "normal." She'd also like to see world peace, an end to poverty, and Australia's eventually winning the World Cup in soccer.

JOE SAMSON, when not walking the dog, listening to music, playing video games, or kicking butt at Boggle, can be found working toward his degree and teacher certification in the San Francisco Bay Area. He lives with his partner, Sondra, their dog, Bela, and cats, Batavia and Perkins Grace. He spends some of his free time with Zevi, age five-and-a-half, and Ari, who is one-and-a-half, and would like to thank Anne and Suegee for making him part of the family. He would also like to thank Crash, Tyler, Drew, and Pup for being brothers to an "other." He would also like to thank his Mistress for making him write this piece. Thank you, Mistress.

APRIL ROSE SCHNEIDER has persisted and persevered as a member of the third gender, despite the vicious onslaught of merciless fate over the course of five decades. A survivor of sex reassignment in Bangkok, she is generally considered quite daffy and completely harmless by her peers (although one may easily discover, by merely scratching the surface, a deep well of profoundly neurotic dysfunction). A consummate authority in the art of avoidance, she blames her parents, her society, public schools, Republicans, right-wing Christians, her dog, and of course estrogen for her beleaguered state of mind.

Shortly after graduation in 1969, Ms. Schneider, who was actually a mister at the time, left Ohio and headed out for parts unknown, eventually residing in Tennessee, Florida, and California twice. During her travels she bravely endured a wide variety of tedious occupations for which she received a mere pittance. A small list of these includes fast-food worker, truck driver, nightclub manager, massage therapist, and radio announcer.

April Rose currently lives in New Mexico where she operates her own commercial and residential cleaning service. One of the most passionate and prolific unknown writers of her kind, she spends her spare time roaming the foothills of the Sangre de Cristo Mountains with her two dogs and her spouse of twenty-two years.

LAURA ANNE SEABROOK is a pagan, goth, writer, cartoonist, and artist, who also reads tarot. Western Australian by birth, she now lives in the Hunter Valley in New South Wales with her pets. She has worked in the public service, has a bachelor of visual arts, and has interests in science fiction and in folk and fringe culture. She has a regular comic feature in a local publication *Out Now,* and has had her prose and poetry published elsewhere. Laura considers herself to be a modern Galla of Cybele and Semnotata of Hecate.

VERA SEPULVEDA lives and works in downtown San Francisco. Shunning the fast lane, she leads a quiet and simple life and doesn't even own a television. Artistic by temperament, she paints and sculpts and has exhibited locally. Although originally from Los Angeles, she has lived in San Francisco for over ten years and now considers the Bay Area her home. Vera occasionally posts her thoughts and experiences on her website, www.underpussy.com. The story in this book is her first published written work.

MASAE TORAI is a freelance writer and postoperative female-to-male transsexual. Because he underwent all his surgeries in the United States, he has a lot of friends there. Having surgeries in a foreign country has led to his being in debt for more than a decade, but it doesn't bother him. He is happy with the result of the surgeries and has a lot of friends. He hopes to have more friends from all over the world. Masae is working vigorously to educate Japanese people about trans-related things. He produces two newsletters, one in Japanese and the other in English. He lectures regularly at such places as elementary schools, junior high schools, high schools, universities, and school festivals, and appears on radio and TV programs. But he never appears on what he calls "silly media," because he thinks that people will see trans people through his image; so he is always poor because serious programs don't pay him much, whereas silly ones pay a lot.

He has written nine books so far, and three more will be published soon. However, he will still be poor, because the Japanese publishing world is in recession. But being poor doesn't bother him much. He is happy to have many opportunities to express his opinions. He hopes that his books will be read all over the world someday. Masae has lived in Tokyo for thirty-eight years in the same house where he was born, with his old, sick mother and some killifish.

ROBYN WALTERS is a retired officer of the U.S. Navy and holds an engineering Ph.D. from the Massachusetts Institute of Technology. Following retirement from the Navy, she continued to work with the Navy both as a male and as a female. She is an occasional author and has been published in *Transgender Tapestry,* the *US Mensa Bulletin,* and various GLBT papers and newsletters. Robyn is an active supporter of the transgendered community. She moderates four TG news lists, is a speaker for Parents, Families and Friends of Lesbians and Gays (PFLAG) transgender outreach, and is vice chair of both the Media Committee and the Veteran Affairs Committee of the National Transgender Advocacy Coalition (NTAC). Robyn transitioned to female in June 2000 on her sixty-third birthday. She and her FTM husband, Emery, share eight children and eighteen grandchildren and live near Seattle, Washington, with their cat, Mouse.

True Selves
Understanding Transsexualism—For Families, Friends, Coworkers, and Helping Professionals

Mildred Brown and Chloe Ann Rounsley

$17.95 paperback

ISBN: 0-7879-6702-5

Filled with wisdom and understanding, *True Selves* paints a vivid portrait of the conflicts transsexuals face on a daily basis—the courage they must summon as they struggle to reveal their true being to themselves and others. This classic resource offers valuable guidance for friends, families, coworkers, and professionals who are struggling to understand these people and their situations. Using real life stories, actual letters, and other compelling examples, *True Selves* gives a clear understanding of what it means to be transsexual and offers practical suggestions for dealing compassionately with these commonly misunderstood individuals.

"*True Selves* is thorough and comprehensive. . . .This is a serious and important book. If you know a transsexual, care about a transsexual, or are interested in understanding transsexuality, *True Selves* should be on your reading list."—*The Transsexual New Telegraph*

"Each chapter poses questions and confronts common misconceptions about transgendered people and offers recommendations to caregivers and family. . . . presented in a simple, straightforward style and is easy to understand."—*Gender Identity Journal*

"With real life stories, letters, poems, and more, this is a first coming-out collection for the TS community."—*Feminist Bookstore News*

MILDRED L. BROWN is a clinical sexologist and therapist in private practice in San Jose, California. She is also professor of clinical sexology at the Institute for Advanced Study of Human Sexuality in San Francisco.

CHLOE ANN ROUNSLEY (www.rounsley.com) is a writer, journalist, and editorial consultant based in the San Francisco Bay Area.

[Price subject to change]